Praise for *Belonging to God:*
Spirituality, Science & a Universal Path of Divine Love

"Helps us to remember what is essential and true, and guides us to live the love that belongs to an awakened soul. Here are keys that we each can use to unlock our own mystic heart."
—**Llewellyn Vaughan-Lee**, founder,
The Golden Sufi Center

"[A] vision of unity that inspires the mind with the perspective of contemporary science; ignites the heart with the mystical fire of divine love across faith traditions; and offers us a path for planetary spiritual awakening."
—**Yogacharya Ellen Grace O'Brian**, spiritual director,
Center for Spiritual Enlightenment

"[With] vast knowledge and deep love of the scriptures and mystics ... [Will's] humble and reverent case for interspirituality can lead each spiritual seeker to the experience of belonging to God. Isn't this exactly what the world needs, and exactly what we need?"
—**Robert McDermott, PhD**, president emeritus
and chair of the Philosophy, Cosmology, and Consciousness
Program at the California Institute of Integral Studies;
author, *The Essential Aurobindo*

"Calls us to something deeper.... Through the framework of three different faiths and that of science, calls on us to love each other's paths."
—**Swami Ambikananda**, translator,
Katha Upanishad and the *Uddhava Gita*

"Weaves the most critical teachings of significant spiritual traditions ... into a majestic tapestry of love. A substantial invitation to open our hearts to the world that needs to be."
—**Rabbi Ted Falcon, PhD**, author, *Journey of Awakening*;
coauthor, *Finding Peace through Spiritual Practice: The Interfaith
Amigos' Guide to Personal, Social and Environmental Healing*

"One has to appreciate the intensive research done in this scientific and faith comparative study.... The path of divine love is available to all humans, so this book is for all."

—**Mary Frost**, deputy chair, Cape Town Interfaith Initiative

"Nothing is more refreshingly relevant than a nuclear physicist writing a riveting book on belonging to God.... Will's great gift is both enthusiasm for the progress in these matters and deep discernment with regard to details."

—**Father Francis D'Sa, SJ**, director,
Institute for the Study of Religion

"A passionate argument for the beauty and profundity of a devotional path to union with the Divine.... A song from the heart (and mind) that calls each of us into a devotional state of prayer for wholeness in our own lives and entices us ever deeper toward union with the Divine."

—**Rory McEntee**, coauthor, *The New Monasticism:
An Interspiritual Manifesto for Contemplative Living*

BELONGING
to GOD

Spirituality, Science &
a Universal Path of Divine Love

WILLIAM KEEPIN, PhD
FOREWORD BY THOMAS KEATING, OCSO

Walking Together, Finding the Way®

SKYLIGHT PATHS®
PUBLISHING
Woodstock, Vermont

Belonging to God:
Spirituality, Science & a Universal Path of Divine Love

2016 Quality Paperback Edition, First Printing
© 2016 by William Keepin
Foreword © 2016 by Thomas Keating

Library of Congress Cataloging-in-Publication Data
Names: Keepin, William, author.
Title: Belonging to God : spirituality, science & a universal path of divine
    love / William Keepin ; foreword by Thomas Keating, OCSO.
Description: Woodstock, VT : SkyLight Paths Pub., 2016. | Includes
    bibliographical references and index.
Identifiers: LCCN 2016009169| ISBN 9781594736216 (pbk.) | ISBN
    9781594736261 (ebook)
Subjects: LCSH: Spirituality. | Love—Religious aspects.
Classification: LCC BL624 .K443 2016 | DDC 204—dc23 LC record available at
    http://lccn.loc.gov/2016009169

10 9 8 7 6 5 4 3 2 1

Manufactured in the United States of America
Cover design: Jenny Buono
Cover art: Irina Pechkareva
Interior design: Tim Holtz

SkyLight Paths Publishing is creating a place where people of different spiritual traditions come together for challenge and inspiration, a place where we can help each other understand the mystery that lies at the heart of our existence.

SkyLight Paths sees both believers and seekers as a community that increasingly transcends traditional boundaries of religion and denomination—people wanting to learn from each other, *walking together, finding the way.*

SkyLight Paths, "Walking Together, Finding the Way" and colophon are trademarks of LongHill Partners, Inc., registered in the U.S. Patent and Trademark Office.

Walking Together, Finding the Way
Published by SkyLight Paths Publishing
A Division of LongHill Partners, Inc.
Sunset Farm Offices, Route 4, P.O. Box 237
Woodstock, VT 05091
Tel: (802) 457-4000   Fax: (802) 457-4004
www.skylightpaths.com

To Cynthia,
with whom I am blessed
to walk this path;

to the Nameless One,
who guides us on this path;

and to all who walk the path of divine love.

Contents

Foreword

Father Thomas Keating, OSCO

In recent times the "interspiritual movement" has been gathering interest and energy from many parts of the world. Interspirituality expands upon traditional interfaith and interreligious dialogue to include a greater emphasis on spiritual experience across diverse faith traditions. There are different understandings of what interspirituality is and what form it might take in the future.

Will Keepin in this book makes a significant contribution to the growing literature of the movement. He clarifies with both scholarship and wisdom the main issues, commonalities, and ultimate goal of this sublime capacity of human nature. He unites the spiritual traditions of the world religions into a single vision of the ultimate purpose of religious practice. Focusing on three major world religions, he presents his thesis that the ultimate experience of God, or Ultimate Reality, is one.

To grasp this insight, it is important to recognize that the experience of interreligious dialogue needs a deeper exploration of the spiritual transformative journey itself, which is the primary purpose of religion in the first place. It is not enough simply to listen patiently to others' presentations of their particular religious beliefs. What is also essential is mutual learning about the transformative experiences of advancing practitioners in other faith traditions, which tends to create bonds of friendship in a common search, despite theological differences. Interreligious dialogue then becomes *interspiritual* dialogue. As the practice of interspiritual dialogue matures, it inspires not only respect but love for other religions. One perceives in them, and in their faithful adherents, the presence and action of Ultimate Reality, or the Holy Spirit, to use Christian terminology. This presence, Source of everything that is, secretly underlies and accompanies each of us in every moment in space and time. The sense of the oneness of all creation, which the spiritual traditions of the world religions are revealing, involves a transcendence of certain aspects of one's own path, without relinquishing its basic teachings. Exploring the commonalties of spiritual wisdom and mystical experience can thus serve to bond spiritual seekers into a greater harmony and unity of purpose, which in turn can help to dispel tension or conflict of various kinds.

Will first outlines the essence of the spiritual path of love as revealed in sacred scriptures—focusing on the Bhagavad Gita, the Qur'an, and the Gospels—demonstrating a remarkable convergence of the essential teachings of Hinduism, Islam, and Christianity. All three scriptures affirm a supreme Godhead, which goes by different names and is perceived in different ways. Next Will summarizes the transformative spiritual journeys of several leading mystics in these traditions, again revealing deep parallels. Particularly important are the common themes emphasizing surrender of self, absolute trust in God, and the gift of divine grace that transforms and divinizes the soul of the seeker. Despite the many theological differences, Will concludes that the underlying path of transformation is strikingly similar across the three traditions.

As Will's presentation unfolds, a new way of understanding the deeper significance of these teachings emerges, drawing upon scientific breakthroughs in the fields of quantum physics and fractal geometry in mathematics. In quantum physics, a single electron is believed to have some form of awareness of the universe. In fractal mathematics, the macrocosm is replicated in the microcosm; for example, neural networks in the brain exhibit a similar structure to galaxies. Weaving these insights together, Will proposes that consciousness itself has a fractal structure, enabling the Infinite to be replicated in the inmost being and heart of every seeker, and offering a new way of understanding the oneness of human and divine consciousness across all divisions.

The fire of divine love, as Will so beautifully explains, is the key metaphor in all the faith traditions. In this cosmic vision there is one divine fire yet many flames, each of which might represent a particular religion or faith tradition. The conclusion culminates in twelve "Principles of Divine Love" that provide a summary of his comprehensive study of paths to divine transformation.

Interspiritual dialogue can serve as a catalyst not only for the growth of interreligious dialogue, but also for the future peace of the world. I believe that Will's book offers a valuable contribution to this vision. It certainly will prove to be a primary resource for those engaged in the transformative process, and in grounding the interspiritual movement. I suggest to the reader that as you delve into this book, you pray for the grace to listen with the ear of your heart.

Introduction

I am a Muslim, a Hindu, a Christian, and a Jew—
and so are all of you!
>—MAHATMA GANDHI

I am neither Christian, nor Jew, nor Zoroastrian, nor
Muslim.
I am not of the East, nor of the West, nor of the land, nor of
the sea;
My place is the Placeless, my trace is the Traceless;
'Tis neither body nor soul, for I belong to the soul of the
Beloved.
I have put duality away, I have seen that the two worlds are
one;
I know none other except God.
>—RUMI

Gandhi belongs to every religion. Rumi belongs to no religion. So it is with all those who belong to God.

This book attempts to articulate the essence of divine love, as revealed through the scriptures, mystics, and practices of three major spiritual traditions, and their relationship to the science of divine love. The spiritual path of divine love is found in one form or another within all the major religious and spiritual traditions, and exists beyond them as well. It is the hidden path of the heart to God, entered through an invisible doorway deep within the heart.

Like Rumi and Gandhi, those who tread the path of divine love belong to all religions—and in a sense they belong to no religion, because they have given themselves utterly and exclusively to the Infinite Supreme

Reality, which is often called "God." Hence they *belong* to this Supreme Reality, aka God, and to nothing else. The path of divine love is thus a kind of universal religion that leads to mystical mergence into the very essence of God (or Brahman, Allah, Yahweh, Nirvana, Tao; there are many names for the Supreme Reality).

After delving into the scriptures and practices of multiple faith traditions for thirty-five years, I have come to the view that the essence of divine love can be distilled into a few key principles and practices that are remarkably consistent across the theistic religions. This foundational path is easily obscured and can be difficult to discern against the backdrop of the rich spectrum of faith traditions—given their diverse scriptures and voluminous commentaries and exegeses; their seemingly disparate and sometimes contradictory theologies; and their broad variety of practices of prayer, meditation, liturgies, institutional structures, and forms of worship. Nevertheless, a universal path of the heart to God can be discerned, and the following pages are an attempt to elucidate the nature and essence of this path, and to offer a glimpse of *why* it is basically the same across the faith traditions.

Differences between religions are widely publicized today, often to the point of proclaiming that the religions are mutually contradictory and fundamentally incompatible. Common ground and similarities across the faith traditions are far less emphasized. Yet the path of divine love suggests that the religions share a universal core. This book seeks to articulate that core, in terms of theology and essential practice, and to offer a scientific perspective on how this Oneness functions at the foundation of spiritual consciousness.

Because each religion or spiritual tradition constitutes a vast and unique domain—an entire sacred world and universe unto itself—the notion of trying to articulate the path of love across multiple spiritual traditions is daunting, if not preposterous. Therefore, the focus here is limited to a few representative traditions, and the conclusions apply strictly to these traditions only. The general results do, however, point toward a universal path of the heart found in all religions. Specifically, I explore the path of divine love as it is articulated in the Christian, Islamic, and Hindu (Vaishnavaite) traditions. I choose these three traditions because they each strongly articulate a spirituality and define a praxis of divine love, and because I have a strong personal engagement with each of them. These three religions include the oldest and youngest of the major world religions, span incarnational and non-incarnational faiths, and embrace the rich diversity of India, the Middle East, and the West. Finally, for sheer practicality, space prohibits detailed consideration of more than three traditions in a single book. I also refer to other traditions, particularly Buddhism, which is dear to my heart and provided my initial training in meditation, as well as Judaism, Native American spiritual paths, Sikhism, Jainism, Baha'i, and Taoism. Appendix 1 briefly addresses the path of divine love in nontheistic traditions.

One of the great advantages of an interfaith exploration like this is that it enables you to clearly discern which elements of your own faith are foundational and universal, and which elements are more tradition-specific. This awareness is extremely valuable as you seek to relate to other traditions, for it lays out the common ground between different traditions and provides a unifying space for further constructive exploration and skillful relating across the faith traditions.

My Personal Background

"I did not write anything concerning theology (*kalam*) until I had memorized twelve thousand pages of the great theologians of Islam," remarked the great Sufi saint Al Ghazali. In the Hindu tradition, according to the French pioneer of Christian-Hindu dialogue Swami Abhishiktananda, one would never even *think* of teaching Vedanta before spending a minimum of twelve years in a cave in solitude, and then only if asked.[1] By these standards, I am utterly unqualified to write this book. Moreover, I am neither theologian nor priest, swami, imam, religious scholar. Nevertheless, I have written this book anyway—out of great love for the scriptures and mystics, and my deep commitment to walk the path of divine love, however inadequately. I also have written it because the path of divine love is available to every human being, and I hope this book might serve to highlight some of the glistening gems of wisdom from across the faith traditions on the spiritual path of love, and articulate for the nonspecialist the exquisite path of divine love as it is set forth in these religious traditions and beyond.

My personal family lineage and cultural conditioning are strongly Christian, although both my parents rejected religion as young adults. My paternal grandfather was a Methodist minister and my grandmother was a Christian mystic interested in Eastern mysticism; she studied the mystics meticulously and was a devotee of Christian mystic Evelyn Underhill's pioneering work, along with other spiritual leaders, including Yoganada, Gandhi, Tagore, and Sri Aurobindo. My maternal grandfather was a devout Irish Catholic who promoted congressional legislation to support the widows of American soldiers killed in World War II. On the morning he was to have an audience with Pope Pius XII, he was found dead from a heart attack in his hotel room in Rome. He had just traveled by train from France, where he had visited for the first time the grave of his only son, who had been killed in the war three years earlier, in 1944. My grandmother from England was originally Anglican, but she later converted to Catholicism because a Catholic priest told her that by so doing, upon her death she would be reunited in heaven with her son and husband.

By training and profession, I am a mathematical physicist, a psychologist, an environmental scientist, and a social activist. The deeper story of my life, however, is that I am profoundly blessed to have been initiated into an interfaith mystical lineage by a spiritual master from India who prefers to remain anonymous.[2] I have been practicing silent meditation and prayer for thirty-five years, and reading scripture for thirty years.

I have attempted to write the book on scripture and the mystics that I wished for when I began a disciplined practice of meditation. I wanted to read scripture and to understand the mystics' journey, but I longed for an overarching articulation of spiritual truth and practice across the religions that could give me an overall sense of what spiritual life is all about, and how it relates to contemporary perspectives at the cutting edge of science. I was seeking something truly grounded in time-tested tradition, and I found plenty of books that promoted one tradition or another as the primary or only valid path. Yet I was seeking an understanding of how the different theological perspectives are interrelated. I also yearned for a theological and disciplined framework that was universal enough to include multiple traditions and did not dismiss or devalue the devotional aspect of spiritual life as somehow inferior. I hungered for nourishment of the devotional side of my nature, yet in a rigorous way that also satisfied the intellectual and philosophical side of my nature—an inclusive nondual path that could encompass both deep intellectual inquiry and devotional abandon of the heart.

Hence this book, which seeks to articulate the universal path of love that holds true in all religions. It is written for the serious spiritual seeker or aspirant who knows or senses in her heart that there is something inherently universal in spirituality and religion, and that this Oneness is a dominant core essence of the religious traditions.

Interspirituality, Multiple Religious Belonging, and Second Axial Consciousness

"Beware of being bound up by a particular religion and rejecting others as unbelief," cautions the Sufi saint Ibn Arabi, "for you will fail to obtain the true knowledge of reality. God is greater and wider than to be confined to one particular religion to the exclusion of others."[3] Archbishop Desmond Tutu emphasizes this same point, "God is not a Christian"—nor a Muslim, a Jew, a Hindu, or a Buddhist for that matter.[4]

God includes and transcends all religions. Every major religion offers a unique pathway to the infinite and eternal Supreme Reality that dwells within and beyond all beings. This book is written for spiritual seekers and contemplative practitioners who yearn for an integral path of divine love—articulated across multiple traditions and uniting them in the fire of love for God in the depths of the heart.

In seeking to articulate a universal path of divine love, this book spans multiple dimensions. It belongs partly within the emerging field of "multiple religious belonging" that bridges two or more religions, as pioneered by authors such as Raimon Panikkar, Swami Abhishiktananda, and others.[5] It also belongs partly in the domain of "perennial philosophy," which posits a universal truth that dwells at the core of all major religious and spiritual traditions.[6] The term *sophia perennis* was first coined in 1540 by Vatican scholar Agostino Steuco, who postulated that there is "one principle of all things, of which there has always been one and the same knowledge among all peoples."[7] The book relates directly to the intersections of "science and spirituality," drawing on numerous recent scientific advances; and, finally, it belongs also within the nascent field of "interspirituality," a term first coined by Brother Wayne Teasdale that refers to the contemporary meeting of the world's major religious and spiritual traditions.[8]

Significant context for this book is further provided by the sweeping historical analyses of "axial transformation," first identified by German philosopher Karl Jaspers and expanded upon in the writings of other religious scholars and historians, such as Robert Bellah and Karen Armstrong. The "First Axial Age" denotes the unique and pivotal shift that took place between approximately 800 and 300 BCE, during which time striking parallel developments in religion and philosophy emerged simultaneously in Persia, India, the Sinosphere, and the Greco-Roman world. Scholars Ewert Cousins, Father Thomas Berry, and others have posited that humanity is now undergoing a "Second Axial Age" in which sweeping changes in spirituality and consciousness are again taking place systemically across the planet.

This book draws from the rich foundations of each of these domains, as it outlines a spiritual path of divine love within three major theistic traditions, which taken together point toward the possibility of a universal path of the heart to God.

Esoteric and Exoteric Spirituality

A crucial distinction must be made at the outset between the esoteric and exoteric dimensions of religion, as identified by Sufi master Frithjof Schuon and religious historian Huston Smith, among others. Simply put, the "esoteric" refers to the innermost essence, or kernel, of religion. It is invisible, hidden inside the outer visible husk—which is the exoteric forms that we know as "religion" in churches, temples, mosques, and synagogues, as well as the mind's encounter with the creeds and scriptures of religion.

The esoteric essence of religion is hidden from view—on both physical and conceptual levels—and can only be realized in the depths of the heart. Such realization is usually precipitated by intensive practice of spiritual disciplines coupled with an ineffable gift of what can only be called divine grace. Perennial philosophy holds that the esoteric dimension of religion is eternal, consistent across all time and cultures, whereas the exoteric dimension is both ephemeral and mutable across different cultures and epochs. In short, religious forms evolve, yet their inner essence is eternal and universal.

Scriptural and Mystical Sources

This book assumes a general familiarity with the Christian tradition, and, to a lesser extent, its parent tradition, Judaism—including their respective scriptures. Most Western readers have far less familiarity with Hinduism and Islam; therefore considerable emphasis is placed on these traditions, particularly in the early chapters.[9]

Many excellent books articulate the profound relationship and overlap between the Christian and Jewish traditions. A smaller number of books address the commonalities among the three major Abrahamic faith traditions, and, among these, it is crucial to distinguish between those books that are essentially partisan—promoting one of the Abrahamic faiths over the others—and the much smaller number of books that present Judaism, Christianity, and Islam in a balanced manner.[10] Even so, we must avoid any naive suggestion that there exists some form of universally accepted theology within these three Abrahamic faiths. Rather, as scholar Kendall Soulen observes, "each of the three religions conceives of its relationship to the other two in ways that are distinctive to its own character and scriptural sources."[11] Thus, there is an Islamic theology of Islam in relation to Christianity and Judaism, and likewise for each Abrahamic faith in relation to the others.[12] Nevertheless, underlying these distinctive theological interpretations, we can discern certain principles of divine love that are shared by all Abrahamic faiths, and extend beyond them as well.

For Practitioners of Divine Love

The intended audience for this book is primarily serious spiritual seekers, contemplative practitioners, and aspiring mystics on the path of divine love. This includes people from all faiths and all walks of life, and specifically includes those who identify as "spiritual but not religious." The key common denominator is a deep personal commitment to realizing God, or to put it another way, a commitment to realizing, serving, and ultimately *becoming* the esoteric essence of one's particular faith tradition. Such practitioners are open or indeed eager to learn from the wisdom of other traditions. They are pursuing a goal of understanding the essence of the universal spiritual path of love. If this speaks to you, you are already aware, perhaps painfully so, of the limitations of exoteric religion and theological analyses, and are striving to realize the unifying truth that lies beyond the seeming contradictions among different faiths.

While this book is not tailored for theologians, religious scholars, or exoteric religious leaders, it certainly does not exclude them, though it may well fail to satisfy them. The focus here is on what seems most essential for practitioners on a path of divine love. In exploring multiple traditions in a single book, there is an obvious risk of creating a superficial analysis that glosses over the rich sacred depths and unique subtleties of each tradition considered. Various theological details and valid perspectives and are necessarily omitted or addressed only briefly. Yet this omission is hopefully outweighed by the inspiring commonalities revealed across the traditions. My purpose here is to ask these questions:

- What are the central inspirations and teachings from the major scriptures for practitioners on the path of divine love?
- What do the scriptures themselves, and leading mystics, tell us are their most important teachings?
- Why do mystics report similar transcendent testimony across the faith traditions? How can finite human beings actually "become one" with the Infinite Godhead, as reported in this transcendent testimony?
- What light does contemporary science shed on these questions?
- What are the universal core principles and practices of divine love, and how can we incorporate them in our own spiritual journey?

There is a great need today for new understandings of how the religious traditions relate to one another, and how their remarkable differences are dwarfed by their even more remarkable common ground. The profound truth of the unifying essence underlying the scriptures and practices of these religious traditions deserves to be clearly articulated and loudly proclaimed—both for its innate glory, and because a universal path of love offers fertile ground for a potential reconciliation across the faith traditions. The transformative path of divine love is the greatness of each of these traditions, and it is their entire purpose in the first place: to transform the human being into a living instrument of divine love and will.

What Is Meant by "God"?

The title *Belonging to God* calls for clarification of what I mean by "God." Some people may object immediately to the use of God language, which is understandable for a multitude of reasons. First is the oppressive conception of God depicted in certain religious texts as a punishing, vindictive, warlike tyrant. Second is the false attribution of the masculine gender to God, and the associated patriarchal oppression that afflicts all major religions (a subject addressed further below). Third is the absence of objective proof that God exists.[13] Fourth is the tragic reality of violence, terrorism, and unjust wars that have been carried out "in the name of God." Fifth is the naive image of God as a wise old man with a white beard floating in the sky. Sixth is that God as Creator or theistic being has little or no meaning for adherents of nontheistic spiritual traditions. Beyond these objections, in the context of interreligious dialogue, there are many different conceptions of God and levels of God experience, so the use of a single word to refer to them all could be seen as creating more confusion than clarity.

Notwithstanding these legitimate concerns, the fact remains that the word "God" is the primary linguistic category and conceptual symbol we have for referring to the ultimate source of existence and all life, regardless of how God is conceived or defined. Moreover, the three religions explored in this book all have "God" strongly at their core, so it makes sense to speak of God in this book, with intent to honor and include different notions of God.

You are encouraged to invoke your own concept of God, and, at the same time, not to take any fixed notion of God too literally, including your own. All concepts of God are inadequate, and fall far short of the living truth or reality or being to which they point.

God as Ultimate Reality

The question still remains, who or what is God? Any attempt to define God seems fraught with peril, but one approach to this inquiry is to draw upon the collective wisdom of a remarkable gathering of religious and spiritual leaders, from all the major world religions, who have been meeting annually for more than thirty years. The Snowmass Interreligious Conference, convened by Cistercian monk Thomas Keating, includes leaders from diverse faiths, including Protestant, Catholic, Eastern Orthodox, Islamic, Sufi, Jewish, Native American, Hindu (Vedanta), Buddhist (including Theravada, Zen, and Tibetan), Taoist, and no tradition. In the course of their extensive dialogues, this group generated a list of eight points of agreement, as follows:

1. The world religions bear witness to the experience of Ultimate Reality, to which they gave various names.
2. Ultimate Reality cannot be limited by any name or concept.
3. Ultimate Reality is the ground of infinite potentiality and actualization.
4. Faith is opening, accepting, and responding to Ultimate Reality. Faith in this sense precedes every belief system.
5. The potential for human wholeness—or, in other frames of reference, enlightenment, salvation, transcendence, transformation, blessedness—is present in every human being.

6. Ultimate Reality may be experienced not only through religious practices, but also through nature, art, human relationships, and service to others.
7. As long as the human condition is experienced as separate from Ultimate Reality, it is subject to ignorance and illusion, weakness and suffering.
8. Disciplined practice is essential to the spiritual life; yet spiritual attainment is not the result of one's own efforts, but the result of the experience of oneness with Ultimate Reality.[14]

These points are not presented as ultimate, definitive, or carved in stone. On the contrary, "We were surprised and delighted to find so many points of similarity and convergence in our respective paths," explains Keating, "and so we present these 'Points of Agreement' as a gift to all who will welcome them, to all who will use them to promote understanding."[15]

Receiving this gift in this spirit, these points comprise a possible conceptual description of God: simply replace "Ultimate Reality" with "God" in the above eight principles. This offers a way of thinking about God that is inclusive across many religions and is consistent with the spirit of this book.

Some might object that describing God in this way is too impersonal, because God is a living "theistic" cosmic Being, with whom intimate relationship is possible, whereas the term "Ultimate Reality" does not seem to carry this implication. Others might question whether Ultimate Reality (or God) even exists.[16] Still others may wish to explicitly include the feminine aspect of the Divine, or some other aspect.

For all such questions and concerns, I encourage you to formulate your own conceptions of God. *Whatever* is responsible for existence, regardless of how it came about, we humans require a way to refer to it, and for this purpose the label of "God" is longstanding and understood by all, regardless of how it is conceived. Of course, we know that every conception of God is woefully inadequate to the Supreme Reality itself. Therefore, in some sense, all conceptions of God are equally valid, and inherently inadequate, as ways to refer to That Which Has No Name, yet which comes into the depths of the heart by whatever name we invoke.

As you invoke your own connection or concept of God, you are encouraged to also release attachment to any fixed concept of God, perhaps cultivating the provocative insight of fourteenth-century mystic Meister Eckhart that our ultimate task is to free ourselves of God altogether.[17]

Divine Love in Other Religions

The basic principles of divine love, and the transformative path of the heart articulated in chapters 4 through 8, can, I believe, be extended to include most other religions. For example, Judaism is the parent tradition of Christianity and bears close resemblance to Islam in many respects. The Jewish mystical process of *devakut* (God realization), the teachings of the Kabbalah and the Zohar, and leading mystics such as the Ba'al Shem Tov and Shimon bar Yochai all correspond closely to what is presented in this book. A wealth of excellent works on mystical and contemplative Judaism is available by authors such as Ted Falcon, Yoel Glick, Arthur Green, Daniel Matt, and Rami Shapiro. Other traditions, including Sikhism, Shinto, Baha'i, and various indigenous shamanistic traditions, also include a mystical tradition of the heart that is broadly similar to what is presented here.

In the case of Buddhism, the path of divine love may seem less applicable at first blush, largely because Buddhism is deemed a "nontheistic" tradition. Although the Buddha remained purposefully silent on speculative issues such as God's existence (because he was focused instead on practical teachings to end suffering), this reticence gave rise over the centuries to a seeming denial of God in Buddhism, which has often been regarded as a serious obstacle to meaningful dialogue between practitioners of Buddhism and theistic religions. Yet remarkable exchanges between Buddhism and Christianity over the past few decades have led to breakthroughs in mutual understanding and discovery of both common ground and differences. Examples include the Gethsemane Encounter series of dialogues between Buddhist and Christian monastics, and dialogues between the Dalai Lama and leading Christian contemplatives, including Father Laurence Freeman, Brother David Steindl-Rast, Father Thomas Keating, and others. Recent interfaith scholarship is even narrowing the theistic/nontheistic gap. "While Buddhism is deemed nontheistic," writes scholar B. Alan Wallace, "the cosmogonies of Vajrayana Buddhism, Vedanta, and Neoplatonic Christianity have so much in common that they could almost be regarded as varying interpretations of a single theory."[18] Wallace further demonstrates that Buddhist Dzogchen and Christian apophatic mystical practice have a great deal in common, and Christian theologian Paul Knitter proclaims that "without Buddha I could not be a Christian."[19] After decades of interfaith monastic dialogue, Zen master Thich Nhat Hanh says, "I do not think there is that much difference between Christians and Buddhists.

Most of the boundaries we have created between our two traditions are artificial. Truth has no boundaries. Our differences may be mostly differences in emphasis."[20]

Meanwhile, Islamic scholar Reza Shah-Kazemi demonstrates remarkable common ground between Islam and Buddhism, in his recent book by that title with an enthusiastic foreword by the Dalai Lama. Shah-Kazemi provides a wealth of compelling scriptural and metaphysical support for his groundbreaking thesis that "the ultimate Reality affirmed by Buddhism is nothing other than what the monotheists refer to as God; or more precisely ... the Essence of God."[21] Finally, core Buddhist meditation practices, the central importance of *bodhicitta* (heart wisdom), the mysticism of Pure Land and Tibetan schools of Buddhism, and Dzogchen in particular, all suggest that Buddhist mysticism accords closely with the transformative path of the heart presented in this book. Although space precludes detailed treatment, the basic outlines of how Buddhism could potentially be aligned with this synthesis of divine love are presented briefly in Appendix 1.

Seeking the Exalted, but Not Ignoring the Shadow

This book deliberately highlights the best and brightest aspects of scripture and religion, rather than the dumbest and dimmest elements that are widely cited today to criticize religion or reject it altogether. The optimistic approach taken here does not deny the negative elements of religion, which I address briefly when necessary, but my primary focus is on the positive aspects of religion—for two key reasons. First, plenty of ink has been spilled and cyberspace is overfilled with the problems and the shadow side of religion. Every religion has its negative side, and the religions do share certain systemic patterns of deep darkness, including religious violence, exclusivism, patriarchy, misogyny, homophobia, intolerance, and the like. I acknowledge all of this, but there is already much information available on these matters. Second, and more importantly, I emphasize the high ground of religions because they call the human soul to a profound path of love that leads to union with God. Despite their problems and failings, religions offer profound potential for human transformation.

Consistent with this approach, I also choose not to dwell on the problematic aspects of scripture here. Again, I do not deny the challenging portions of scripture, as well as various passages of scripture that seem less inspired, if not altogether misleading, irrelevant, or mistaken. Such difficulties are found in all scriptures, as well as religious institutions. Other contemporary writers address these challenges skillfully and their critical work enables us to choose a different tack here. If you are interested in learning about these challenging dimensions of religion for the three major Abrahamic faith traditions, an excellent recent book is *Religion Gone Astray: What We Found at the Heart of Interfaith*.[22]

There is another even more compelling reason for setting aside the negative and contradictory aspects of scripture. The spiritual similarities between the scriptures and mystics of the religions are deep, and these parallels are far more profound and illuminating than the religious differences. Taken together, these religious parallels point to something universal and uplifting that the faith traditions share in common. To make this clear is a primary goal of this book.

The true purpose of religion is not only to show the pathway *to* God, and *in* God, but also to guide and empower human beings to actually walk the path of radical spiritual transformation. Failing this, religion fails its true purpose. As Father Thomas Keating puts it, "the sole purpose of Christianity is transformation into Christ—nothing else."[23] Similarly, we can say that the sole purpose of Buddhism is transformation into Buddha, the sole purpose of (Vaishnavite) Hinduism is transformation into Krishna, and so forth. Tragically, many religious institutions, churches, congregations, and fellowships seem to have failed utterly in this primary purpose. This is unconscionable, but it is certainly not a new phenomenon. Jesus chastised the Pharisees for posing as wise spiritual leaders, parading their vestments and rituals, yet failing to enter the kingdom of heaven themselves and not allowing others to enter. The Buddha chastised the Brahmanic priests of his time for similar corruption of the true heart and purpose of religion, for masquerading as wise elders yet proffering only empty ritualism. The situation has changed little over the centuries.

No doubt some will regard the entire approach of this book to be naive or unrealistic, perhaps invoking arguments like those in Reinhold Niebuhr's trenchant classic on human evil, *Moral Man, Immoral Society*.[24] To all such, my reply is that love is stronger than evil and ignorance. As Martin Luther King said (in response to Niebuhr), "If we do not balance our pessimism about human nature with optimism about divine nature, we will overlook the cure of grace."[25] God and love existed long before humanity was created. Those who, in the depths of the heart, stand on love for God stand on something that existed before the universe was ever born. Love and truth predate and permeate every religion, and are therefore independent of all religions; "perfect love casts out fear" (1 John 4:18). Let us therefore take our stand *on*, *in*, and *for* love.

The Nondual Path of Divine Love

The path of divine love leads to the highest levels of supreme spiritual realization, including nondual realization of the Absolute (that is, the spiritual realization that the human being and the Absolute are a single reality, not dual entities). There are multiple pathways to spiritual realization, including the path of love (*bhakti*) and the path of spiritual awareness or wisdom (*jnana*)—both of which lead to the same supreme goal. The path of love is a gradual path that works with the mystic power of love in the heart as the fuel that propels the disciple into radical transformation and full spiritual realization.

In some contemporary and historical Hindu (Advaita Vedanta) and Buddhist schools as well as certain nondual schools of spirituality, the path of divine love and devotion is mistakenly considered to be limited or inferior. The assumption is that the path of love is inherently dualistic and inclined toward theistic devotion or religiosity. It is therefore deemed less advanced than the nondual paths of spiritual realization. This bias is nothing new; Sri Aurobindo describes the attitude clearly in his wry observation that seekers on the path of knowledge "seem often, if not to despise, yet to look downward from their dizzy eminence on the path of the devotee as if it were a thing inferior, ignorant, good only for souls that are not ready for the heights of the Truth."[26]

This attitude is based on two factors: a mistaken understanding of genuine *bhakti*, and a preferential bias toward the *jnani* path because it is considered the more direct path to realization. These factors, taken together, can lead to a kind of prejudice or unspoken nondual fundamentalism that dismisses *bhakti* as a less evolved spiritual path. Regarding the first factor, the path of love is widely misunderstood as inherently dualistic because the path begins with the human devotee focusing on an object of spiritual veneration or worship. The notion of an individual self, or "I," is recognized as an ontologically inadequate or mistaken view; hence, the *bhakti* path is dismissed as an ignorant or simplistic approach. Here we might perhaps ask the nondualist: Do you regard Jesus to be less spiritually evolved, because he "stooped" to dualism in the Garden of Gethsemane when he asked God if it was possible to take the cup of crucifixion from his lips? In any case, the true process of *bhakti* moves beyond the early dualistic stages into supreme love or *prema bhakti*, which culminates in a sustained nondual merging of lover and divine Beloved. This abiding in oneness with God is called *baqa* in Sufism, and could also be called "nondual" *bhakti*.

The second factor, the notion that the *jnani* path is superior because it is more direct, relates to a sectarian bias or rivalry that dates back to Hindu philosopher Shankara (eighth century) or earlier. Shankara advocated the path of knowledge over the path of love, even though when he reached a certain impasse in his own spiritual progress, he was able to overcome it only after engaging in intensive devotion to the Goddess, as expressed in some of his great hymns. More recently, Sri Ramakrishna has advocated the path of love as much easier for most people than the path of knowledge, which is also consonant with the teaching of the Bhagavad Gita. The "best" path is not the same for all, nor even the same for a given disciple at each stage of his spiritual life. Different spiritual methodologies and pathways are suited for different human temperaments, and also for different stages in a disciple's spiritual journey.

Hermeneutics of the Heart

In this inquiry we strive to approach the scriptures and the mystics with an open, humble heart, characterized by a gracious sensitivity and receptivity, coupled with an appropriate skepticism. The Qur'an is a "shy bride," says Rumi, who will not reveal her secrets to a demanding interrogation or antagonistic scrutiny. This is no less true of other scriptures. Therefore we expand our being inwardly to receive the fullness of the spiritual transmission that comes through the sacred scriptures, without abandoning our critical intellect, and thereby cultivate a discerning "hermeneutics of the heart."[27] We embrace the scriptures—whether Hindu, Christian, Islamic, Buddhist, or others—for what they actually intend to inspire and impart and transform, and not merely for what they say, and still less for what the various religious institutions say about them.

All scriptures are regarded here as the "word of God," yet with various degrees and forms of human error and confusion mixed in, including certain outdated passages, which constitute an inevitable part of any scripture. This necessitates the daunting task of having to recognize which parts of scripture are the genuine, indispensable essentials of the spiritual transmission—something that can only be done properly in the depths of the heart. We are aided in this process by considering multiple scriptures together, for certain striking themes and core messages emerge that are clearly emphasized across the traditions. These take on a shining radiance when viewed in the resplendent light of multiple faith traditions.

Esoteric Universalism: Divine Love in Perennial Philosophy

The type of perennialism advanced in this book might be called "esoteric universalism," referring to the Absolute Godhead that constitutes the mystical core of all religions. This is both hidden and universal, transcending all finite conditioning. Outer forms of religious traditions, on the other hand, are very different from one another and are often contradictory or mutually exclusive. This form of perennialism has the advantage of preserving the exoteric distinctions, thus honoring the uniqueness and integrity of the different religious traditions. We can celebrate the rich diversity of religions, and uphold the unique particularity of each, while also highlighting their universal esoteric oneness. Esoteric universalism differs from certain other schools of religious pluralism, such as those espoused by John Hick and others, which posit that religious differences are simply a consequence of sociocultural constructs and are therefore dispensable. Such an approach denies each religion its own uniqueness and self-definition in order to advance an overarching universal truth that all religions express. The irony of this type of religious "inclusivism" is that in denying the particular historical forms of religions and their unique divine origins, it becomes itself exclusivist, thereby also alienating potential allies within the traditional religious communities themselves. Esoteric universalism, on the other hand, fosters a deep recognition of the underlying universal substance of all religions, yet also honors the uniqueness of each. This approach supports practitioners of any given faith in becoming ever more firmly rooted in their own tradition, while simultaneously honoring all the others. As the ancient hermetic principle puts it, "Each contains all, and all contain each."

God Is Beyond Gender

God has been constructed as male in most religions, coupled with male domination and strong patriarchal norms in religious institutions. This has wrought profound damage, particularly to women and non–hetero-conforming people, but also to men. Even religions that uphold a balance of masculine and feminine deities in their theologies (such as Hinduism and Vajrayana Buddhism) remain male dominated in their customs and institutions. As Buddhist teacher Jetsunma Tenzin Palmo observes, "Patriarchy is entrenched in all religious traditions, where one might have hoped that more wisdom, compassion and sheer empathy would have manifested over the ages. But alas …"[28] This pervasive form of gender injustice is beginning to receive far more attention than ever before, and transformative changes are slowly beginning to emerge.

God is inherently beyond gender, or rather God contains and transcends all possible genders. In the book of Genesis, as humanity is first created, God says, "Let *us* create humanity in *our* image … male and female …" (Gen. 1:26–27). At the very outset of the Bible, God identifies as male and female, but this androgynous nature of Divinity seems to have quickly disappeared as the tradition developed (although St. Paul intimates that there is neither male nor female in Christ [Gal. 3:28]).

In this book I endeavor to avoid the purely masculine association for God whenever possible. When translating from scripture, gender-inclusive translations are chosen if possible, except in cases where it renders the translation too awkward. "He" and "him" are translated as "God" if possible, which sometimes results in its own awkwardness because the word "God" is repeated excessively, but I accept this limitation rather than attributing a gender to God. Occasionally, I deploy the dual pronoun "him/her," which has its own awkwardness and implies that God is dualistic, which even if partially valid is certainly not the truth. I use masculine and feminine pronouns alternately throughout the text, and I usually stick to one gender within a given paragraph, in hopes of achieving an overall gender balance in the text as a whole. Finally, there are places where none of the above approaches or fixes seems adequate, and I leave the original quotation as it is, patriarchal warts and all. I beg understanding in such cases, knowing that God him/herself is quite beyond all these human mischaracterizations.

Transforming Patriarchy in Religion

The world religions are all afflicted by gender injustice. Women have been systematically regarded as intrinsically inferior, leading to gender-based

oppression and exploitation in religious communities. The female prophetic voice has been repressed in all religions, and a strong masculine
bias has marginalized women's spiritual experience, which differs mark-
edly from men's in certain ways.[29] A plethora of sex scandals involving
religious leadership in recent decades has afflicted many faith traditions,
and underscores theologian Elizabeth Johnson's observation that "the truth
about God, the human dignity of women, and the transformation of institutional structures are profoundly interconnected."[30] Although this issue
is not the focus of this book, my other primary life mission is developing
programs and training in gender equity and reconciliation to help cultivate
skillful transformation of gender dynamics in society, both within and outside religious institutions.[31]

The Prophet Muhammad and the Qur'an did much to alleviate horrific
oppression of women in seventh-century Arabia, but the Islamic tradition
nevertheless adopted pre-Islamic patriarchal customs and tribal attitudes,
many of which persist to this day. A similar process took place in other
religions, which replicated the crippling patriarchal structures of the societies in which they emerged. Even in religions such as Sikhism and Baha'i,
laudable for their noble proclamations of gender equality in their founding
scriptures, realities on the ground have fallen far short.

On the positive side, profound change is afoot. Women are ordained
in twelve out of the seventeen largest Christian faith traditions in the
United States.[32] There are sixteen hundred female Hindu priests in India
today,[33] and interfaith projects in India to support destitute women and
bridge religious and caste divisions are emerging, such as the inspiring
Maher project.[34] Islamic feminist scholarship has highlighted sharp discrep-
ancies between Qur'anic support for women and gender equality with the
entrenched patriarchal injustice in Islamic law and societies. More recent
scholarship suggests that feminist conceptions of justice are not as fully
reconcilable with the Qur'an as originally envisioned, but a thriving school
of feminist *tafsir* (Qur'anic exegesis) is rapidly growing and changing the
face of Islam in ways unthinkable just two decades ago.[35]

Theologian Beverly Lanzetta has developed a new pathway of feminine spirituality called *via feminina*. In traditional Christian mysticism, *via
positiva* and *via negativa* refer to the kataphatic and apophatic mystical paths,
first articulated by the sixth-century monk Dionysius. The kataphatic path
entails affirmation of God and spiritual presence (Divine Word), whereas

the apophatic path entails the negation of all concepts of God (Divine Silence). Lanzetta proposes a third way, *via feminina*, that "extends the apophatic process not only to language and conceptual ideas about God, but also to the gender disparity codified within its spiritual practices and contemplative paths." Lanzetta analyzes the spiritual suppression of women in religion, and the need for women to pass through a "dark night of the feminine" stage in their spiritual development "in order to 'un-say' and 'un-become' the internalized inferiority that oppresses or denigrates her soul." The *via feminina* thus heals and restores women's dignity and worth, and "maps out a spiritual path to women's divine humanity."[36]

Despite the systemic gender bias in religion, in the chapters that follow I encourage you to be circumspect in considering the scriptures and mystics explored here, for three reasons. First, the time for transforming gender oppression is only now arriving; its time had not yet come when the scriptures were written. The masculine gender bias is, of course, present in the ancient scriptures and testimonies of mystics, both male and female, and is thus discernable in the texts explored in this book. Second, despite this patriarchal bias, the three scriptures examined here all made crucial strides to uplift the status of women in their day, and were extremely progressive at the time they were written. In the Bhagavad Gita, Krishna proclaims, in radical departure from brutally repressive norms of the time (around 500 BCE), that women and people of the lowest caste are capable of the highest spiritual attainment and realization. The Qur'an gave remarkable rights to women, such as the right to own and inherit property, and to retain property in divorce—rights that were denied to Western women for at least another thousand years. Jesus repeatedly defied the gender bias of his day, and, according to biblical scholar Walter Wink, he "violated the mores of his time in every single encounter with women recorded in the four Gospels."[37] Finally, despite rampant patriarchy, many male mystics (such as Ibn Arabi) recognized gender injustice far ahead of their time and skillfully overcame it within their own spheres.[38]

Without denying the gender bias in these religions, there is nevertheless a profound light and wisdom in these traditions—let us harvest this deep wisdom. And rather than finding fault with the ancient scriptures for gender discrimination, let us instead forge new pathways to transform *today's* religious institutions that continue to perpetuate these injustices.

Toward that end, the Gender Equity and Reconciliation International project (co-founded by Rev. Cynthia Brix and myself) recently led an entourage of twelve religious leaders from six countries to the Parliament of World Religions, where we jointly presented a panel session titled "Transforming Patriarchy in Religion: The Promise of Gender Reconciliation." It was a small gesture compared to the vast need, but an important step in a promising direction.

The Key to Spiritual Life

The mind is the source of all analyses of religious distinctions, yet the thinking mind is also the essential obstacle to be overcome in spiritual life. "I think, therefore I am [stuck]" is a potential stumbling block for all of us. We are identified with our minds and thoughts, and this is the primary challenge that must be surmounted. Identification with the mind is the normal unenlightened human condition, and the mind cannot be overcome by means of the mind itself. This is why theology and scripture alone, for all their value, are inadequate to the task. Something "higher" is required.

Identification with thought is one of three fundamental knots of the heart, and in genuine spiritual life we strive to untie this knot and liberate ourselves from this identification. This is a deep task of spiritual life and should not be misconstrued here as anti-intellectual bias—far from it. We honor the mind for its remarkable talents and capacities, and indeed we rely heavily upon the mind—but as servant, not master. The normal human condition has it the other way around: We are the unwitting slaves of our mind and thoughts, which create our world and cover our hearts. We don't see this, and so we mistake our mind-created world to be reality.

Because the mind is the primary obstacle to be overcome in spiritual realization, the various products of the mind—ideas, books, paradigms, philosophies, and theologies—however essential, are all potential traps. The key to authentic spiritual life is direct connection to the Spirit deep within the heart—and following this connection precisely and unwaveringly, rather than any outer prescription or formula. The truth is written in our hearts, not carved in stone. Without this deep connection to Spirit from within, authentic spiritual life is ultimately futile. The mind must be trained and disciplined, to be sure, but in its quest for complete understanding on its own terms the mind may interfere or complicate spiritual matters unnecessarily. There is a significant danger in religious life of becoming overly enamored of the scriptures or theologies as inspiration, philosophy, literature, teachings, or whatever—and missing the One Thing most essential: intensive practice that leads to direct, humble connection to the living Spirit. This is not to deny the importance of proper intellectual training and understanding, but rather to relinquish the mind's insistent demand that everything must be understood on its terms, in cogent concepts and tidy logical frameworks. In spirituality and mysticism the mind *cannot* fully understand; an altogether different kind of mastery is required. As the Sufis put it, "to understand the *in*ability to understand is true understanding."[39]

This caveat may seem ironic at the outset of a book that focuses extensively on the scriptures and the traditions, seeking to outline a grand universal path of divine love. Yet we focus on scripture and mystics precisely because they illuminate a profound wisdom, one that human beings desperately need and that our contemporary society has largely rejected. Moreover, the scriptures of different traditions are often profoundly aligned in their foundational teachings. This alignment provides even greater support and clarity to this timeless wisdom, which constitutes a powerful inspiration and motivation in itself. Nevertheless, the approach adopted here should not be construed as an implicit recommendation for exhaustive study of diverse scriptures and mystics as the essence of the spiritual path—not at all. What is absolutely essential is to connect with God directly, through the heart; everything else is secondary.

Enough preliminaries. Let us begin!

> Oh Beloved! How can I ever know You, when You are the inwardly hidden who is not known?
> How can I not know you, when wheresoever I turn, there is Your Face!
>
> —Ibn Arabi

Scriptures of
Divine Love

The Yoga of Divine Love in the Bhagavad Gita

The Unreal has never existed. The Real never ceases to be.

—Bhagavad Gita 2:16

"Almost *nobody* knows the deep secret of the Gita!" exclaimed my spiritual teacher one day. She spoke in a forceful whisper, as if to suggest that this disclosure itself was a secret. Her exasperation came after I had been pummeling her with questions, nonstop, for months, in my struggle to unravel the deeper meaning of this most revered of Indian scriptures, the Bhagavad Gita (often called simply "the Gita"). As she expounded further, it became clear that included in this "nobody" were many pundits, scholars, and even spiritual leaders who illustriously quote and comment on the Gita. Indeed, even the great yogi Sri Yukteswar, when asked if he knew the spiritual meaning of the Gita, had the humility to reply, "No, even though my eyes and mind have run through its pages many times."[1]

Let me hasten from the outset to include myself among those who make no claim to know the deep secret of the Gita, or of the Gospels or the Qur'an for that matter—despite my aspiration to realize and live their truth. So it may seem imprudent, or worse, for me even to set fingers to keyboard on this topic. However, I write this book not from any claim to special knowledge, authority, or spiritual insight, but out of great love for the scriptures, and a burning desire to follow where they lead us. Like all profound scriptures, the Gita is not to be understood and digested as information, but rather to be absorbed, practiced, and experienced as a living transformation at the core of one's being.

The Gita is the most celebrated and widely read scripture of Hinduism, both inside and outside India. In the short space of this chapter

I hope to impart something of the resplendent beauty and magnificent depth of this scripture, focusing on selected passages and verses that relate most directly to the path of divine love.[2] It is important to begin with a brief glimpse of the theology and metaphysics, as well as the content and flow, of several Gita chapters to convey a sense of this scripture and the deeper context of its remarkable teaching on divine love. References for quoted verses are provided in parentheses, but I encourage you at first reading to ignore these and the quotation marks, and simply drink in the flow of ideas, narrative, and inspiration.

Approaching the Bhagavad Gita

"I will not fight!" (2:9) declares Arjuna at the beginning of the Bhagavad Gita—bitterly defying the will of God. Arjuna casts down his bow and arrows as he faces the opposing Kauravas army in the battlefield. His charioteer, Krishna, is an incarnation of God, but Arjuna does not yet realize this. Krishna is asking Arjuna to fight to defend his people from annihilation, but Arjuna refuses, presenting a full range of compelling rational and moral arguments. In this high-stakes drama of an impending war, Arjuna eloquently justifies his refusal to fight. Yet in so doing he makes the very mistake that we humans are constantly making, which is to righteously assert our human will in defiance of the pathway ordained for us by divine will that leads us to our highest destiny and spiritual realization. The profound struggle between Arjuna's human will and the divine will enjoined upon him by Krishna is all the more poignant in the tense battlefield drama of an incipient brutal war in which Arjuna is called to defeat his own kith and kin. By the end of the scripture, however, after all that transpires in the interim, Arjuna finally concedes to God, "I will fulfill thy command" (18:73). The intervening chapters of the Gita articulate the major practices and stages in the process of spiritual transformation that leads a human being from normal egoic identity and willfulness (*my* will, not Thy will) to the radical stance of full surrender to God (*Thy* will, not my will).

It is crucial to interpret Arjuna's call to "fight" very carefully in this scripture. First, on the level of society and human morality, this battle is one of self-defense for the virtuous minority of the Pandava clan, whose rightful half of the kingdom was effectively stolen from them in a rigged dice game, and who are now threatened with total annihilation.

All attempts to mediate a peace agreement have utterly failed. Even God himself, incarnated in human form as Krishna, has pursued every available avenue to negotiate peace and avoid war—all to no avail because Duryodhana, leader of the opposing Kauravas army, will have nothing of it. Not only is the evil Duryodhana bent upon the destruction of Arjuna and his brothers' clan, but Duryodhana earlier swindled them out of all their property, and then won them and Arjuna's wife, Draupadi, as slaves in the dice game. To top it off, the guffawing Duryodhana attempts to disrobe Draupadi in the royal court, in full humiliating view of all the senior statesmen and religious leadership of the kingdom. Although Draupadi eloquently defends herself, her pleas for help to the elders of the royal Kuru court fall on deaf ears, and her honor is saved only at the last minute by the miraculous intervention of Krishna. For all these reasons, war has become inevitable—even Krishna can't stop it—and at the beginning of the Gita, it seems the likely outcome might well be the total destruction of the Pandavas, whose small army is vastly outnumbered by the Kauravas army. Given this background, the impending war in the Gita must be understood as the self-defense of an innocent, exploited people facing total annihilation. In this sense and this sense only, can the Bhagavad Gita be regarded as "justifying" war.

There is another, much deeper interpretation of the significance of Arjuna's call to "fight," which Mahatma Gandhi and most other commentators have emphasized. The Gita is to be understood and applied in symbolic terms as representing the essence of the human journey of spiritual transformation. The war poignantly symbolizes the time-honored inner struggle between the lower and the higher dimensions of human nature. "There must be war in this life" remarked St. Teresa of Avila,[3] and she did not mean just ordinary warfare or human conflict, although she had plenty of that to contend with in her own ministry. More importantly, she was referring to the fundamental human struggle against our own lower nature, which is an essential battle undertaken by every sincere human aspirant to manifest our highest purpose and spiritual destiny in life. This is the inherently challenging process of spiritual transformation, the inner struggle that is known as the "greater *jihad*" in Islam. Our highest spiritual destiny is often difficult for us to see, and even more difficult to manifest. The transformative process requires tremendous commitment, determination, and perseverance, and it is generally opposed by our ego's cherished attachments or desires for its version of our life. Therefore, an inner struggle ensues, and the Bhagavad Gita lays out the various challenges and dangers of this transformative struggle, coupled with a range of effective practices and progressive stages of spiritual realization. The Gita emphasizes the central importance of being guided by the divine light or essence within us, here symbolized by the incarnation of God in the form of Krishna.

Multiple Spiritual Paths in the Gita

The Bhagavad Gita articulates the essential stages on the path of spiritual realization. Several different spiritual pathways are articulated in the Gita, each suited for a different human character type. This is one reason the Gita has enjoyed such wide appeal: It offers a broad spectrum of spiritual pathways. The usual delineation includes three primary pathways: *karma yoga* (path of selfless service or action), *jnana yoga* (path of knowledge), and *bhakti yoga* (path of devotion). Sometimes *raja* yoga, the "royal path of meditation," is counted as a fourth path, but it is generally viewed as a key methodology particularly for the *jnana yoga* path. These categories of spiritual path are not rigid; there is considerable overlap among them, and each path encompasses the others to a significant degree. These various paths accommodate a broad variety of human character types, and a similar diversity of paths can also be found in other traditions. The Dalai Lama has observed, for example, that the Buddha offered contradictory teachings at times, not because he was confused, but because he was addressing different temperaments among his disciples.

Regardless of the path, the goal is the same; "All paths lead to Me" (4:11), says Krishna. The multiple paths articulated in the Gita all lead to union with God, and their distinct methodologies do not necessarily conform to a single logically consistent framework. This has sometimes confused Western scholars, a few of whom have criticized the Gita as internally inconsistent and therefore an inferior work. The problem is not with the Gita, however, but with the scholars' twofold misunderstanding. First, they fail to recognize that multiple spiritual paths are advocated to suit diverse temperaments, and second, the nature of spiritual teachings themselves cannot always be articulated in conceptual, purely rational, or linguistic frameworks, but inevitably entail paradox—hence the inevitable apparent contradictions.

Stages of the Spiritual Journey in the Gita

There are distinct stages in the spiritual journey that all disciples must pass through, and the structure of the Gita as a whole is organized into these stages. The Gita can thus be viewed as a progressive revelation of the path to union with God, and it broadly accords with the classical stages of mysticism: purification, illumination, and union with God. Chapters 1 through 6 address the process of spiritual purification, and introduce the basic spiritual teachings and practices. Chapters 7 through 11 address spiritual illumination and revelation, progressively revealing to Arjuna what and who Krishna is. Chapters 12 through 18 deal with the path of divine love, cosmology, the encounter with darkness, faith, renunciation, and the ultimate secret to union with God. This is an oversimplification, but the key elements and stages of the spiritual journey are all represented.

As Gandhi observes, the Gita sets out in "scientific" form what Jesus puts forward in rhetorical form in his parables and in the Sermon on the Mount. The teachings of the Gita are in many ways remarkably close to those of the Gospels, and they also closely mirror the central teachings of mystical Islam. As a whole, the Gita can be viewed as a scripture on the spiritual path of love, and also the path of knowledge, and also the path of selfless action, as well as an integration of all these paths, which is the "integral yoga" approach adopted by the twentieth-century Indian sage Sri Aurobindo.

Cosmology and Levels of Consciousness in the Gita

The Gita's "developmental model" of spiritual consciousness, if we might call it that, is summarized succinctly in one verse: "The senses are higher than the body, the mind is higher than the senses; above the mind is the *buddhi* (intuitive integral perception), and above the *buddhi* is the *Atman* (soul)" (2:42). Human consciousness "rises" through these different levels or stages as we develop spiritually, and each level becomes subsumed or "dissolved" into the next higher level.

The lowest level is the dense physical body; next comes the level of the physical senses (*indriyas*), which are in turn subsumed into the next higher level of the mind (*manas*), which means that the mind is able to exercise control over the senses. This stage is familiar to all of us, for example, when we choose to forgo that next sumptuous cookie. At the next higher level, the mind is similarly subsumed or dissolved into the *buddhi*, a subtle perceptive faculty that is described more fully below. The *buddhi* is in turn eventually subsumed into the *Atman*, the highest inner essence of the human being, which as the Upanishads tell us, is one with God: "Atman is Brahman."[4] This description is an oversimplification, to which there are various refinements, but these are the basic levels of consciousness: *indriyas, manas, buddhi, Atman.*

The *buddhi*, a crucial concept in the Gita, refers to higher visionary intelligence or a keen intuitive perceptive faculty that all human beings possess, yet relatively few develop or apply to any significant degree. The *buddhi* is sometimes translated as "intellection," but it is well beyond what we normally think of as intellect; the *buddhi* is both the capacity to perceive a larger whole, as well as the higher or unitive reality that is perceived through such seeing. It can be likened to the awakening of a keen spiritual sensitivity and intuition that directly perceives the inherent oneness of all reality. The *buddhi* synthesizes and illuminates what the *manas* divides and analyzes. The Gita refers frequently to *buddhi yoga* or *buddhi-yukta*, meaning the inner condition of being fully united with or actually "yoked" to the *buddhi*, which is the crucial developmental step that must take place as the precursor for any spiritual development beyond normal egoic consciousness. "Hence the extreme importance of the buddhi yoga," observes Krishnaprem, "for this union, when achieved, brings about a liberation from the 'knots of the heart,' the fetters which had bound the Soul within the prison of separate individuality."[5]

Purification and Spiritual Practice

The early chapters of the Gita focus on key spiritual teachings that inspire and orient the disciple, and include the essential processes of purification. The opening chapter deals with the dejection that every disciple feels to some degree at the beginning of the true spiritual journey. Prior to this stage, there has often been an ecstatic awakening or some key visionary inspiration or breakthrough that inspires one to embark upon the spiritual journey, called "entry into the stream" in Buddhism. However, as one gets going, soon the inevitable process of purification begins, and the disciple begins to realize the demands of the path: that it will cost much that one has held dear, and requires the eradication of certain aspects of oneself to which there may still be strong attachments. Friends, family, cherished preoccupations, and even supportive teachers from the past often become obstacles on the path, and one way or another they have to be renounced. Jesus expresses this dilemma when he says, "Your enemies will be members of your own family" (Matt. 10:36), and this is illustrated dramatically in Arjuna's case as he faces his own cousins, uncles, and former revered teachers arrayed against him on the battlefield.

The Self Does Not Die

"There has never been a time when you and I and everyone gathered here have not existed, nor will there ever be a time when we shall cease to exist" (2:12). Thus Krishna opens his magnificent teachings about the eternity of the human soul in chapter 2. "Unborn, eternal, immutable, immemorial, you do not die when the body dies" (2:20). Krishna then expounds upon the *Atman*, which is generally translated as "soul," or the "Self"—referring to the innermost essence of the human being. "The Self cannot be pierced by weapons or burned by fire; water cannot wet it, nor can the wind dry it.… The Self is everlasting and infinite, standing on the motionless foundations of eternity. The Self is unmanifested, beyond all thought, beyond all change. Knowing this, Arjuna, you should not grieve" (2:23–25).

Krishna continues to bring forth one spiritual gem after another. "The Unreal has never existed; the Real never ceases to be" (2:16).[6] This teaching is found across many religious and metaphysical traditions, particularly in their mystical dimensions. The Real is understood to be the Eternal, which does not manifest but endures supreme, beyond time; whereas the passing forms of manifestation are collectively deemed to be "unreal," precisely because they come and go.

"Just as a reservoir is of little use when the whole countryside is flooded, scriptures are of little use to the illumined person, who sees the Lord everywhere" (2:46). This is the crucial teaching that the spiritual path must be realized in the heart and lived in the everyday life of the disciple. Spiritual life is not a conceptual or intellectual endeavor, and scriptures are at best an aid, which become superfluous for those who are spiritually realized. The Gita goes even further: "When your intelligence crosses beyond the thicket of delusion, then shall you become indifferent to scripture heard, or that which you have yet to hear. When your consciousness, fed up with bewildering scriptural doctrines and their interpretations, settles [finally] into stable deep meditation [*samadhi*], unwavering, then shall you attain to real union [*yoga*]" (2:52–53).

This remarkable teaching flies in the face of religious orthodoxy—revealing that spiritual realization and union with God effectively supersede the scriptures. "So offensive is all this to conventional religious sentiment," observes Sri Aurobindo about these verses, "that attempts are naturally made by the convenient and indispensable human faculty of text-twisting to put a different sense on some of these verses, but the meaning is plain and hangs together from beginning to end."[7] Krishna repeats the same point in a later passage (6:44), but it's important to affirm that the Gita is not dispensing with scripture altogether—far from it. Krishna is making the salient point, found also in Christian scripture, that the Spirit of the living God is not to be found carved in stone, but is written in the heart; "The letter kills, but the Spirit gives life" (see 2 Cor. 3:3–6). In later chapters the Gita extols the scriptures (Vedas and Upanishads) in several places, but the real point here is that God, rather than scripture, is the one true goal of spiritual life. "All the scriptures lead to Me," says Krishna, "I am their author and their wisdom" (15:15). The living God is to be found in the depths of the heart—here and now—in daily life. Otherwise spiritual life is a chimera.

Freedom from Freedom

Arjuna asks the very appropriate question: How does a person of true wisdom or enlightenment walk, sit, and behave in life generally? In short, what makes her "tick"? Krishna's reply to this question in the last eighteen verses of chapter 2 presents a foundational teaching emphasized throughout the Gita, and indeed throughout all Eastern religions. Turning the lens of consciousness inward, the disciple becomes free from being driven by the senses and the mind's incessant stream of desires and aversions, and thereby gradually settles into a serene, steady wisdom (*prajna pratisthita*). "One who is unattached, neither elated by good fortune nor disturbed by misfortune, achieves steady wisdom" (2:57). Ascetic renunciation of sense experience is not advocated here. Not only is it entirely impractical, but more importantly as the Buddha discovered, it does not lead to true wisdom.

A moment of self-reflection reveals how profoundly we are conditioned and motivated in our thought and action by things we want, and by what we wish to avoid. The path advocated here is not a radical renunciation of all this; rather, the renunciation to be practiced is an inner detachment or withdrawal from *identification* with sense experience and mental machination, while still participating in both outwardly. The key is to decouple one's identity from sensation and thought, so that the essence of one's inner self becomes pure awareness itself—more subtle than any thought or sense experience could ever be. Over time this enables a profound inner peace and freedom to emerge, which in turn naturally leads to an outer calm and mastery. This is the beginning of true yoga.

This transformative process takes time and persistent practice, and requires patience and perseverance for genuine mastery to develop. There are pitfalls along the way. The senses and mind, habituated to dominating the person, are not happy to be superseded, and they fight back, sometimes with a vengeance. "Even the mind of a wise person striving for perfection can be swept away by the stormy senses" (2:60). This reveals yet another challenge: it is pointless and even dangerous to detach from outer sense experience, while still indulging in or craving for sense experience inwardly. The detachment must be both outward and inward, supported and inspired by a strong and abiding aspiration for God. "Aspirants abstain from sense pleasures, yet they still crave them. But these cravings disappear when they see the highest goal" (2:59).

Consumer society today strongly conditions us to chase after material benefits and outer rewards and pleasures in life, which desensitize us to the refined intangibles in life and subtle "gifts of the spirit." Spiritual life cultivates a reversal of our desires, for without a profound yearning for God, or ultimate reality, it is difficult to follow the spiritual path of the heart.

Buddhi

The crucial concept of the *buddhi* was introduced earlier as a higher integral perception beyond the mind. To achieve union with the *buddhi* in practice, the mind must be freed from being driven by desire and aversion, a process sometimes referred to as purification, that is found in all schools of mysticism. Otherwise, the obstinate mind will never consent to this higher union. Hence the mind must be trained to withdraw from the pull of the senses, and aspire to something higher. This does not mean ascetic refusal to engage with outer sense activity, as is sometimes mistakenly believed. Rather, it entails a withdrawal from being compulsively driven by outer forces of attraction and aversion that constitute the normal condition of the human being. The shift is best facilitated by adopting specific practices that harmonize the mind, such as meditation and selfless service. The mind is then trained to detach from the constant push and pull of the senses, and by turning inward achieves harmonious mastery over the senses, "just as a tortoise can draw in its limbs at will" (2:58). This results in a luminous peace that descends upon the mind. Then only, not before, the *buddhi* begins to come subtly into view.

Moving Beyond Desires

The next several chapters in the Gita (3–6) develop the above themes further. Chapter 3 begins training the aspirant to detach from being driven by desire (and also aversion, which is just the negative form of desire). "Knowing the *Atman* to be higher than the *buddhi*, and restraining the lower self by the *Atman*, slay the enemy in the form of selfish desire, which is difficult to overcome," declares Krishna (3:43). This may sound extreme, and we might object at first because desire seems innate in us, and even necessary to keep us motivated and engaged in life. Yet we must learn not to automatically follow the call of our senses and whims, and this is in fact the beginning stage of practicing "not my will" (but Thy will), though still hidden in its fullness.

Detaching from desire is an essential first step toward building the strength required for the act of full surrender, which comes later and is not yet asked for by Krishna. Some may object that relinquishing desire will render us sterile and bereft, unmotivated and empty. Yet precisely the opposite is the case. "The true *vairagi* [renunciate] is not a dull, dried up 'holy' person, but a tireless fountain of joyful and inspired life."[8] We can witness many contemporary examples, such as Archbishop Desmond Tutu, Jetsunma Tenzin Palmo, Father Thomas Keating, Sister Lucy Kurien, and so many other great mystics who are anything but dried-up holy people!

Mystic Sacrifice

As we decouple from personal desire, our actions that were previously rooted largely in self-centered pursuits shift toward service and benefit to others. "The eternal, infinite Godhead is present in every act of selfless service" (3:15). How exquisite! Even the simplest gestures of loving kindness bring the Infinite divine presence into our troubled world. This is the key principle of mystic sacrifice. Although "sacrifice" often carries a negative connotation in our contemporary society, all life flows and functions by virtue of this principle. The etymology of the word "sacrifice" is to "make sacred." Every morsel of food we eat is taken from the life of another being, who sacrificed its life for our life. We, too, are to offer ourselves as "food," or nourishing benefit to the life of other beings. In the process, we are "made sacred" without even realizing it.

How do we accomplish this sacrifice in practice? We begin by cultivating discernment of the inner voice or impulse of our higher self under all circumstances. "The disciple must always listen for that voice, and having heard it must always act in accordance with it.... This must be achieved before the next stage, union with the *buddhi*, becomes possible."[9] Here again, the essential training is to relinquish our selfish inclinations and predilections, which are slowly supplanted with more profound and selfless actions.

Avatar: Incarnation of God

Early in chapter 4, Krishna proclaims the remarkable doctrine of the avatar, divine incarnation in the Hindu tradition. In Christianity, God incarnated only once in human form, in Jesus Christ, whereas in Hinduism the avatar refers not to one but to a series of incarnations of God, coming "down" to earth across the ages.

"Whenever righteousness [*dharma*] declines and vice is on the rise, I incarnate Myself on earth. I am born in every age to protect the good, to destroy evil, and to reestablish righteousness [*dharma*]" (4:7–8).

Here the Gita stands right in the middle between the Qur'an and the Gospels. On the one hand, the Gita affirms, as does the Qur'an, that God sends down messengers or prophets to protect the good and establish righteousness—thus proclaiming, just as the Qur'an does, that every people in every age has its divine messenger or prophet, sent from God. On the other hand, the Gita affirms here that God him/herself incarnates on earth, which is absolutely anathema in Islam, yet is affirmed by the Gospel teaching, with the major caveat that Christianity insists that such incarnation took place only once in Jesus the Christ, whereas the Hindu tradition says it has happened a number of times. Nevertheless, on the notion of incarnation, the Gita and the Gospels are closely aligned in a unique manner that other religious traditions do not share.[10] The avatar is "the great Mystery, the birth of the Birthless, the action of the Actionless," and each time the avatar comes, "the Light of the World is revealed to them who walk in darkness."[11]

Meditation Practice

In chapter 6 Krishna gives the basic instructions for silent meditation, which is a foundational practice in all Eastern traditions. The form of meditation is essentially the *dhyana* practice, as set forth by Patanjali, and consists of sitting quietly in an alert but relaxed posture, focusing one's awareness on God as the only goal.

"When meditation is mastered, the mind is unwavering like the flame of a lamp in a windless place" (6:19)—an eloquent metaphor for the quintessential goal of virtually every Eastern meditation practice. "In the still mind, in the depths of meditation, the Self reveals itself" (6:19–20), just as a perfectly still lake reveals the splendor of the sky above. To actually achieve this stilled mind condition is another matter—as difficult for the untrained mind as trying to steady a candle flame in a blustery wind. Stilling the mind is virtually impossible to achieve by working at the level of mind alone; something more, or higher, is required. "No true yoga is possible by the unaided personal will. Thought may be stilled to the point of trance, but unless the self is surrendered to the *Atman* there can be no yoga in the true sense."[12]

This "something more" that is needed is love—the fuel that propels us right through the *manas* and beyond it, into the *buddhi*, and again further beyond into union with God. "By love, God can be gotten and holden, by thought never!" proclaims *The Cloud of Unknowing*, the fourteenth-century Christian mystical text that speaks of the "sharp dart of longing love" that springs from the human heart, passes straight through the "cloud of "unknowing," the veils of obscurity that cover the heart, to pierce the very heart of God.

When the stilling of the mind finally takes place, "the center of consciousness withdraws its attention from the world of outer phenomena, whether of sense or thought, passes through the central point [which is itself], and emerges into the spiritual world of the *buddhi*."[13] This is the all-important "union with the *buddhi*" that is emphasized throughout the Gita, and constitutes the prerequisite for further progress to eventual union with the *Atman* (or enlightenment). The requisite discipline applies not just in the quiet hours of meditation, but entails a constant, twofold practice throughout the day of both "detachment and practice" (6:35), detaching from desire and aversion, and uniting with what is higher than the thinking mind. Another way to think of this discipline is essentially the practice of "not my will, but Thy will"—cultivating continual alignment with the inner voice of spirit, rather than blithely following the whims of personal desire. This is also effectively the practice of the presence of God (a phrase from Christian friar Brother Lawrence, explored in chapter 5), and requires considerable effort, especially in the early stages. Yet when truly followed, "by firmly adhering to the *buddhi*, the disciple gradually attains tranquility in the Self" (6:25). "Among all yogis, the one who worships Me with perfect faith, completely merged into Me, is the most devoted of all" (6:47). Union with the *buddhi* is the first glimpse of oneness beyond individuality, "Wherever they live, they abide in Me" (6:31).

Illumination and Revelation

In the next five chapters (7–11), God reveals himself in stages to Arjuna, who is increasingly opened to ever deeper levels of awe and reverence. The speaking God (Krishna) emphasizes that all worship should be directed to the one true God alone, but God does not proclaim this in any exclusivist sense. Other forms of worship are accepted, yet God makes it clear that worshippers of other gods are actually worshipping the one true God, though without realizing it. "Others whose discrimination is misled by various desires, following their own natures, worship other gods, practicing various rites. Endowed with faith in such gods and performing worship, they obtain the fruits thereof, which are granted by Me alone. But temporary is the fruit for those of small understanding. Those who worship the gods go to the gods, but My devotees come to Me" (7:23–24).

Inclusiveness and Monotheism of the Gita

Krishna enjoins unwavering devotion to the one God alone (*ekabhakti*). "Good people worship Me for different reasons.... The *jnani* who is eternally united with Me, unwavering in devotion, surpasses the others" (7:17). "Even those who worship other gods, with deep faith, they also worship Me alone, though contrary to religious injunctions" (9:23). As translator Winthrop Sargent points out, "All religions are subsumed here, and the speaking God explains that all worship, of whatever kind, comes to him, and that all boons, begged from whatever gods, are granted by him alone. This is an instance of the strong monotheistic element in the Gita, also of its religious tolerance."[14]

Universal Salvation

"All those who take refuge in Me, whatever their birth, race, sex, or caste, will attain the supreme goal; this realization can be attained even by those whom society scorns" (9:33). "Even a sinner becomes holy when he worships me with firm resolve" (9:30). Here we find the same promise of universal salvation from God that we find in the Qur'an and the Gospels, for those who take refuge in God.

Death and Destiny in the Afterlife

Krishna gives a remarkable teaching on death in chapter 8. "Those who remember Me at the time of death will come to Me. Do not doubt this. Whatever occupies the mind at the time of death determines the destination of the dying" (8:5–6). The state of mind of the dying person—in the depths of her thought and heart—actually determines where she goes in the afterlife. Hence the importance of developing a disciplined practice, and always cultivating the divine aspiration, because for "those who remember Me continuously, whose thoughts are never on anything else, I am easily attained" (8:14). Moreover, "Those who worship me and meditate on me constantly, without any other thought, I will provide for all their needs" (9:22). "Never forget this, Arjuna: no one who is devoted to me shall perish" (9:31). This last promise expresses the gift of eternal life, as Jesus also promises (John 3:15).

The Supreme Abode of God

Krishna speaks for the first time of the supreme Godhead in chapter 8, and how it may be attained. "Beyond this unmanifest state there is another, unmanifested Reality, which is eternal, and which, when all beings perish, does not ever perish. Know that Reality, which is called the Unmanifested and Imperishable, to be the ultimate goal. That is my supreme abode" (8:20).

This ultimate abode of God can be attained by human disciples: "This is the supreme Spirit, Arjuna—within which all beings stand, and by which this entire universe is pervaded—and can be attained by one-pointed devotion to the supreme Spirit" (8:22). This is Krishna's profound testimony and promise that to follow earnestly the path of love will lead to the highest Abode of God (*Purushottama*). "Those whose souls are great, abiding in divine nature, worship Me with one-pointed focus, having realized that I am the eternal source of all" (9:13).

The First Commandment and the *Sh'ma* in the Gita

At the halfway point of the Gita, Krishna concludes chapter 9 with a verse that summarizes the whole first half of the Gita, and which he later reveals is part of the supreme secret of the entire scripture. He proclaims to Arjuna,

> Fill your mind with Me, give yourself in love to Me, sacrifice to Me, prostrate yourself before Me. Having thus united your whole self [to Me], with Me as your Supreme Goal, you shall come to Me. (9:34)[15]

Notice how strikingly close this comes to the first commandment in the Gospels, which is also a key component of the *Sh'ma* ("Hear O Israel…") in the Torah: "You shall love the Lord your God with all your heart [*madbhakto*], and with all your soul, and with all your mind [*manmana bhava*], and with all your strength" (Mark 12:33, Deut. 6:4–5). This is the very foundation of the spiritual path of divine love. It is also the first hint of the close correspondence across the scriptures explored in this book.

Why is love such a profound force on the spiritual path? Loving devotion is the power by which human beings can transcend their limitations, and go beyond themselves altogether. "The reason that love and devotion have this power is that they have their roots in the *buddhi*"—the oneness beyond the illusion of separation—"and thus they have the power to pull the disciple right through the "dead-center" of the higher ego where so many others stop, subtly magnifying self with every effort to diminish it."[16] Love is the greatest transformative power. The "higher emotions" elicited by love entail cognitive and intuitive faculties that impart a refined spiritual sensitivity and knowledge, quite beyond the analytic knowledge of the mind. We have all sensed this at least once, when falling in love, and divine love harnesses this exalted power in the heart and directs it toward God.

Revelation of God: Immanent and Transcendent

Revelations of God—both immanent and transcendent—are unveiled in chapters 10 and 11, for which the Gita is perhaps most famous. Krishna first displays his divine immanence, and proclaims that He dwells within all creatures and every manifested form, whether animate or inanimate. "I am the Source of everything; all creation comes from Me. The wise, awe-struck by this realization, worship Me" (10:8).

Immanent Divine

"Whoever knows Me as the Lord of all Worlds, without birth or begin-ning, knows the truth and frees himself from all evil" (10:3), declares Krishna, expounding on divine supremacy. "I am the beginning, middle, and end of creation. I am imperishable Time, I am the Sustainer, whose face is seen everywhere" (10:32–33).

Almost identical declarations are found in the Qur'an about Allah: "Wheresoever you turn, there is His Face." Allah is "Lord of the Worlds," "Most High and Most Great" (2:255), "higher than heaven" (67:16). Allah "arranges every affair from the heavens to the earth" (32:5). "God the One, the Eternal, Absolute … There is none like unto Allah" (112:1–4).

Krishna continues: "I am the Feminine qualities of glory, prosperity, speech, remembrance, intelligence, endurance, and forbearance…. I am the silence of the unknown, and the wisdom of the wise. I am the seed of all exis-tences. [Always] remember that I am, and that I support this entire cosmos with only a fragment of my being" (10:34–42). This last declaration reveals that the immensity of God includes yet greatly exceeds the entire universe.

Similar superlative declarations about Christ are found in the Christian scriptures, in both immanent and transcendent forms. For example, in immanent form:

> Christ is before all things, and in Him all things hold together. Christ is also head of the body, the church; and He is the beginning … [and] first place in everything. (Col. 1:17)

And in transcendent form:

> Christ is the image of the invisible God, the firstborn of all creation. For by Him all things were created, both in the heavens and on earth, visible and invisible. (Col. 1:15–16)

He is the radiance of His glory ... and sustains all things by the word of His power. (Heb. 1:3)

Transcendent Divine

Before Krishna can reveal his transcendent form, he says to Arjuna, "These things cannot be seen with your eyes. Therefore I give you spiritual vision, to perceive my majestic power" (11:8).

Then "Krishna revealed to Arjuna His supremely glorious divine Form. Arjuna saw the infinite Lord, decked with many divine ornaments, possessing many mouths and eyes, wielding many uplifted divine weapons, source of all wonders, whose Face is everywhere. If a thousand suns were to rise simultaneously in the heavens, the blaze of their light might resemble the splendor of that supreme Being" (11:9–12). And further, "I am death, shatterer of worlds" (11:32), a verse that burst into the mind of physicist Robert Oppenheimer, director of the Manhattan Project, when he witnessed the first successful detonation of an atomic bomb in July 1945.

Arjuna is at once awestruck and terrified. He proclaims this overwhelming vision in ecstatic stupor: "O Lord, I see within your body all the gods and every kind of living creature.... I see the ancient sages and the Celestial serpents. I see you everywhere, without beginning, middle, or end. You are the Lord of all creation, and the cosmos is your body. You are the supreme, changeless reality, the one thing to be known.... Your presence fills the heavens and the earth, and expands in every direction" (11:15–20).

Arjuna's vision is reminiscent of a similar ecstatic vision of Plotinus: "For there everything is transparent, ... every being is lucid to every other, ... light runs through light. And each of them contains all within itself, and at the same time sees all in every other.... While some one manner of being is dominant in each, all are mirrored in every other."[17] Thus are unveiled to the mystic, in resplendent glory, all the great beings and powers that humans have worshipped as gods, "not as if standing side-by-side in space, but each a facet mirroring the Whole, and so interfused in being each with each." Christ, Krishna, Buddha, Muhammad, Moses, and all the great teachers of humanity are there, and "whoever worships one draws near to them all."[18]

Power of Devotion

Krishna emphasizes to Arjuna how rare such a vision is:

> "Through my grace, you have received this vision of My radiant, universal form, without beginning or end, which others have not seen."

Exhilarated yet still terrified, Arjuna implores Krishna to assume once again his human form. Krishna complies out of compassion for Arjuna, and continues:

> "It is extremely difficult to obtain the vision you've just seen; even the gods long always to see me in this aspect. Neither knowledge of the Vedas, nor austerity, nor charity, nor sacrifice can bring the vision of Me you have seen. But through undistracted devotion alone [bhaktya ananyaya] can I be known, and seen in truth, and be entered into, Arjuna." (11:52–54)

This is one of several passages throughout the Gita where Krishna unequivocally affirms the superlative power of devotion. If the devotee's heart is entirely and unswervingly directed in love to God alone, then she can not only *know* and *see* God, but most importantly, *enter into* God. In the final verse of chapter 11, according to Shankara, Krishna sums up the entire essence of the Gita:

> Those who do all actions for Me, with Me as their only goal, are devoted to Me, abandoning all attachments, and free from enmity toward any other creature, they come to Me. (11:55)

The Gita's Path of Love and Devotion

Chapter 12 is titled "The Yoga of Loving Devotion," and here Krishna articulates the path of *bhakti*, or divine love and devotion. Various aspects of this path have been introduced in earlier chapters, and now Krishna puts it all together.

The chapter opens with an important practical question from Arjuna. By this point Krishna has laid out a number of spiritual paths, and Arjuna wants to know, "Which is better, the path of direct knowledge or the path of divine love?" Krishna responds by affirming both paths as legitimate; the goal of spiritual realization is the same, and the characteristics he describes of disciples on both paths are essentially the same (verses 3–4 compared to verses 13–19). Nevertheless, "The difficulty of those whose minds are set on the Unmanifest is much greater. The [direct] path to the Unmanifest is indeed a difficult one for those who are embodied" (12:5). In short, the "manifested" path of divine love is easier, especially for those who are identified with their physical bodies.

The neophyte spiritual seeker is naturally tempted to charge ahead on the quickest and most direct path to spiritual realization; why settle for anything less? But as in all serious mountain climbing, the direct route to the summit is often the steepest and most dangerous, and rarely the wisest choice. This caution given by Krishna thousands of years ago applies equally today, and perhaps even more so in the West, where people are strongly conditioned to identify with the physical body and mind. As spiritual teacher Eknath Easwaran observes, the direct path is appropriate "for those who meet the qualifications—giants like Meister Eckhart, Shankara, or Anandamayi Ma…. But if you believe in your heart that you are essentially physical … this path is very tough going."[19] In other words, those who are identified with their mind and physical body—nearly everyone!—will find the path of divine love to be far more practical and achievable. The direct path of spiritual knowledge is steep, with unique hazards that carry major risks for the seeker, and little to hold on to along the way.[20] On the path of love, by contrast, every experience of life is an aid to the path, and God as divine lover accompanies the disciple the whole way.

Spiritual Evolution by Stages

The path of divine love is one of gradual liberation by stages, and the aspirant realizes these different stages by *becoming* each stage herself. Giving herself in devotion and service to God, the disciple ascends the mystic ladder rung by rung, until she finally attains full spiritual realization or mergence into God. In Hinduism this gradual path is called *krama-mukti*, and it has long been widely misunderstood because it was shunned by Shankara, who favored *sadyo-mukti*, or the path of immediate liberation (although Shankara was also a master of spiritual devotion, as demonstrated in his magnificent hymns of praise to the Divine Mother). Most contemporary seekers on a path of Advaita Vedanta, and its offshoot neo-Advaita, have followed Shankara in pursuit of the direct path of *sadyo-mukti*, "at least in theory," observes Krishnaprem. "Whether they get satisfactory results in practice is a matter that can be left for them to judge, but ... much easier it is to climb step by step the Ladder of Being" on the path of divine love.[21]

Perhaps this is why Sri Ramakrishna, Sri Aurobindo, Krishnaprem, and many others have upheld *para bhakti* (or supreme divine love) as the most effective path in this challenging epoch of the Kali Yuga, when the forces of ignorance and darkness are in ascendancy and threaten spiritual life at every turn, rendering the direct path even more difficult. Yet "How different it is for those who ... meditate on God with a Yoga which sees none else," exclaims Sri Aurobindo, because "God meets them at every point, in every moment, at all times, with innumerable forms and faces, holds up the lamp of knowledge within, and floods with its divine and happy lustre the whole of existence." Aurobindo's description closely resembles the ecstatic account given by the Christian mystic Brother Lawrence (explored further in chapter 5): "God gives me the Key to his treasures, feasts with me.... God meets his divine lover at every point, in every moment, at all times."[22]

"God as the supreme Will meets the [human] will of sacrifice, takes from it its burden and assumes ... the works of the divine Nature in us," continues Aurobindo. "Swiftly the Supreme comes to [the disciple] as the saviour and exalts him by a happy embrace ... into the secure bosom of the Eternal.... This then is the swiftest, largest, and greatest way."[23]

Of course, like all paths, there are dangers. "For there is the lower nature with fierce or dull downward gravitation which resists and battles against the motion of ascent.... There are nights of long exile from the Light, there are hours or moments of revolt, doubt, or failure. But still by the practice of union and by constant repetition of the experience, the divine consciousness grows upon the devotees and takes permanent possession of their nature."[24]

The Practice of Divine Love

Krishna summarizes specific details of the practice of divine love, depending on the spiritual maturity and temperament of the disciple. The optimal practice is to constantly focus the mind and center the intuitive faculty (*buddhi*) one-pointedly on God, which will unite the disciple's consciousness with the eternal divine consciousness. However, this is an advanced level that generally requires extensive practice before it is attained. So Krishna encourages yoga practice of devotional meditation on God and self-identification with inner levels of witnessing awareness, thereby cultivating divine presence within. If this practice is found to be overly difficult, disciples may devote themselves to selfless service to other beings and to life, performing all actions for Krishna's sake. If even this is beyond their capacity, disciples are enjoined to renounce the fruits of all actions for Krishna's sake, and take refuge in Krishna (12:6–12).

These different levels of devotional practice describe, in reverse order, the stages of consciousness that the disciple will move through on the path of divine love. The beauty is that the first (highest) stage encompasses them all, and the last leads naturally to the first. Relinquishing the fruits of one's actions into the hands of God brings peace to the heart. In this peace the flower of divine love blossoms, which lifts the disciple into ever higher levels of spiritual consciousness as she ascends the stages of mystical union.

What then unfolds in the devotee is the cultivation of profound qualities of genuine love, articulated beautifully by Krishna in the final verses of chapter 12, which are reminiscent of St. Paul's eloquent words on love in 1 Corinthians 4–8. The lover of God becomes, over time, compassionate to all, devoid of arrogance and possessiveness, alike in honor or insult, heat or cold, praise or criticism, evenhanded to friend and foe, free of agitation from disturbing emotions of anger, fear, envy; beyond "I" and "mine," harboring no ill will, returning love for hate, inwardly and outwardly pure, neither elated by good fortune nor depressed by misfortune, content with life and unattached to the world. The sole concern of such disciples is love for the One, their Beloved. "For love they act, for love they speak and think, and so *by* love they rise swiftly"—into the heart of God.[25]

Toward the Supreme Secret

The remaining chapters in the Gita (13–18) address various aspects of the spiritual path, culminating in the "supreme secret" addressed below. Given our special focus on divine love, and space limitations in this chapter, detailed consideration of these intervening chapters must be omitted, despite their importance for a comprehensive understanding of the Gita. Touching briefly on what we will miss: Chapter 13 introduces the key cosmic principles of *prakriti* and *purusha*, roughly translatable respectively as "mind/matter manifestation" and "unmanifest spirit." The next two chapters delve into each of these principles in greater depth. Chapter 16 addresses the dark side of human nature, contrasting it with benevolent spiritual qualities. Chapter 17 explores the critical issue of faith, or *shraddha*, the deep inner convictions of the heart that are crucial for walking the path. The final chapter, 18, addresses renunciation, and gives an exquisite summation of the entire teaching, culminating in the "supreme secret" to which we turn shortly.

The Absolute Godhead

Before addressing the supreme secret, it is essential to explore the deepest identity and true abode of Krishna, which is revealed at the end of chapter 15. "There are two orders of spirit [*purusha*] in the world: perishable and imperishable. The perishable is all beings; the imperishable is the transcendent witness [*kuthastha*]" (15:16). Krishna here makes the key distinction between the mutable spirit of all manifest beings, and the timeless unmanifest spirit that is ever changeless. This same distinction is found in virtually every spiritual and metaphysical tradition.

Consciousness manifests in the form of individual creatures and beings, all flowing in the stream of time. Beyond these, yet embracing them all, is an altogether different realm or order of consciousness, outside of time, that silently witnesses (*kuthastha*) everything as if situated in eternal repose upon a mountain summit. This immutable spirit, sometimes called the unchanging witness, is frequently mistaken in practice for God him/herself. Yet this is not the case, as Krishna makes clear: "But there is yet *another* imperishable, the unexcelled Highest Spirit, called the Supreme Self, who is the Eternal God, pervading the three worlds and supporting them" (15:17). This is the Absolute Godhead, to which Krishna referred briefly earlier (8:20–22), saying it was attainable by one-pointed devotion.

Krishna now reveals this Absolute Godhead as his true identity, beyond all that is manifest and unmanifest, yet fully pervading both: "I am that Supreme Self [*purushottama*]," declares Krishna, "praised by the scriptures as beyond the changing and the changeless" (15:18). Krishna's supreme abode was described earlier as a realm of light beyond the light of the sun (15:6), and now for the first time, Krishna reveals his identity as the supreme Godhead. "Those who, thus undeluded, know Me as the Supreme Spirit have found the source of all wisdom, and they worship Me with their entire being" (15:19).

These few verses succinctly summarize the metaphysics of the Gita, although the deepest implications are not yet disclosed. In summary, Krishna is the immanent Divine (chapter 10) *and* the transcendent Divine (chapter 11) *and* beyond both as Absolute Godhead (chapter 15).

The Supreme Secret of the Bhagavad Gita

What is the deepest teaching of the Bhagavad Gita? Most people familiar with the scripture will respond that it teaches a highly refined spiritual philosophy and practical training on how to act and serve in the world without any attachment whatsoever to the fruits of our actions. This is certainly true, and for good reason the Gita is often called the "gospel of selfless service." Yet if we put this question to the Gita itself, we find that Krishna gives a clear yet different answer at the end of the final chapter.

Some might object that we should not jump to the end of the scripture, skipping over some of the detailed earlier stages to arrive here. I am sympathetic to this view. Aurobindo, for example, stresses that the Gita must always be interpreted as a whole, in its entirety, because otherwise it is all too easy to highlight particular verses, interpret them in isolation, and misread the whole essence of the scripture.

Acknowledging this risk, it is nevertheless still appropriate to highlight the supreme secret of the Gita for several reasons. First, the Gita itself underscores these two verses, which represent the whole spirit of the Gita in its entirety. The supreme secret is repeated in different forms several times throughout the Gita, without naming it as such, so its emphasis at the end does not misrepresent all that has gone before, but rather encapsulates the essential thread woven throughout the Gita.[26] Second, the supreme secret includes the *caramasloka*, a radical verse (18:66) that points to a remarkable doorway into divine union, and which has been the focus of voluminous commentaries and entire lineages of spiritual practice down through the centuries, as revealed further in chapter 5.

So what is this supreme secret? Krishna tells Arjuna, "Hear again My supreme word—most secret of all. Thou art dearly loved by me; therefore shall I disclose [this secret] for thy good" (18:64). The secret is:

Fix thy mind upon Me; devote thyself to Me;
Make every action a sacrifice to Me; hold thyself as nothing
    before Me.
You shall come to Me truly,
I promise, for you are dear to Me.
Abandon all dharmas,
Take refuge in Me alone.
I shall liberate you from all sins,
Do not grieve. (18:65–66)

The meaning of the first two lines is extremely deep, and their importance is underscored by the fact that Krishna has already given this same teaching at the midpoint of the Gita (9:34). These lines encapsulate the entire yoga of divine love, integrating the principal branches of *jnana*, *bhakti*, and *karma yogas*.[27] We consider each line of the supreme secret separately.

Fix thy mind upon Me; devote thyself to Me. This is the very essence of the spiritual path of divine love. God pours out love to us, and we are to give our unconditional love back to God, thereby completing this profound circle of love. Recall why Krishna is sharing this secret. He is saying, in effect, "I share this secret of secrets with you, Arjuna, because you are my beloved." Indeed, this is what lovers do; they share deep intimacies together! And what is the secret? "Make Me *your* beloved," says Krishna. "You are *My* beloved, Arjuna; now make Me *your* beloved, and you shall enter into full, intimate union with Me."

Make every action a sacrifice to Me; hold thyself as nothing before Me. This is the great mystic sacrifice that is the very essence of spiritual life. Here "sacrifice" is not to be understood in the dutiful or morbid sense of obligation so often associated with this term in the West, but rather as engaging in the profound self-giving that is the very foundation of life itself. Meister Eckhart put it eloquently: "It is not what we do that makes us holy, but we ought to make holy what we do."[28]

When we truly offer ourselves in surrender to God, we bow down to the Divine with every last fiber of our being—in joyful submission. This is the apophatic mystical path of becoming nothing, and merging into oneness with the Divine. This line is equivalent to Jesus's testimony (with "friend" interpreted as "God"), "No one has greater love than this; to lay down one's life for a friend" (John 15:13).

You shall come to Me truly, I promise you, for you are dear to Me. This is the promise of union with God. Krishna again repeats here something he had just said in the prior verse (18:64), that he is offering this gift of union because Arjuna is very dear to him. He later enjoins Arjuna not to share this secret with any who are unfaithful, or who scorn Krishna.

Abandon all dharmas. This is one of the most astonishing and profound lines in the Bhagavad Gita. It is also one of the most controversial, as it directly addresses the long-standing tension between religious tradition and spiritual freedom. This line stands not alone, but takes its fullest meaning in conjunction with the subsequent line ("Take refuge in Me alone"), which together are called the *caramasloka*, the "final verse" or key verse.

The well-known Sanskrit term "dharma" has several meanings and nuances, and in the plural form used here, "dharmas," refers to spiritual pathways, practices, and injunctions that support and guide the disciple to realization of God. The startling directive to abandon these, at the end of a scripture that has just carefully laid out several specific dharmas, is a paradoxical shift in the teaching that must be interpreted very carefully. It is no accident that this teaching is given only once in the Gita, and then only at the end of the entire training and transmission from Krishna. This final secret is divulged to the advanced disciple who has engaged deeply in the *sadhana* (spiritual disciplines) and earnestly followed the disciplines of purification and the injunctions of the dharma and scriptures, and is now fully prepared to realize the *Atman*, or (borrowing from Christian terminology) to "enter the Kingdom," where human laws and institutions are necessarily transcended altogether. As Bede Griffiths observes in his extensive commentary on the Gita, *River of Compassion*, "*Dharma* is the law. This is a call to go beyond the law, to enter into a state of grace."[29]

Sri Aurobindo summarizes the essential message of this *caramasloka* verse as follows:

> The supreme, the faultless largest law of action is therefore to find out the truth of your own highest and inmost existence and live in it, and not to follow any outer standard and Dharma.... Know then your self; know your true self to be God and one with the self of all others.... Offer, first, all your actions as a sacrifice to the Highest and One in you; ... deliver last all you are and do into his hands for

the supreme and universal Spirit to do through you his own will and works in the world.[30]

The injunction to "abandon all dharmas" makes explicit the deeper implications of the earlier teaching, because to fully "bow down" exclusively to the Supreme Divine necessarily requires the abandonment of all other dharmas, and surrendering to God as sole refuge. Hence the disciple doesn't actually abandon *all* dharmas, but replaces them with this one supreme dharma. This entails totally entrusting the human soul to the heart of God.

Take refuge in Me alone. This is the very foundation of the spiritual life. We abandon our own ideas, preferences, plans, and modes of being, and take deep refuge in the unfathomable intimacy and infinity of That Which Has No Name, but which comes by whatever name we call It. This is total surrender, or submission, to God—or using perhaps more appealing terminology, "unconditional consent" to God. This total self-giving to God is the fundamental practice on the path of divine love for all devotees and seekers, in each moment of life.[31]

The abandonment of all dharmas has a deeper significance, for it is not actually the disciple who does the true abandonment. The advanced disciple performs the abandonment of dharmas outwardly, but it is the Divine who releases the disciple from bondage to all lower dharmas, and this takes place precisely and only because the disciple takes refuge in God. Otherwise, the disciple cannot just willfully "abandon all dharmas" without suffering serious karmic consequences, to say nothing of the practical and worldly consequences. The dharmas, or spiritual practices and paths referred to, are universal and necessary for ordinary human existence, and for advancement on the spiritual journey. Release from these lower dharmas and laws is an act of divine grace—or rather, necessity—and it is coupled with divine gifts, including higher faculties of subtle sensitivity and vision that are essential for the disciple to be lifted up into spiritual consciousness and discernment. Only by divine grace is spiritual consciousness bestowed upon the disciple, and then only when the requisite stages of purification and advancement have been reached. Even the very cells of the physical body are transformed and function at a higher vibrational frequency as the divine alchemy proceeds within the serious devotee. All this is activated by divine grace, after taking refuge in God.

Krishna concludes by promising Arjuna peace and full forgiveness of all sins (discussed in chapter 3), and then immediately enjoins Arjuna in the very next verse, "Do not share this wisdom with anyone who lacks in devotion or self-control, lacks the desire to learn, or scoffs at Me" (Gita 18:67). Jesus gives the same admonition "not to cast your pearls before the swine" (Matt. 7:6), and he speaks in parables to conceal his deeper teaching from those who are unprepared or might abuse it (see Mark 9:10–12).

Significance of the Supreme Secret

The supreme secret isn't the real secret, nor is it really secret. Krishna spells it out in plain Sanskrit, for all to see, so it hasn't been a secret since at least 500 BCE or thereabouts, when the Gita was written down. But more to the point, the real secret Krishna speaks of is not the scriptural text of the supreme secret itself (to love God and surrender absolutely). The real secret is what takes place after the devotee fully surrenders, and enters into direct communion with God. This is nowhere spelled out, nor can it be. The *caramasloka* is but the doorway to the real secret. One must go through that doorway and walk the path of surrender to discover the true supreme secret.

The text of the supreme secret nevertheless gives a specific prescription for how the human disciple is to proceed to implement unconditional love for God; that is, to give oneself entirely and utterly to God, to give up one's very identity in total surrender of self, to consecrate one's entire mind and heart and every action and very life as a sacred offering to God. To facilitate this supreme surrender or submission in practical terms, the devotee is to abandon entirely every practice, belief, thought, and reliance of any kind on any outside support, philosophy, person, or practice—in a total, one-pointed radical act of taking absolute refuge in God, and relying on nothing else whatsoever. This is the radical demand, and the gateway to the supreme secret.

An objection arises immediately: How can anyone possibly live up to and follow this path in practice? Don't we necessarily rely constantly on other things, other people, other principles—even the very laws of nature, for instance—rather than depending solely and entirely on the invisible mystery of God? In some sense yes, in terms of how we experience human life through the senses and movements of mind and body, all of which are sacred in their own right. Yet the teaching here is to see and discern the universal invisible Spirit, in its immanence and transcendence, which stands within all beings and underlies everything that exists (and all that doesn't exist). This is the supreme ineffable Godhead, to which we are called to make our surrender because it is the one Supreme Reality. All else is inherently ephemeral, or unreal, or incommensurable with That.

The supreme secret entails two interlinked parts, reflected in its two verses. The first verse marks the end of separation from God; the second verse (*caramasloka*) marks the beginning of merging with God. The disciple is first lifted out of herself and into oneness with God (first verse). At this point, all earlier dharmas make no sense anymore, and are to be abandoned—for they were all predicated upon the assumption of separation from God. The divine "rules" now change radically. Divine union, having been attained, is now to be sustained. Taking refuge in God is the sole practice, because it keeps the disciple "diving back" into God, which stabilizes and reinforces the union whenever it is perturbed. Sustained abiding in God is the result.

As Meister Eckhart describes this condition, "God must become me and I must become God, so entirely one that 'God' and this 'I' become one 'is' and act in this '*is*ness' as one."[32] In the disciple's new identity as this "isness" in God, there is no longer a disciple, no longer God; there is only this oneness, or "isness."

Although "isness" is a more awkward word than oneness, it is more accurate, because rather than a static noun it contains the eternal dynamic verb *is*, which connects directly to the present moment, the infinite silent now. God *is*. Union with God means the disciple becomes this "isness" in God, a full and free mergence into the radical freedom and infinity of God's own dynamic essence.

This entails a shift from dualistic *bhakti* to nondual *bhakti*, or *para bhakti*, which is the highest form of love for God. It is a love so great that we give up our very "I" to God. It goes beyond the usual concepts of surrender, because there is no "I" left to surrender. The "I" itself has been surrendered, and dissolved into God. Hence there is no more "I" and "God," no more "my will/Thy will"; only the one "isness."

Now there is only one practice, which is to remain in this "isness." It is an inner "isness," for only the innermost essence of the human being is fully one with the transcendent essence of the Godhead. Outwardly, the world will not recognize it; people will respond to the disciple the same as before, believing her to be the same separate person she was before. This can disorient or tempt the disciple to fall back into the illusion of separation, and whenever this happens, the sole practice is to take refuge in God. As long as the disciple remains in this "isness," "Thy will, not my will" no longer applies, because there is only one will. Nothing else. There is no separation, no duality. As Dante expressed it in the last line of his trilogy, "My will became one with the will of Love, the Love that runs the stars and the planets."

If any factor or circumstance arises that begins to cause the slightest separation from God, the disciple's sole response is to return to the *is*ness by taking refuge in God. This is the only "practice" that is ever needed, and it is needed only when there is a breach of the oneness. And there will be, as long as the disciple is incarnated in a body. Consider Jesus in the garden of Gethsemane. He had already lived the oneness with God profoundly, for years, yet he experienced once again the human experience and separation from God when facing the crucifixion, yet then immediately surrendered and took absolute refuge back into God. Thus he was following this practice, to remain in union with God. Then it happened again on the cross, "My God, my God, why hast thou forsaken me?" and again the complete surrender.

The first verse marks the completion of the journey *to* God, and the second verse the beginning of the journey *in* God. The second verse therefore connotes the beginning of true spiritual life; everything prior to this was but preparation for "union with God." Many people believe that this union is the glorious and triumphant culmination of the spiritual journey, but it is just the beginning. The supreme secret then begins to unveil its untold splendors.

> Almost *nobody* knows this secret.
> Only by becoming "nobody"
> Can it be known.

2

The Compassion and Majesty of Islam

Come, come whoever you are!
Even if you have broken your vows a thousand times, come
  yet again!
Come! Let yourself be silently drawn by the stronger pull
  of what you really love.
　　　—RUMI

Lovers don't finally meet somewhere;
they're in each other all along.
　　　—RUMI

Have you ever been inspired by Rumi? We all have! Perhaps no greater poet of divine love has ever lived; Rumi is in a class by himself. Yet few people realize that when they are inspired by Rumi, they are in fact inspired by the sacred essence of Islam. The source of Rumi's endless fountain of inspiration and wisdom is the very wellspring of the Islamic spiritual tradition.

Rumi and other great poets such as Rab'ia and Hafiz are expressing, or rather transmitting, the remarkable depths and beauty of this sacred religion.

If you love Rumi and Hafiz, then you already love the real Islam, whether you know it or not. And you also love the profound beauty and essential wisdom contained in the Qur'an and the aHadith (plural of Hadith), the two canonical sources in Islam. Rumi's masterpiece, the *Mathnawi*, is regarded by many Sufis as the Persian Qur'an. In the *Mathnawi*

32

there are more than two thousand instances in which the verses of the Qur'an are cited, or meanings and words derived from it. Rumi also drew heavily on the aHadith, the sayings of the Prophet.

The close connection between Rumi and the Qur'an and the aHadith may not be immediately obvious, even to the seasoned Muslim or Islamic scholar. This is because, according to scholar Nargis Virani, "Rumi's use of the Qur'an and his insertions of Qur'anic verses and allusions are so natural and intertwined with such skill that it is almost impossible to detect them.... Rumi's arguments run thus: the Qur'an says such and such which in reality means 'this.' He goes even further ... and fuses his interpretation so completely with the Qur'anic quotations, that to draw a distinction between the two is impossible."[1]

For this reason the deep source of Rumi's inspiration is hidden. Nevertheless, by Rumi's own admission:

> I am the slave of the Qur'an while I still have life,
> I am dust on the path of Muhammad, the Chosen One.
> If anyone interprets my words in any other way,
> I deplore that person and I deplore his words.

To love Rumi is thus to love the essence and wisdom of the Islamic tradition. This should never be forgotten, especially in light of today's tragic Islamophobia.

Several excellent books are available that outline the essentials of the Islamic faith, so there is no need for a general introduction here.[2] My purpose here is more specific: What does the serious student on the path of divine love need to know about Islam, and the Qur'an in particular, especially in relation to the Sufi path of love? With such a practitioner in mind, I focus specifically on the spiritual path of love in Islam, how the Qur'an and the aHadith articulate teachings relevant to this path, and how these teachings relate to similar or parallel teachings in other religions.

One important caveat: I make no claim to know the Qur'an in depth, and despite having delved into the Qur'an over the past few years, I have not worked deeply with the Qur'an as a spiritual text or path in the same manner I have with other scriptures, such as the Bhagavad Gita and the Gospels, both of which I've worked with for decades. In that time I also read much Sufi literature and spent a couple of years living in a Sufi community. I also attended various Sufi conferences and gatherings. So when

I first began reading the Qur'an, I assumed this background would stand me in good stead, and that I could grasp the essence of the Qur'an fairly quickly. How mistaken I was! The Qur'an is a profound, dense, and mysterious book, not something to be grasped quickly. What I thought might take a few months has taken me years, and even now I know that I've only barely scratched the surface of the Qur'an. For one thing, I don't speak or read Arabic and thus I cannot understand the recitation of the Qur'an (apart from the first sura), which is the only authentic way to receive it. Nevertheless, I have made some important discoveries that bear directly on the spiritual path of divine love, as beautifully articulated in the Qur'an. My purpose in this chapter is to share these insights and discoveries with others who, like me, are committed to the spiritual path of love, and would like at least an introduction to how this path is articulated in the Qur'an and the aHadith. I have also been blessed by wonderful friendships with my Muslim friends and colleagues in this process, which has been the greatest blessing throughout, and my respect and love for this venerable tradition have grown immensely.

Another caveat: I do not address the complex issues of Islamophobia and extremist "Muslim terrorism" here, which are two sides of a tragic coin. Suffice it to say that such terrorism is perpetrated by a tiny minority of "Muslims" who profoundly betray the very heart of Islam, violate the entire thrust of the Qur'an, and evidently pay no heed to their own Prophet Muhammad's ominous warning that "He who wrongs a Jew or a Christian will have myself as his accuser on the Day of Judgment" (*Al-Bukhari*). For those interested in pursuing the phenomenon of Islamophobia further, two valuable up-to-date resources are recommended: For an analysis of how terrorism violates the Qur'anic teachings, the true meaning of *jihad*, and related issues, see Reza Shah-Kazemi's book *The Spirit of Tolerance in Islam*, which draws upon compelling historical illustration and theological exposition to make a powerful argument that the Islamic faith is inherently and emphatically tolerant by nature and disposition.[3] For an engaging treatment of the "problematic" verses in the Qur'an that relate to *jihad*, violence, the treatment of women, homophobia, and other contemporary issues in Islam, see the important book *Religion Gone Astray* by Imam Jamal Rahman and his colleagues Rabbi Ted Falcon and Pastor Don Mackenzie, which addresses these questions in detail, and also includes parallel chapters addressing similar thorny issues in Christianity and Judaism.[4]

Before leaving the topic of terrorism and Islamophobia, let us give the last word to H. H. the Dalai Lama, whose writings on Islam constantly stress the Qur'an's repeated emphasis on compassion. The Dalai Lama sums up today's tragic situation with his usual clarity:

> Once we have a recognition of compassion as a key spiritual value in Islam, we will not be swayed by those who wish to portray Islam as inherently violent.... A handful of mischievous Muslims cannot represent the tradition as a whole.... There is a view, both within and outside Islam, that the concept of *jihad* defines Islam as a more militant faith than others. But I have been told by expert Islamic thinkers that ... other interpretations take *jihad*—the concept of a Holy War—to be an internal spiritual struggle. The literal reading [as war against infidels], it seems to me, is incompatible with the Qur'an's repeated invocation of Allah as merciful and compassionate.
>
> Historically speaking, some of the most open and pluralist moments in world culture have taken place under Islamic rule. Whether one thinks of Spain in the Middle Ages, or the Caliphate of Baghdad, or Akbar's India, literary culture and scientific learning flourished along with a notable tolerance of religious multiplicity.... The perception of Islam as narrow, intolerant, and even open to terrorism is a false one and a very unfortunate consequence of 9/11. To take the insane acts of a misguided handful as representative of anything but their own depravity is to make a generalization that simply has no basis. In the religious community worldwide we must work unceasingly to reverse this wrong image.[5]

Before proceeding further, is important to begin with a brief introduction, or rather orientation, to the Qur'an. This is essential because the Qur'an is so widely misunderstood in contemporary times, and also because the Qur'an is an entirely different type of scripture that holds a radically different place in Islam compared to the Jewish and Christian scriptures within their respective traditions.

"I usually advise my non-Muslim friends who are interested in Islamic spirituality not to rush out and buy a translation of the Qur'an," counsels my friend Imam Jamal Rahman. "For a variety of reasons, the Holy Book might come across as confusing and bewildering."[6] Of course a few years ago I *did* rush out and buy not one but several translations of the Qur'an, plus some guidebooks, and I can attest to the wisdom of Jamal's advice. It was quite a challenging journey at first, and, despite being deeply inspired by Sufi literature and wisdom and poetry, like so many other Western seekers, I can see now why there are fewer who delve into the Qur'an and the aHadith to uncover some of the roots of this tradition. The journey has been well worth it, however, and some of the fruits of this exploration are presented below to make them more accessible to fellow students on the path of divine love.

Approaching the Qur'an

The Qur'an is the great theophany of Islam, and provides spiritual guidance and wisdom to nearly one-quarter of the human race. The Qur'an describes itself as a "discernment" (*furqan*) between truth and error. The first common error that must be cleared up at the outset is that, despite being a revealed scripture in the form of a sacred book, the Qur'an is not the equivalent of the Torah in Judaism, or the Christian scriptures. Although the monotheistic theology of Islam is similar in broad terms to that of its two Abrahamic forerunners, the scripture of Islam is radically different from the Bible. The Qur'an for Muslims is more akin to the place of Christ in Christianity than the Bible. For Muslims the Qur'an is the uncreated word of God, and the model perfection of language.

"Qur'an" means "recitation." It is meant to be recited aloud in Arabic, and was originally spoken through the angel Gabriel to the Prophet Muhammad over a twenty-three-year period. It still speaks today directly to the hearer when recited. Thus the Qur'an does not merely recount the glories of Muhammad's revelations; it is also a vehicle of luminous transmission that reverberates with God's living word and presence. Like all scriptures, the Qur'an expresses profound or divine truths that exceed the capacity of human language to convey. Its deeper levels of meaning are therefore imparted by transmission to those with ears to hear—not just the outer ears of the flesh, but more importantly the "inner ear" of the heart. The Arabic words are said to penetrate the soul and body of the Muslim hearer, even before they reach the mind. "The implicit meaning is everything, and the obscurities of the literal meaning are so many veils highlighting the majesty of the content."[7] The beauty of the Arabic verses when recited aloud is legendary, and in Muslim countries public recitations of the Qur'an are frequently major cultural events, something like grand opera or theater performances in the West, or perhaps closer to a glorious and majestic performance of Handel's *Messiah* or Bach's *B Minor Mass*, in which the divine scriptures are glorified in sacred music.

Let's face it: the Qur'an is a challenging book. First, it's written in Arabic, and even native speakers of Arabic find it a challenging document. But this is no reason to shy away from the Qur'an. More than 80 percent of Muslims don't speak Arabic either, and only 10 percent of Muslims speak Arabic as their native tongue. Therefore, even most Muslims study the Qur'an in translation, although they all recite their daily prayers in Arabic. In its structure, the Qur'an consists of 114 chapters, called suras, and these are not arranged chronologically (the earliest revelation to Muhammad occurs in sura 96, verses 1–5). The first sura is called *Al-Fatihah*, "the Opening," and all remaining suras are arranged in order of decreasing length (hence the longest sura is no. 2, the shortest is no. 114). The suras, in turn, are divided into shorter sections, each of which is called an *ayah*. The word *ayah* is often translated as "verse," but actually means "sign," which is significant because *ayah* actually refers to anything in the universe that conveys the presence or message of God, including all natural and human phenomena, scriptures, the actions of the prophets, and the Qur'an itself.

All Muslims have memorized at least some Qur'anic verses in Arabic, which are recited daily in *salat*, their daily prayers. There are some nine million Muslims who have memorized the Qur'an in its entirety—a remarkable feat given that the Qur'an contains eighty thousand Arabic words, and is about 80 percent the length of the Christian scriptures.

Much of the content of the Qur'an is similar to the Tanakh (the Hebrew Bible) and the Christian scriptures, with many of the same persons and events figuring prominently, although often with significant differences in narrative accounts and interpretation. Previous prophets are venerated highly; the most frequently mentioned are Adam, Abraham, Moses, and Jesus. Moses is mentioned by name most often in the Qur'an, followed by his great enemy the Pharaoh, who is depicted as the archetype of human evil. This has a deep significance beyond the historical account, because "Moses" and "Pharaoh" are reflected in every human being as our divine and egotistical tendencies, respectively, and the outer conflict between the historical personages mirrors the inner struggle between these two tendencies within each human being.

Jesus is highly venerated in the Qur'an, even more so than the Prophet Muhammad in some ways, and Jesus and Adam are said to be the only two human beings who were born free of the stain of Satan (the Prophet was purified of this stain after birth). The Qur'an upholds Jesus as the "Messiah" and affirms his resurrection, though it denies that he was the Son of God and denies the crucifixion. The Virgin Mary is highly revered, and there are more references to Mary in the Qur'an than in the entirety of Christian scriptures. The Qur'an affirms the Annunciation through the angel Gabriel, and narrates the virgin birth of Jesus several times, which is considered one of the greatest of God's miracles. Mary is the only woman mentioned by name in the Qur'an, and she holds a cherished place in Islamic tradition.

The picture of God that emerges in the Qur'an is an awesome, all-powerful lord of stupendous power, compassion, and mercy. Mercy is repeatedly emphasized by Allah himself—"My mercy surpasses My wrath"[8]—and this is borne out in the Qur'an where God's compassion and mercy are cited 192 times, compared to 17 references to his wrath and vengeance. "The merciful are shown mercy by the All-Merciful. Show mercy to those on earth, and He Who is in heaven will show mercy unto you."[9]

There are multiple levels of meaning in the Qur'an, as in all sacred scriptures. To understand the full scope of the Qur'an, Frithjof Schuon says three elements must be taken into account: its doctrinal content, its narrative content, and its divine magic, or mysterious and, in a sense, miraculous, power. "These sources of metaphysical and eschatological doctrine, of mystical psychology and theurgic power lie hidden under a veil of breathless utterances, often clashing in shock, of crystalline and fiery images, but also of passages majestic in rhythm, woven of every fiber of the human condition."[10] The Qur'an addresses many subjects, including history, various beliefs and customs, tales of the prophets, the Day of Judgment, Paradise and Hell, the legal rulings, spiritual teachings, and much more.

The earliest translations of the Qur'an into English from the seventeenth century are wholly unreliable and replete with errors, because they were undertaken by Christian missionaries who sought to repudiate Islam and convert Muslims to Christianity. Later translations from the eighteenth and nineteenth centuries were similarly motivated and are also very poor. So it was not until the twentieth century that the first decent English translations of the Qur'an appeared, initially by Muslims in India under British colonial rule. Today there are many English translations available, some of which are excellent.[11]

Muslims maintain that the Qur'an cannot be translated accurately into other languages; any translation is, at best, an "interpretation." For example, in the introduction to one of the better translations, we read of "the complete impossibility of adequately conveying the meanings of the Qur'an in English or indeed in any other language. Allah, may He be exalted, chose pure classical Arabic as the linguistic vehicle for His final Revelation to mankind because of its unique capacity of retaining and conveying great depth of meaning in a multi-faceted way which is beyond the scope of any other language."[12] Like all sacred languages, there is a profound beauty and transmission that can only come through in the original. Nevertheless, according to the Qur'an itself, the wisdom and message conveyed in the Qur'an is basically the same that God has vouchsafed in other revelations. The Qur'an explains that:

> We sent this down as an Arabic Qur'an so you people will understand. (12:2)

> We never sent a messenger who did not use his own people's language to make things clear for them. (14:4)

> We have made this Qur'an easy to understand—in your own language. (44:58)

> If we had made it a foreign [language] Qur'an, people would have said, "If only its verses were made clear! What?—why this foreign speech to an Arab?" (41:44)

The Qur'an as a whole conveys a consistent message to worship God, and to submit to God's will. However, as in any major scripture, there are many instances of contradictory verses throughout the Qur'an. In some cases, a particular verse is intended to "abrogate" (*naskh*) an earlier verse that is evidently deemed to have been limited in scope, or require improvement or updating in some way. The Qur'an itself introduces the notion of abrogation by saying, "And for whatever verse We abrogate or cast into oblivion, We bring a better or the like of it; knowest thou not that God is powerful over everything?" (2:106). Elsewhere, in relation to earlier scriptures, the Qur'an says, "God erases or confirms whatever He will, and the source of Scripture is with Him" (13:39). Some scholars say the Qur'an abrogates only other Qur'anic verses, whereas other scholars maintain the Qur'an sometimes also abrogates the Sunnah or vice versa. The infamous "sword verse" (9:5) that has sometimes been cited as terrorist justification for killing "infidels" is considered to be abrogated by at least 113 other verses in the Qur'an that call for compassion, tolerance, and proactive peacemaking from Muslims toward their adversaries; for example, "Repel evil with what is better, and your enemy will become as close as an old and valued friend" (41:34). There are numerous instances of Qur'anic verses that are contradicted by another verse not intended as an abrogation; this is a phenomenon (also found in any other major scripture) for which there are complex reasons. In the case of the Qur'an, when its message was presented to the Arabs it was something very new and different from their way of life, so important changes were introduced gradually to allow the people to adjust to the new prescriptions. This resulted in later abrogations of earlier verses; as one example, there are three verses in the Qur'an concerning the drinking of wine, which was widespread and highly esteemed in pre-Islamic times. The three verses that finally led to the prohibition of intoxicating substances were revealed in stages (4:43, 2:219; 5:93–94).

The Qur'an upholds the revelations of both the Christian and the Jewish traditions, and also repudiates certain aspects of both. As a new revelation it cannot help but do so, and then present itself as an "improvement" upon both Christianity and Judaism. We see the same pattern in the relationship of Christianity emerging out of Judaism, and Buddhism emerging out of Brahmanic Hinduism, and more recently in Baha'i emerging out of Islam. In each case, the new tradition has the awkward task of upholding the timeless spiritual truths and the unassailable prophets and celebrated sages of the previous tradition while also finding sufficient fault or error in the earlier tradition to justify the birth of a whole new religion. As Frithjof Schuon remarks, "By the logic of things the later tradition is 'condemned' to the symbolic attitude of superiority, on pain of non-existence."[13]

A similar process takes place within each tradition, as different sects and divisions are created, which not infrequently have led to significant intrareligious tension or even violence. The age-old conflict between

Catholics and Protestants has a close parallel in Islam between Sunni and Shi'ite Muslims.

Suffice it to say, as Rumi put it, "the Qur'an is a shy and veiled bride," and must be approached with great respect, patience, and reverence, before its secrets can be revealed.

The *Shahadah*

The profession of faith in Islam is the *shahadah*, which is the first of the Five Pillars in Islam (the other four being the daily *salat* prayer five times a day, the alms tax, fasting during Ramadan, and the pilgrimage [*hajj*] to Mecca for those who are able). The *shahadah* has two parts: *la ilaha il Allah*, usually translated as "There is no god but God," and *Muhammadan rasul ullah*, "Muhammad is His Messenger." This dual *shahadah* is the central article of faith for Muslims, and to proclaim both these articles of faith makes one a Muslim. The first part of the *shahadah* is essentially the same as in all other monotheistic religions, which proclaim there is one supreme God, so we are to worship this God alone. The second part is specific to Islam, affirming that Muhammad is the Messenger of God. We shall revisit the *shahadah* and its deeper meanings below when we explore Sufism.

It is interesting to note that in Muslim countries, particularly among people untouched by Western education, there is widespread belief that all religions accept the first part of the *shahadah*, and that the second part is adapted to their particular religion.[14] Thus it is thought that Christians would say "There is no god but God, and Jesus is the spirit of God," or Jews would say "There is no god but God, and Moses is God's speaking companion" (because God spoke directly to Moses at the burning bush). An informal "confirmation" of this vernacular perspective is found in 1 Timothy 2:5, which could be viewed almost as a Christian *shahadah*: "For there is one God, and one mediator also between God and [humans], the man Christ Jesus."

Tawhid—Making One

Tawhid is a core principle of Islam; the affirmation of God's oneness. *Tawhid* is usually translated as "oneness" or "asserting unity," and is the first principle of Muslim faith, expressed succinctly in the first part of the *shahadah: la ilaha il Allah.*

Tawhid means not just oneness but also refers to the actual process of realizing this oneness. "It could be translated as 'the realization of oneness' or 'making real' of the actual reality of oneness, through the elimination of all multiplicity."[15] *Tawhid* proclaims the oneness of an Infinite Reality, and the Sufis have developed practical pathways for mystical union with this Reality, which constitutes full realization of *tawhid*. There is a close parallel to *tawhid* in the Hindu philosophy of Advaita Vedanta. *Advaita* means "not two," or nondual, and affirms the same fundamental oneness of God that *tawhid* does.

Tawhid has different interpretations in different contexts. "Theological *tawhid*" affirms that there is only one God, whereas "ontological *tawhid*" affirms that there is only one Reality. Sufis sometimes interpret the *shahadah* as "There is no reality but God." Legendary Sufi masters such as Ibn Arabi, Junayd Baghdadi, and Al Ghazali identify different steps of *tawhid* associated with the rejection of concepts relating to the world of multiplicity. Junayd "distinguishes four steps, starting from the simple attestation of unicity which is sufficient for ordinary believers, and culminating in the highest rank reserved for the elite, when the creature totally ceases to exist before his Lord, thus achieving annihilation in unity."[16] Al Ghazali explains that the fruit of spiritual ascent of the Sufi is to witness that there is no existence in the world except God, and cites the Qur'anic verse "Everything is perishing except His face" (28:88), a favorite of the Sufis.

A Positive Approach to the Qur'an

The Qur'anic excerpts assembled below highlight something of the majesty, beauty, and universalism of Islam. In adopting a deliberately positive approach to the Qur'an, I do not deny that there exist less exalted portions of the scripture, and that some verses are qualified or contradicted by other Qur'anic verses; such is the nuanced complexity of any scripture. The purpose here is not to attempt an exhaustive exegesis that covers the many rich and varied dimensions of the Qur'an. Nevertheless, taken together, the remarkable verses gathered below illuminate the sweeping profundity of the Islamic revelation, yet they remain largely unknown to non-Muslims today, even among the spiritually informed.

Broadly speaking, study of the Qur'an can be divided into two types: *tadhakkur* (remembrance) and *tadabbur* (contemplation), after the Quranic verse: "That people may ponder over its revelations and ...

may take them to heart" (38:29). In this book we adopt the *tadhakkur* approach to the Qur'an, in which "you try to grasp the general messages and teachings being conveyed by the Qur'an, to find out what they mean for you and what demands they make upon you, to take them to heart, to bring forth corresponding responses of heart and mind and attitudes, ... and finally, to determine what message you have to deliver to your fellow human beings."[17] This is the sense in which the Qur'an has declared itself easy to understand: "Indeed we have made this Qur'an easy for understanding and remembering. Is there any, then, that will take it to heart?" (54:17). This approach to the Qur'an is legitimate for our purposes, and is distinct from the more rigorous and scholarly approach of *tadabbur*.[18]

To sum up briefly: "In a very deep sense, the Qur'an is Islam, and Islam is the Qur'an.... The Qur'an itself is Light, as it tells us in several verses, and to embody the Qur'an through faith and practice is to become transmuted by this light and to actualize all the qualities of light, which are the divine qualities."[19]

There are a number of verses in the Qur'an that criticize the other major revelations of Christianity and perhaps even more so Judaism, and make corrections to what are presented as mistaken or corrupted views, and which uphold Islam as the best and perfect religion. Several excellent books explore these challenging and nuanced issues.[20] Nevertheless, the Quran actually affirms the previous revelations and scriptures, and uplifts Jews and Christians who follow their divine paths appropriately:

> They are not all alike; among the People of the Book there is an upstanding community. They recite God's revelations through the night, and they fall prostrate. They believe in God and the last day. They advocate good and forbid evil, and they hasten to do good works. These are among the righteous. Whatever good they do will not be denied. God knows those who are reverent. (3:113–115)

Key Messages of the Qur'an

Let us now ask: What is the essence of Islam as revealed in the Qur'an? To address this, we delve into some of the key verses in the Qur'an that relate directly to the universal path of divine love. One important caveat before we begin: The interpretation of scripture is always multivalent; the "meaning" of a particular verse has multiple interpretations, and any given interpretation often bears multiple levels of meaning, ranging from the exoteric literal rendering of the words to deeper esoteric levels. This is the very nature of all scripture, due in large part to the limitations of language itself. Therefore, this multivalent principle applies to any attempt to present spiritual truth in human language.

Hence the interpretation of the verses selected below is only one of several possibilities, although it is strongly supported by these verses. Ibn Arabi has emphasized that any interpretation of a verse that is supported by the precise wording of that verse has to be considered one of the valid interpretations. In what follows, I have sought to provide a straightforward, noncontroversial reading of these verses, especially because I am not a Muslim in the formal sense, nor do I read or speak Arabic, so I want to be especially careful not to "read into" these verses a meaning they do not clearly convey. To this end, I have also drawn on multiple translations of the Qur'an, to help get a better sense of the meaning by "triangulating" from multiple translators, which, of course, is still highly inadequate compared to reading in the original Arabic, but nonetheless is better than relying upon a single translation alone.

The *Fatihah*

The first sura of the Qur'an is *Al-Fatihah* (the Opening). The *Fatihah* is one of the earliest revelations received by the Prophet, and it was probably the first sura to be revealed in its entirety at one time. It is formulated as a prayer, which is repeated several times a day by all Muslims. According to the Qur'anic translator Muhammad Asad, the *Fatihah* encapsulates the essence of the entire Qur'anic teachings, including that God is one, and utterly unique, and God is the Creator and Sustainer of the universe, the Source of life-giving grace, the One to whom humanity is ultimately responsible, and the only power that can truly guide and help humanity. The *Fatihah* expresses the call for righteous action in this world, the principle of life after death, divine accountability for all human actions, the principle of continuity of all true religions, and the need for voluntary surrender to the will of the Supreme Being, and thus for worshipping God alone.

Here is one translation of the *Fatihah*:

In the Name of God, the Lord of Mercy, the Giver of Mercy! Praise belongs to God, the Lord of the Worlds, the Lord of Mercy, the Giver of Mercy, the Master of the Day of Judgment. It is You we worship; it is You we ask for help. Guide us to the straight path: the path of those You have blessed, those who incur no anger and who have not gone astray. (1:1–7)[21]

The first line of the *Fatihah* is of paramount importance, and is invoked again at the opening of all but one of the 114 suras. The transliteration in Arabic is *Bismillah ir Rahman ir Rahim*, a phrase familiar even to many non-Muslims. *Rahman* refers to the quality of grace or mercy inherent in the essence of God, whereas *Rahim* expresses the active manifestation of that mercy and grace within the creation.[22] The words *rahman* and *rahim* both derive from the noun *rahmah*, which means "mercy," "compassion," "loving tenderness," or, more comprehensively, "grace." The etymology of *rahmah* is related to *rahm*, meaning "womb." Thus there is a profoundly intimate and precious quality to God's love and mercy, something akin to a mother's protective and nurturing love for her young.

The Essence of Islam: Submission to the Will of God

The core of the Islamic faith is profound devotion for and surrender to God—nothing else and nothing less. In this regard Islam is one of the most exalted religious traditions, because it goes straight to the very heart of spiritual life. The word *islam* is Arabic for "surrender," or "submission," or the "peace that comes in submission" to God.

A key verse in the Qur'an that is of paramount importance, yet widely misunderstood, is the following:

Behold, the only true religion in the sight of God is self-surrender. (3:19)

The meaning of this verse is straightforward and clear, even if challenging to put into practice! The translation given here is an accurate rendering of how the verse would have been understood by the Prophet's contemporaries at the time it was written. However, one detail renders this verse widely misunderstood today: The Arabic word for "self-surrender" is *islam*. Hence this verse is often mistranslated—and thereby turned completely on its head—to read: "Behold, the only true religion in the sight of God is *Islam*." Right there begins the battle! Notice how easily a profound misunderstanding has been propagated. What is crucial to understand is that fourteen hundred years ago, when the Qur'an was revealed and written down, "Islam" was not yet an institutional religion, and the word *islam* was simply the Arabic word for "surrender," or "submission to God."[23] The Qur'an is therefore *not* saying that Islam is the only true religion; it is saying that self-surrender is the only true religion—a key point that the other theistic religions also affirm emphatically. Moreover, the Qur'an actually upholds the truth of other religions, as we shall see below. A closely related verse, to which this same point applies, is this:

> If anyone goes in search of a religion other than self-surrender to God, it will never be accepted (3:85).

Again, this verse and indeed all verses in the Qur'an with the word *islam* must be situated as the Prophet's contemporaries would have heard them, in which *islam* means "self-surrender" to God, and nothing else.[24] There are only eight verses in the Qur'an that mention the word *islam*, and none of them refers exclusively to the religion itself.

Another word that has been similarly widely misunderstood is "Muslim." At the time of the Qur'anic revelation, the word "Muslim" was an Arabic word denoting a person who submits to the will of God. By this definition, all the prophets were "Muslims," long before the Islamic religion even existed—including Abraham, Moses, Jesus, and his disciples—all of whom are called "Muslims" in the Qur'an. This has been another source of endless confusion and debate, yet need not be. We just need to understand that only well *after* the Qur'an was written down did the words "Muslim" and "Islam" begin to acquire the more specific, institutionalized meanings they have today that apply specifically to the followers of the Qur'an and the Prophet Muhammad.

We encounter a similar problem in the translation of the *shahadah*, *la ilaha il allah*. It should be translated "There is no god but God," but sometimes it is translated: "There is no god but *Allah*." This lends itself to an exclusivist misinterpretation that would posit a specifically Islamic God, which is not what the Qur'an is saying. On the contrary, the Qur'an affirms that the God of the Muslims and the Christians and the Jews is one and the same God.

Worship God Alone, and No Other

> You shall maintain your devotion absolutely to God alone. (22:31)[25]

> It is We who sent down the Scripture to you with the Truth, so worship God with your total devotion: true devotion is due to God alone. (39:2)

Here is the clear command to give our love and devotion to God alone. This instruction follows naturally from the *shahadah*—because there is no god but God, our devotion and worship must go only to God, who is the only God there is.

> Those who do good in this world will have a good reward—God's earth is wide—and those who persevere patiently will be given a full and unstinting reward. (39:10)

> He guides therewith whomever wills [to be guided]—whereas he whom God lets go astray can never find any guide. (21:29–30)[26]

All Qur'anic references to God letting people go astray must be understood against the backdrop of 2:26–27:

> None does He cause to go astray save the iniquitous, who break their bond with God. Hence those who go astray freely choose to do so according to their attitudes and inclinations; they are not arbitrarily preordained to do so.[27]

God's Message Is the Same Across All Ages and Religions

The Qur'an affirms that God has given one basic message to humanity, over and over again, to every community and society across the globe. This message was given by *all* the prophets—not just Muhammad, but also every prophet from Abraham to Moses to Jesus, and many others. The message was given as a revelation that included a mix of inspiration, teachings, and warnings about the perils awaiting those who do not follow the guidance.

In essence, this one universal message from God to humanity can be summarized in this one verse:

> There is no God but Me, so worship and serve Me. (21:25)

There is one supreme God, who has a universal message for all times and ages: We humans are to bow down to, serve, and surrender to this God alone. This is perhaps the most fundamental message of the Qur'an. It aligns precisely with the theme of this book: there is one God, and there is one supreme path of divine love; we are to love, serve, and surrender to God.

The path of love may manifest in many different expressions, but in essence the path is one of surrender to God. This message has been given to humanity time and again, through the prophets and messengers of God:

> We never sent any Messenger before you [Muhammad] without revealing to him: "There is no God but Me, so worship and serve Me." (21:25)

God Is One; God Is the Supreme "Lord of All the Worlds."

> Say: He is the One God. God the Eternal [the Uncaused Cause of all Being]. He begets not, and neither is He begotten; and there is nothing that could be compared with Him. (112)

This is the entirety of sura 112, titled *Al-Ikhlas*. Many of the later suras in the Qur'an are much shorter and more mystical than earlier suras. A casual reader might miss these, and thereby miss some of the most significant and profound parts of the Qur'an. Like any canonical scripture, the Qur'an must be read in its entirety, and each sura and verse must be considered not only in context, but also in light of the rest of the book.

The first verse of sura 112 is highly revered, and said to be equal to one-third of the Qur'an. The Arabic term *as-samad* (Eternal Refuge) in this verse is applied only to God, and appears only once in the entire Qur'an. One of the Prophet's companions, Abu Said Al Khudri, recounts the story of a man who was heard during prayers reciting this verse repeatedly. The next morning, the Prophet Muhammad was told of this by someone who assumed such recitation was inadequate. The Prophet replied, "By Him in Whose hand my life is, it is equal to one-third of the Quran."[28] According to Muhammad Asad, *as-samad* comprises the concepts of Primary Cause and eternal Independent Being, coupled with the notion that everything is sourced in God and is therefore dependent on God for its beginning and continued existence.

The oneness of God is absolute in Islam. In particular, there can be no "partner with God." To deify anything other than God, or to ascribe any form of "partner" with God, explicitly or implicitly, human or otherwise, is considered *shirk*, the gravest possible sin. *Shirk* is regarded as the only sin that cannot be forgiven in Islam.

The Qur'an Proclaims the Truth of All Revealed Religions

> Say: "People of the Book, let us arrive at a statement that is common to us all: We worship God alone, we ascribe no partner to God, and none of us takes others besides God as lords." If they turn away, say, "Witness our devotion to God." (3:64)

Contrary to widespread popular misconception, Islam validates and upholds the other great religions of the world. This fundamental doctrine is stated in several crucial verses in the Qur'an, and God even offers a form of universal salvation. It is true that there are also certain verses in the Qur'an that proclaim Islam to be the best and perfect religion (as other religions also proclaim); we address these exclusivist verses below. But far more significantly, the following verses are of paramount importance:

> Truly those who believe, and the Jews, and the Christians, and the Sabeans—whoever believes in God and judgment day, and performs virtuous deeds—surely they shall have their reward with their Lord: they shall have no fear, neither shall they grieve. (2:62, see also 5:69)

This key doctrine guarantees salvation to all righteous believers, regardless of their faith. Notice that only three requirements are specified to guarantee salvation; no special doctrines must be believed to receive God's grace. This is a foundational principle of Islam that is repeated several times in the Qur'an. Islamic scholar Reza Shah-Kazemi observes that "the verse stands out as one of the most significant proof-texts in the Qur'an for the principle that access to salvation is not the exclusive preserve of the particular religion of Islam."[29]

This magnanimous verse affirms unambiguously the validity and salvific efficacy of the earlier Abrahamic religions, and it heralds not merely religious tolerance, but a deep interreligious respect and inclusivity. And the verse doesn't stop there; it goes even further to offer what amounts to a profound promise from God of universal grace and salvation to anyone who believes in God, is virtuous, and is accountable for his actions. This is a remarkable offering of divine grace from God to the human soul, and it does not even require the person to be a Muslim, or to follow the prescribed Islamic rites of the Five Pillars or the *sharia*.[30] This expansive and inclusive spirit continues in several more key verses below.

The Qur'an Calls for Constructive Interfaith Dialogue

Call unto the way of thy Lord with wisdom and fair exhortation, and hold discourse with them [the People of the Book] in the finest manner. (16:125)

And do not hold discourse with the People of the Book except in that which is finest, save with those who do wrong. And say: We believe in that which hath been revealed to us and revealed to you. (29:46)

Here is a call for the very finest of interfaith exchange and dialogue—precisely the kind of skillful conversation and cross-cultural exchange among the Abrahamic faiths that could go such a long way to alleviating and reconciling much of today's tension and misunderstanding between Islam and other religions. The Qur'an itself is calling for this! How many contemporary Westerners realize that the Qur'an has been asking for skillful interfaith exchange for more than fourteen hundred years?

The Diversity of Humanity Is Divinely Ordained

For each We have appointed a Law and a Way. Had God willed, He could have made you all one single community. But [God willed otherwise] in order to test you by means of what He has vouchsafed unto you. So vie with one another in doing good works! Unto God you all must return, and He will inform you of that wherein you differed. (5:48)

The diversity in human communities is divinely ordained by God; it is not the result of some anthropological accident, evolutionary process, or social construct. We humans are created with diversity—culture, language, race, gender, and the like—for a divine purpose. Here the Qur'an enjoins us all to learn from each other, and learn how to get along and appreciate our differences. Diversity is a divine gift; let us learn to embrace it as such!

God Is One Across the Religions

We believe in what has been sent down to us, and in what has been sent down to you. Our God and your God is one, and to Him we surrender. (29:46)

Despite human diversity, God is one. Here the Qur'an affirms the universal truth of all divine revelations, and upholds the one God from whom all these revelations come. The second line is clear and unambiguous: Christians, Jews, and Muslims all worship the same God. Although the Qur'an does dispute certain aspects of Jewish and Christian theology in other verses (discussed below), here we have an unmistakable affirmation that the God worshipped in all the Abrahamic faiths is one and the same God.

Every Human Community and Civilization Has a Messenger from God

Every community (*umma*) has its [own] Messenger (*rasul*). (10:47)

We have sent Messengers before.... There was a Scripture for every age. (13:38)

We sent Messengers before thee, among the ancient peoples. (15:10)

Every people has had its guide. (13:8)

Every community has had its warner.... Messengers came to them with clear signs, scriptures, and enlightening revelation. (35:26)

Some Messengers we have told you about, and some we have not. (4:164)

These proclamations are repeated multiple times in the Qur'an (see also 17:15, 23:44, 30:47, 35:22). Across the globe, in all cultures and ages, the Qur'an affirms that every human society has been sent a divine messenger from God who gives, or has given, the divine dispensation to that community, as well as a warning about the consequences of not following divine guidance.[31]

This verily is the word of an illustrious Messenger. It is not the word of a poet ... neither is it the word of a soothsayer—how little you reflect! It is a revelation from the Lord of the Worlds. (69:40–43)

God Makes No Distinction Between Any of the Prophets or Messengers

We believe in God, and that which has been revealed to us, and that which was revealed to Abraham, Ishmael, Isaac, Jacob, and the tribes, and that which was given to Moses and Jesus and the prophets from their Lord. We make no distinction between any of them; to God we are resigned. (2:136)

Messengers believe in that which has been sent down from the Lord. We make no distinction between any of His Messengers. (2:285)

What a remarkable revelation! Above we heard that every human community and civilization has had its prophet or messenger from God—all human civilizations throughout history have been blessed by divine revelation. And here we find that God makes no distinction between any of these prophets.

This is one of the strongest possible affirmations of a universal spiritual path to God. It appears at least four different times in the Qur'an. God makes no distinction between any of his prophets (2:136, 3:84) or any of his messengers (2:285, 4:152).[32]

Moreover, God says we are not free to choose to believe in some prophets and not others. They must all be taken seriously:

As for those who ignore God and His Messengers, and want to make a distinction between them, saying, "We believe in some but not in others," seeking a middle way, they are in truth disbelievers. (4:150–151)

Tradition says there are 124,000 prophets, although only twenty-five are mentioned directly by name in the Qur'an. Here the Qur'an is basically telling us that God makes no distinction whatsoever between all 124,000 prophets—they all brought the same essential message to humanity, in various different languages to many different communities. "Allah directed the believers to refrain from differentiating between the Prophets, and to believe in them all," explains the feminist Tafsir Ibn Kathir.[33]

The verse above seems almost tantamount to repudiating religious exclusivism. That is, a person who believes that her religion's messenger or prophet is the only true one, and dismisses all the others, would be "in truth a disbeliever" if this verse is taken literally. One wonders if the verse could be applied to exclusivists of any religion, or even Muslim exclusivists. According to Muhammad Asad, "In Islam the rejection of any or all of God's apostles constitutes almost as grave a sin as a denial of God himself."[34]

The Qur'an tells us there are other prophets it has not told us about, who are not mentioned by name. Indeed—there are evidently some 123,975 of these unnamed prophets! Among these we can most likely include the prophets and avatars from other religions, including the Eastern religions, the nontheistic religions, such as Buddhism and Jainism, and many smaller religions and indigenous traditions.

Nothing Was Revealed to Muhammad That Was Not Revealed to Earlier Prophets

> We have revealed to thee as to Noah and the prophets after him. Nothing has been revealed to you that was not revealed earlier to them. (5:68)

This is yet another startling revelation: Nothing new was revealed to the Prophet Muhammad. The foundational message from God to humanity remains unchanged with the birth of Islam. This is not to deny the uniqueness of the Qur'an or Muhammad's mission, which together created a whole new religion. All prophets bring forth their revelations in unique ways under specific cultural circumstances and in particular historical epochs.

Nevertheless, here we find Allah himself proclaiming that the essential divine message to humanity has not changed, and is not new with Islam. It remains the same as it had been for thousands of years.

Allah Tells Muhammad to Quell His Doubts Through Earlier Scriptures

> If you [Prophet Muhammad] are in doubt about what We have revealed to you, ask those who have been reading the scriptures before you. (10:94)

This is another remarkable statement from God to his prophet. Allah is effectively saying to Muhammad, "If you don't believe Me, check it out with the believers of Christian and Jewish scriptures, where you will find this same teaching." This counsel from Allah himself offers a key validation of the fundamental unity of the Abrahamic scriptures in the eyes of God. Otherwise, how could Allah recommend that Muhammad consult the earlier scriptures, unless they were consistent with the Qur'an?

This verse may also have implications for another issue, *tahrif*, which refers to the supposed corruption of the Hebrew and Christian scriptures. This claim, sometimes made by Muslim scholars, is offered as an explanation for the different accounts of Jesus and Mary in the Qur'an, the crucifixion, and other biblical stories. One wonders, why would Allah instruct Muhammed to quell his doubts by consulting earlier scriptures, if those scriptures had been corrupted? This verse (10:94) and other Qur'anic verses that uphold the earlier scriptures perhaps cast doubt on the notion that the Christian and Hebrew scriptures had been corrupted.

There are numerous extant versions of the Christian scriptures, dating back well before Muhammad's time, that correlate closely to the Christian scriptures of today. So there is little reason to suspect that Muhammad had access to Christian scriptures that differ significantly from what we have today. The same holds for the Tanakh; there is little physical manuscript evidence of alteration to the biblical texts. Devotion of the Jewish people to the Torah and the meticulous copying of the text by the Masoretes also supports the idea that the Torah has changed little since Muhammad's time. For example, the oldest Dead Sea Scrolls versions (c. 280 BCE–68 CE) match current usage with only minor variations.

According to the Qur'an, God (or Muhammad under God's orders) appealed to the Torah and Gospel more than twenty times. The Psalms of David and the Torah are frequently quoted, and at certain points, Muhammad asks the Jews to bring a copy of the Torah to settle a dispute. People of the Book who are non-Muslims are encouraged to read their own scriptures, the Torah and the Gospels, and to abide thereby. On certain occasions, the Prophet Muhammad actually invites Jewish and Christian leaders to perform their worship services in the mosque, a remarkably generous gesture on his part. All these facts seem to imply a larger theological consonance among the scriptures, and at least general agreement on the major issues.

A Universal Religion Is Proclaimed in the Qur'an

> Unto each community We have given sacred rites which they are
> to perform; so let them not dispute with thee about the matter, but
> summon them unto thy Lord. (22:67)

> He hath ordained for you of religion [*din*] that which He commended
> unto Noah, and that which We reveal to thee [Muhammad], and
> that which We commended to Abraham and Moses and Jesus, say-
> ing: Establish the religion, and be not divided therein. (42:13)

Here and in several other verses the Qur'an proclaims a universal religion,
or *din*, that dwells at the heart—or *as* the heart—of all religions. This
is a profound contribution from the Qur'an that is rarely found in other
scriptures. It harkens back to the Rig Veda: *Truth is one; sages call it by many
names.* This spiritual universalism is a direct consequence of *tawhid* (oneness) and the *fitra*, the essential nature of the human being. God ordains
all the prophets to establish one absolute religion, and to be undivided in
this endeavor.

The fourteenth-century Sufi commentator Abd al-Razzaq Kashani,
who wrote a profound esoteric commentary on the entire Qur'an, observes
that the difference between the "absolute religion" and the various manifest
forms it acquires is a matter of permanence versus mutability. "The right
religion is tied to that which is immutable within knowledge and action;
while the revealed Law is tied to that which alters in respect of rules and
conditions."[35] Here Kashani is mirroring the distinction between the esoteric essence of religion, which is eternal and permanent, and its exoteric
formulations, which are inevitably mutable and ephemeral.

> So set thy purpose for religion as one with pure devotion—the
> nature of God, according to which God hath created humankind.
> There is no altering God's creation. That is the right religion, but
> most people know it not. (30:30)

Kashani comments on this verse, "Set thy purpose for the religion of *tawhid*,
and this is the path to the Real.... That which is other than this is not 'religion.'" Following Kashani, Reza Shah-Kazemi summarizes the essence of
this essential religion as follows: "The deepest meaning of Islam is extinction
of selfhood within God," a process called *fana* in Sufism. *Fana* is the gateway
of self-transcendence that leads to the sustained abiding in the heart of God,

called *baqa*. "The innermost substance of the soul resonates harmoniously with the transcendent truths conveyed by the revealed Word. It is on the basis of this reverberation, together with the imponderables of divine grace and human effort, that spiritual affinity is transformed into mystical unity: the realization, through *fana*, of the deepest meaning of Islam."[36]

Prayer and Remembrance of God

Remember Me, and I will remember you. (2:152)

The Qur'an repeats this command to remember God fifteen times, which shows the key importance of this practice. The primary practice of remembrance is the *zhikr*, repetition of the name of God, or repetition of the *shahadah*. According to the Naqshbandi Sheikh Khwaja Muhammad Parsa (d. 1420), "The root of being a Muslim is 'No god but God,' words that are identical with remembrance."[37] Repetition of the divine name is described as the best practice by the Prophet. In the Bhagavad Gita, Krishna says this same thing (Gita 10:25).

Remembrance of God means to maintain communion with God from within, through invoking God's name. Mere mental remembrance, or chanting the names of God without a connection through the heart to God, is of little value. The whole point of *zhikr* is to strengthen the intention and aspiration to connect directly with God, and to invoke God's presence in every moment of life. Nothing less will suffice for the serious devotee. This covenant for remembrance of God was established even prior to the creation of humanity:

And when their Lord brought forth from the Children of Adam, from their reins, their seed, and made them testify of themselves [saying], Am I not your Lord? They said, Yes, verily. We testify. That was lest ye say on the Day of Resurrection: Truly, of this we were unaware. (7:172)

Over time "remembrance of God" evolves from being a duty and discipline in the early stages of practice to becoming a blessing and privilege, as the sacramental power and blessing of the practice evolves. Eventually, it becomes more of an abiding presence or inner communion than a practice, in which the name of God is continually invoked as an aspiration or yearning from the heart, and the presence or grace of God suffuses (or drenches!) the heart in response. Over time the invocation and presence are gradually interwoven into a seamless whole.

The Light of God

One of the most subtle and profound verses in the Qur'an is the famous "light verse":

> God is the Light of the heavens and the earth. The Parable of God's Light is as if there were a niche, and within it a lamp: the lamp enclosed in glass: the glass as it were a brilliant star: lit from a blessed tree, an olive [tree], neither of the East nor of the West, whose oil is well-nigh luminous, though fire scarce touched it: Light upon light! God guides whom God will to God's Light. God speaks in parables to the people, for God has knowledge of all things. (24:35)

Let us close this chapter with a meditation on this verse from American Sufi Sheikh Nur (Lex Hixon):

> The Light of Allah is the window [niche].... On the sill of this window rests the precious lamp of the human soul ... protected by the transparent crystal of the heart that glistens delicately, like a star, with the soul's light. This lamp, ignited by Divine Love alone, burns aromatic oil from the Tree of Life ... [which is] found nowhere on earth, neither in the East nor in the West. This fragrant oil of wisdom radiates spontaneously, not touched by any earthly fire. The light of the soul and Source of Light behind it blend, merge, and reappear in the mystery of eternal companionship, as the Light of Allah within the Light of Allah.[38]

3

Divine Love in the Gita, the Qur'an, and the Gospels

"God can be realized through all paths," proclaimed the nineteenth-century Bengali saint Ramakrishna. "God has made different religions to suit different aspirants, times, and countries.... One can reach God if one follows any of the paths with whole hearted devotion."[1]

This chapter reveals the scriptural basis for Ramakrishna's prescient declaration by examining several remarkable parallels between the Bhagavad Gita, the Qur'an, and the Gospels. At this point, we do not concern ourselves with *why* these parallels exist, or what their deeper significance is—these are key issues taken up in later chapters. The focus here is to explore the parallel teachings themselves, and to ask: What does this apparent harmony and synergy between the Gita, the Gospels, and the Qur'an tell us about the essence of the spiritual journey, and about the path of divine love in particular? What does this mean for contemporary spirituality?

Similarities between the teachings and lives of Christ and Krishna have long been noted, with different scholars drawing widely divergent conclusions from these commonalities. Some analyses focus on the striking parallels in the life stories of Jesus and Krishna, and others on the surprising correspondence of their teachings. Similarities between the Gospels and the Qur'an are also extensive, which is perhaps less surprising because they are scriptures of two Abrahamic faith traditions. What might seem more surprising are the striking similarities between the Qur'an and the Bhagavad Gita, which are also remarkably numerous.[2]

In exploring such parallels, it is very important to be mindful of key differences between these scriptures and their respective theologies, religious institutions, and cultures. This is vital for at least two key reasons. First, we need to respect the traditions themselves and the unique character of each. The intent here is not to make a comparison of the traditions in an evaluative or preferential manner. Second, it is important not to superficially fuse distinct traditions or theologies that do not belong together, or directly contradict one another. For example, the Christian tradition regards the fully human incarnation of Jesus as ontologically distinct from what it calls the docetic nature of Krishna's incarnation as an avatar of Vishnu, whereas the Islamic tradition categorically rejects all possibility of incarnation of God in human form whatsoever. While striving to respect these and other crucial differences, it is also important to allow for the possibility of an underlying unity of teaching or revelation that is common to two or more traditions. This unity may inadvertently appear to be significantly different simply because of its expression through dissimilar theological concepts and frameworks. We seek to be sensitive on these accounts in what follows below.

There are several ways we could structure this inquiry, and the approach chosen below is to utilize Krishna's final teaching in the Bhagavad Gita as a backdrop, because it offers a simple framework that helps to organize the information. Krishna describes this teaching as his supreme word and the most secret teaching, so in what follows we can be confident that the essence of the Gita is included in the analysis. We proceed through each verse of this teaching, and explore parallels in the Gospels and the Qur'an, as well as certain key parallels from Sufism. To the extent that the Gospels and the Qur'an are found to concur more or less with the supreme secret of the Gita, then we have found significant common ground across these three scriptures.

Common Ground in the Gospels, the Qur'an, and the Gita

Let us now consider each verse of the "supreme secret" of the Bhagavad Gita (see pages 25–29), and explore parallel or related teachings in the Christian scriptures (especially the Gospels) and in the Qur'an and the aHadith. The correspondences are so numerous and rich that there are several ways this comparison could be carried out. What follows is just one possible (and highly abbreviated) formulation.

Fix Thy Mind upon Me; Devote Thyself to Me

This is the very essence of the spiritual path of divine love. God pours out love to us, and we are to pour our love back to God, thereby completing this profound circle of love. This verse is essentially identical to the first commandment given by Jesus and the *She'ma* of the Jewish tradition: "You shall love the Lord your God with all your heart, and with all your soul, and with all your mind, and with all your strength" (Mark 12:30; Deut. 6:4–5).

The Qur'an is also explicit on this point: "You shall maintain your devotion absolutely to God alone" (Q 22:31),[3] and "There is no God but Me, so worship Me" (Q 21:25). "Celebrate the Name of your Lord and devote yourself wholeheartedly to Him" (Q 73:8). Such exhortations appear throughout the Qur'an, and the *shahadah* also implies this foundational covenant between the human being and God; nothing is worthy of our deepest devotion and worship—except God.

Krishna does not impose. Several times throughout his teaching he reminds Arjuna of his free will to do as he chooses. Similarly in the Qur'an, "There is no compulsion in religion" (Q 2:256), a key point oft repeated. Yet God is inviting us into this profound love affair, if we choose. Krishna invites Arjuna to complete this circle of love, and thereby enter into full and intimate union with God. Krishna says, in effect, make God your greatest treasure, as Jesus also said, "Where your treasure is, there shall your heart be also" (Matt. 6:21).

As human beings, our love and devotion for God is the one thing God does not inherently possess. Everything else we are and have already belongs to the Divine, even before it's manifested. All our theologies and philosophies, scientific inventions, artistic creations, our social and cultural innovations—all these belong intrinsically to the Divine, because they were created through the instruments of human mind and body, which were given to us by God. However, because we have been given free will, we have the freedom to direct our love to whomever and wherever we wish. God asks us to turn our love and devotion back to him/her.

Just as Krishna proclaims his love for the human disciple (represented by Arjuna) and on account of this love discloses to the disciple the greatest spiritual secret (which is to requite God's love by giving devotion back to God), so, too, the very foundation of Sufism is precisely this same completion of the circle of love. This is revealed in the Qur'anic verse, "God loves them, and they love God" (Q 5:59). This short verse, so easy to gloss over in a quick reading, contains the key to the Sufi path of divine love:

> The whole of Sufism can be summed up in the saying in the Qur'an, "God loves them, and they love God" (Q 5:59). Within the heart the lover knows that this is the essence of her relationship with God: His love for us awakens our love for Him, His love draws us back to Him. The whole path is this drama of love being enacted within our heart and within our whole life.[4]

This reciprocal love from the disciple back to the Divine is not a static exchange, but rather a dynamic mutual intimacy and symbiosis of loving communion between the soul and the Divine. A closely related verse is "To God we belong, and to Him we shall return" (Q 2:156), which Sufi master Martin Lings also said sums up the whole of Sufism.[5] These verses speak to a living relationship, something that takes place moment to moment, not just after death. Nor is it some grand breakthrough that happens only once. In each moment of our existence—the eternal now—the exquisite invitation and promise is: "Draw near to God, and God will draw near to you" (James 4:8). "In whatever way persons take refuge in Me, so I share my love with them," says Krishna (Gita 4:11). "Therefore remember Me, and I shall remember you" (Q 2:262); "Allah supports those who support Allah" (Q 22:40). All three scriptures are here inviting us into this direct intimacy with God, in every moment, and God promises the same intimacy with us. The more intensely we draw near to the Divine—in love and devotion, offering ourselves utterly and surrendering with complete abandon—the more closely will the Divine approach us.

Moreover, this circle of love is heavily lopsided with disproportionate grace and benevolence from God toward the human devotee who steps toward God. All three scriptures make this explicit. In the Gospel this is powerfully depicted in the story of the prodigal son, whose Father (God) rushes out to welcome his wayward son's return home, and instead of rebuking him hosts a grand feast and celebration in his honor. Similarly: "If you take one step towards Krishna, He takes one hundred steps towards you."[6] And Allah promises: "Whoever approaches Me by the length of a hand-span, I will approach him by an arm's length. Whoever approaches Me by an arm's length, I will approach him by the length of two outstretched arms. Whoever comes to Me walking, I will approach him running."[7] "The likeness of those who expend their resources in the way of God is as the likeness of a grain of corn that sprouts seven ears, in every ear a hundred grains. So God multiplies unto whom He will" (Q 2:261).

Make Every Action a Sacrifice to Me

This is the great mystic sacrifice, which is the very foundation of spiritual life. It is eloquently expressed in Matthew 16:25: "Whoever seeks to save their life will lose it, but whoever will lose their life for My sake shall find it." The great Sufi Junayd affirms this in a matter-of-fact fashion: "The great *wujud* [finding, experience, ecstasy, existence] of the Real occurs through the loss of your self."[8] In witty jest Meister Eckhart makes the same point: "God is on sale at bargain-basement prices! The only price is your self!"

Rumi expresses this same principle in a magnificent poem:

> This Love sacrifices all souls, however wise, however
> awakened—
> Cuts off their heads without a sword, hangs them without a
> scaffold.
> We are the guests of the One who devours his guests;
> the friends of the One who slaughters his friends.
> Although by his gaze, He brings death to so many lovers,
> Let yourself be killed by Him. Is He not the water of life?
>
> Never, ever grow bitter. He is the Friend who grows gently.
> Keep your heart noble, for this most noble Love
> kills only kings near God, and those free from passion.
> We are like the night, Earth's shadow. He is the sun.
> He splits open the night with a sword soaked in dawn.[9]

This principle is reiterated dramatically in John 15:13: "No one has greater love than this: to lay down one's life for a friend." The sacrifice to be made is in devotion and service to God, or to Sri Krishna, or to Allah. What or who is sacrificed? Nothing except what we are not; nothing real is sacrificed, only the false self we believe ourselves to be. Yet this sacrifice entails all the sense of dread and foreboding if we are strongly identified with the false self, which is inevitably the case for the vast majority of human beings.

Like Christ, Krishna is seated in the hearts of all beings, and hence the profound teaching, "That which you do unto the least of my brethren, you do unto me" (Matt. 25:40), could also be said of Krishna. A key aspect of the sacrifice is to serve God, something oft repeated in the Qur'an. The Arabic word *budni* means either "worship" or "service," perhaps suggesting that to worship *is* to serve, or vice versa.

Ultimately, we must be prepared to face death, if necessary, in our service to God, which Arjuna certainly does on the battlefield, and Jesus implies in "Take up your cross and follow Me" (Matt. 16:24). However, the death involved is generally understood to be the "mystic death" that is incumbent upon the sincere aspirant seeking full spiritual realization. "Die before you die" declares the famous Hadith, calling for the death of our small self and identity, including all worldly attachments. We are explicitly admonished not to wait until physical death for spiritual liberation and salvation, but rather to undergo the radical purification and transformation of identity here and now, in this life. This process entails the "death" or sacrifice of our self as we have known it, and we are then "reborn" or remade into a life centered on, and in, God.

Bow Down Before Me; Hold Thyself as Nothing Before Me

This is a call to give our life for our Beloved, to become nothing, and consecrate all credit for our works to the Divine alone. First and foremost, this entails profound humility before God, as demonstrated by Jesus: "Why do you call me 'good'? None is good but God alone" (Luke 18:19); and earlier by Job (42:6): "Wherefore I abhor myself, and repent in dust and ashes." Jesus bows down to the Father: "The Father is greater than I" (John 14:28), even though he also affirms oneness with the Father—both are true. Notice the close parallel here to the Islamic injunction never to ascribe any partners to God; Jesus ascribes all goodness to God alone, disavows any inherent goodness for himself, and acknowledges that God is greater than he is.

This injunction expresses the essential spirit of *islam* ("submission") as profound humility before God. "Less than the dust are we, beneath

Thy foot Divine!" exclaims Hafiz. "So glorify the praises of your Lord, and be of those who prostrate themselves [to God]" (Q 15:98). "The servants of the Merciful are those who walk on the earth in humility and calmness" (Q 25:63).

> Whoso bows his head to the King of Kings
> Will receive a hundred kingdoms not of this world;
> But the delight of bowing down before God
> Will seem sweeter to thee than countless glories.
>
> —RUMI *MATHNAWI* 4:2

Concomitant with this injunction to bow down to God is that we bow down to nothing else whatsoever. There is a wonderful Sufi story of a humble wayfarer who was invited as part of an entourage to meet with the king. The group was ushered into the royal palace and presented before the king and his retinue in full regalia. Everyone bowed deeply before the king, except the Sufi wayfarer, who remained standing. The king was furious. "How *dare* you not bow down to me!" he roared. "Everyone in the entire kingdom bows down to me! Even when royalty visit from other kingdoms, near or far, they too bow down to me. There is *nobody* who does not bow down to me! Who then are you!?" demanded the king. "I am that nobody," replied the wayfarer.

This story illustrates that we are never to bow down or surrender to anything other than the Supreme Divine itself, by whatever name we call it. This is one of the deeper implications of the *shahadah*, "There is no god but God." We do not settle for any of the myriad treasures or glamorous powers that are offered us along the way. We neither serve nor bow to any worldly sovereigns or temptations, nor to the majestic deities and expansive spiritual consolations—but only to God alone.

You Shall Come to Me Truly I Promise, for You Are Dear to Me

Herein lies the profound gift of the Gita and the Gospels: both scriptures promise direct union with God for those who are true to the path. This union is not reserved exclusively for the exalted Arjuna or Jesus ("I and the Father are one," John 10:30). The promise here is that every true devotee of God will also be made one with God. This promise is explicit and unambiguous in the Gita, and it is expressed also in the Upanishads in a different form, as the supreme identity of Atman and Brahman. Union with God is sanctified by Christ's remarkable prayer, not only for his disciples and followers, but for all who believe in him:

> I pray for those also who will believe in me through their word, that they all may be one, as you, Father, are in me, and I in you, that they may also be one in us.... I in them and you in me, that they may become perfectly one, so that the world may know that you sent me and loved them even as you loved me. (John 17:20–23)

But how is it that ordinary people like you and me can become one with the Divine, like Christ? We can't! You and I cannot "become God." What we can do, or rather allow to happen, is to become nothing. Unless a seed dies, it cannot bear fruit (see John 12:24). The "I" in us must die, in order for the divine Beloved to be born. As Ramana Maharshi describes it, "A perfect self-surrender leaves a residuum of God in which the 'I' is lost.... The 'I' casts off the illusion of 'I' and yet remains as 'I.'"[10]

Ravi Ravindra helps to explain the subtlety here: "No man can make himself God, but he can empty himself so he will be filled with God."[11] This is the process to which the scriptures East and West call us: Empty yourself of your self, and become nothing. "Kenosis" is the term for this process in Western mysticism. In Sufi terms, "When Truth takes hold of a heart, it empties it of everything except Itself."[12] Once emptied, adds Meister Eckhart, "where and when God finds you ready, God must act and overflow into you, just as when the air is clear and pure, the sun must overflow into it and cannot refrain from doing so."[13]

A beautiful Hadith expresses this same principle in Islam: "My servant never ceases to draw nigh unto Me by works of devotion, until I love him, and when I love him I become the eye by which he sees, the mouth through which he speaks, the ear by which he hears."[14] Note that in Islam the human devotee does not become God, but rather is filled with, or "divinized" by, God's attributes, called the Ninety-Nine Names of God. According to Islamic scholar William Chittick, Sufism originated from early Muslims who yearned to become intimate with God by following in the Prophet Muhammad's footsteps. They too sought to come as near as possible to God, just as the Prophet did in the *Miraj*, or night of power, when he ascended through the seven heavens. Sufis aspire to this same process of ascending to ultimate intimacy with God.

It is instructive to compare the Hadith in the previous paragraph with the testimony to Christian mystical realization attributed to St. Teresa of Avila:

> Christ has no body now but yours; no hands, no feet on earth but yours. Yours are the eyes through which he looks with compassion on this world; yours are the feet with which he walks to do good; yours are the hands through which he blesses all the world; you are his body.[15]

Christ "inhabits" the very inward being and body of the Christian mystic, just as Allah becomes the devotee's seeing, hearing, walking, and so forth. This suggests that the subjective phenomenology of mystical realization, based on the experiences of Sufi and Christian mystics, is basically the same in both cases. The Sufi mystic becomes the human instrument for Allah's voice, hands, and feet, and the Christian mystic becomes the human instrument for Christ's voice, hands, and feet. Both are emptied of themselves, and "divinized" as instruments for channeling divine love and will. This is the very fulfillment of the sacred purpose of the mystical journey. The differences between their respective traditions in terms of contradictory theologies or prayer practices seem to be rendered irrelevant in the experience of mystical realization.

Intimacy with God: union or nearness? The above Hadith illustrates how unconditional devotion to God eventually leads to the experience of supreme intimacy with God. The notion of actual union with God has no theological place in Islam, because God is necessarily other—utterly incommensurable with anything that is created. In Islam, the human devotee, or servant, does not become "one with God"; indeed, such a claim would be blasphemy, or *shirk*, the worst and only unforgivable sin in Islam. Yet the distinction between devotee and God becomes ever more subtle at the depths of mystical realization.

There is a certain tension within the Islamic tradition regarding the realization of oneness with God, especially in Sufism. As Muslims, Sufis are generally very careful to distinguish between God and human devotees. On the one hand, the foundational principle of *tawhid* holds that there exists one supreme Reality, which is God, and nothing can exist outside of God. God alone exists. On the one hand, God is utterly other—incommensurable with all of creation—and to affirm identification or ontological equivalence with God is *shirk*. So Muslims speak of "nearness" to God as a way to characterize deep intimacy with God, and it seems the distance can be very slight, infinitesimal, while still maintaining the distinction between the human soul and God. As one commentator puts it, "The mystic does not become one with God, he becomes conscious of his oneness with God."[16]

However, Ibn Arabi and certain other Sufis have proclaimed a kind of oneness with God, similar to what we find in other traditions, which of course has been controversial. When Al Hallaj proclaimed *An al Haqq*, he was claiming his oneness with *Haqq* (Truth, or the Real), which is one of the Ninety-Nine Names of God. The Sufi term *fana* refers to the extinction or annihilation of the human identity, and total absorption in God. When this condition is fully established and stabilized, it becomes *baqa*, or abiding in *fana*.

Ibn Arabi distinguishes between two types of *gnosis*, or knowledge of God: knowing God through knowing yourself (the lower type, which is to know one's Lord), and knowing God "through you *as* Him, not as yourself," the higher type, which is attainable exclusively through being the Absolute Godhead. The latter form of knowing "is possible only insofar as one already *is* the Absolute, on the one hand, and insofar as one's specific contingency is negated, on the other."[17] In the latter case of higher knowing, it is difficult to see how one can maintain the claim to a distinction between devotee and God, except perhaps to note that in this supreme state of realization the human devotee has ceased to exist (*fana*), so the point may be moot. Even so, Ibn Arabi has proclaimed that "when you know yourself, your 'I' ness vanishes and you know that you and Allah are one and the same."[18] This declaration is virtually identical to similar statements from Meister Eckhart, and mystics in other traditions. "The highest stage of *fana* is reached when even the consciousness of having attained *fana* disappears. This is what the Sufis call 'the passing-away of passing-away (*fana al-fana*).' The mystic is now wrapped in contemplation of the divine essence."[19]

As Sufi scholar Reza Shah-Kazemi describes the foundation and highest goal of the mystical path, "the inmost essence of the individual is not other than the transcendent Essence of the Absolute."[20] This affirms the ontological identity of the deepest essence of the human being with the transcendent essence of God. It is difficult to discern any substantive difference here between this and, say, the Hindu mystical assertion that "Atman is Brahman."[21] Indeed, it seems that St. Paul's declaration, "I live, yet not I, but Christ liveth in me" can be equally applied verbatim to realized mystics in Hinduism or Islam, by simply replacing the word "Christ" with either "Krishna" or "Allah." The intimate process of divinization in the heart of the mystic is the same in every case. Regardless of what position one takes on these fine points of mystical theology, the divine promise to the human soul is clear: If we truly give our love to God, then God promises to confer the realization of profound intimacy with God, regardless of whether we conceive of it as "union" or infinitesimal "nearness."

Returning to the Gita text, Krishna repeats here something he had just said in the prior verse (18:64), that he is offering this gift of union because Arjuna is very dear to him. He later enjoins Arjuna not to share this secret with any who are unfaithful, or who scorn Krishna. "The wise should not disturb the ignorant" (3:26), and we find this same selective process with Jesus and the Prophet. Despite the popular religious notion that "Jesus loves you," he prays not for the entire world, but for those God gave him and for those who believe in him through their word (John 17:9, 20), and he presents his teachings in parables "lest [the unbelievers] should understand and convert" (Matt. 13:15). Similarly for the Prophet, "When you recite the Qur'an, We put an invisible barrier between you and those who do not believe, ... We put covers on their hearts to prevent them from understanding" (17:45–46). Allah makes frequent distinction between the faithful and the unbelievers, and promises [God's] reward only to the former, whereas the latter will suffer. This is not ungracious on God's part, as it might seem at first to the uninitiated. God offers divine grace freely to all. "Of the bounties of thy Lord, We bestow freely upon all [believers and unbelievers]" (7:20). Although "We have bestowed more on some than others" (7:21), the bounties "are not closed [to anyone]" (7:20), and "My loving compassion encompasses all things" (7:156). Nevertheless, many withdraw from God's grace, into themselves, and then God can do nothing because the human being has free will. "Seeing they do not perceive; hearing they do not listen" (Matt. 13:13), and the ensuing suffering is caused by human ignorance and insistence on separation from God, rather than allowing union or nearness.

Abandon All Dharmas

It is no accident that this teaching is given only once in the Gita, and then only at the very end of the entire training and transmission from Krishna.

This final secret is divulged to the advanced disciple who has engaged deeply in the *sadhana* and earnestly followed the injunctions of the dharma and scriptures, and is now prepared to "enter the kingdom," as it were, where human laws and institutions of every form are necessarily transcended altogether. As Bede Griffiths observes in his extensive commentary on the Gita, *River of Compassion*, "Dharma is the law. This is a call to go beyond the law, to enter into a state of grace."[22]

The resulting state of spiritual perfection is exemplified in the case of mystics such as St. John of the Cross. On his famous schematic drawing of the spiritual journey symbolized by the ascent of Mt. Carmel, John scribbles across the summit of the mountain: "Here there is no longer any way because for the just man there is no law; he is a law unto himself."[23]

There is a close parallel to this in the long, mixed history between Sufism and orthodox Islam. Many Sufi mystics over the centuries, including preeminent leaders like Rumi, Ibn Arabi, Al Hallaj, and others, have departed from Islamic law at times and said and written things that branded them as heretics or apostates. Response was varied and in some cases entailed persecution or death, like Al Hallaj's execution. Nevertheless, a number of antinomian Sufi lineages (called *Bi-Shara*, lawless) emerged; these maintained that following the *sharia* law of Islam was unnecessary for those on the esoteric (*batin*) path, and this led to a division between *Bi-Shara* Sufi communities and *Ba-Shara* communities, which follow the *sharia* law.[24] Ibn Arabi and other great teachers said that realized Sufis, although exempt from repetitious religious observances because of their attainment, would maintain outward observance for the public good, or else would be exonerated by legal decision, as often happened and still does. According to Idries Shah, even a thousand years ago Islamic jurists upheld the notion that certain things said and done in nonordinary states of ecstatic consciousness could not be judged by ordinary criteria, and this helped legitimize the Sufis in Islamic opinion.[25]

There is a story that Rumi told about the great Sufi Bayazid Bistami, who, in states of ecstatic rapture, sometimes proclaimed himself to be God. Afterward, his students would challenge him fiercely for this outrageous blasphemy, and he was shocked and dumbfounded, and agreed with them that this was absolutely unacceptable. He instructed them, if it ever happened again, to draw their swords and kill him on the spot. The very next evening, Bistami entered into a state of profound spiritual ecstasy, and once again ecstatically proclaimed his oneness with God. The students drew their swords and dutifully attacked their master, but their blades bounced back, as if from an invisible shield. The swords harmed only the attackers, but Bistami could not be harmed, and remained in ecstatic communion with, or as, God.[26]

The metaphysical principle in these traditions is that higher realms of spiritual consciousness confer greater freedoms, and those who attain those higher realms follow higher laws. St. Paul gives essentially the same teaching, "If you are guided by the Spirit, you are not under the law" (Gal. 5:20). Many are the occasions when Jesus invokes this exemption from traditional religious law, such as healing on the Sabbath, forgiving sins, and proclaiming himself one with the Father. Jesus is living the direct union with the Father, come what may, and he calls us to the same.

In the apocryphal Gospel of Mary (discovered in 1896, one of the noncanonical "gnostic gospels"), there is a remarkable moment when Jesus tells Mary Magdalene, who is arguably his most senior and beloved disciple:

> The Son of Humanity already exists within you. Follow him, for those who seek him there will find him.... Beyond what I have already given you, do not lay down any further rules nor issue laws as the Lawgiver, lest you too be dominated by them.[27]

Here Jesus counsels Mary to follow her direct connection to Christ within, and not to establish any other rules or laws. The parallel here with the supreme secret of the Gita—to take refuge in Krishna alone, and abandon all other dharmas—is remarkable.

The divine gift is expressed in distinctive ways in different traditions, but the subtle nature of the mystical process is essentially the same. In Aurobindo's integral yoga, there is a "supreme grace from above" that responds to sincere aspiration "from below" in the heart of the aspirant.[28] In the Gospels Jesus says, "I am the light of the world" and he also declares emphatically, "You are the light of the world." In the *Ayat an-Nur* of "Light upon light" in the Qur'an (24:35), the divine light descends and merges with the light rising up from the soul. And the psalmist confirms, "In Thy Light we see light" (Ps. 36:9). In all these cases, there is an aspiration or "light" of prayer from the human soul, to which the Divine responds by infusing the soul with a supreme "Light" or higher grace, and the two merge into one Light. Words fail us here when trying to describe something so subtle and glorious, far beyond what language or concepts can express.

Take Refuge in God Alone

This line, together with the previous line—"Abandon all dharmas, take refuge in God alone"—is the *caramasloka* of the Bhagavad Gita. It is the injunction to abandon all reliance on anything other than God. From an Islamic perspective, this could be seen as the inevitable consequence of the first *shahadah*. Precisely because "there is no god but God," we should abandon every practice except taking absolute refuge in the one God. This is the foundation of spiritual life, and is consistent with the essence of both the Qur'an and the Gospels, which repeatedly affirm that God is the sole source of all power, all knowledge, all mercy, and all salvation, and thus humans are to submit utterly to God. In short: Belong to God, and to nothing else.

This is the Gita's supreme secret, and it spells out in unambiguous terms what it actually means to love God with all your heart, soul, mind, and strength (in Christian and Jewish terms), or to totally submit (*islam*) to God (in Islamic terms). It reflects the deepest meaning of what is enjoined as well in the Qur'an, *la ilaha il Allah* ("There is no reality but God"), and by Jesus in the garden of Gethsemane ("Let it be as Thou, not I, would have it"). Nothing less than absolute surrender is required, and this entails the "death" of our human identity; the end of who we have believed ourselves to be.

Nevertheless, it is important to acknowledge a potential distinction between the traditions, depending on how the injunction to "abandon all dharmas" is interpreted. If it is taken as an explicit call to go beyond the religious law, this would be inconsistent with the requirement for all Muslims to abide by the *sharia*. However, Sufis such as Ibn Arabi and Al Ghazali "shared the view that Islamic law was only a temporary means to a higher goal, and they eschewed the heavy focus on worldly matters such as financial transactions and regulations regarding clothing. Ibn Arabi ... was known for his view that religiously binding consensus could only serve as a source of sacred law if it was the consensus of the first generation of Muslims," who were companions of the Prophet Muhammad.[29] This is another area of controversy in Islam, particularly in Sufism.

There are multiple examples in the Gospels of taking refuge in God. At the obvious level, Jesus promises refuge: "Come to Me, all who are weary and heavy-laden, and I will give you rest. Take my yoke upon you, and learn from me, for I am gentle and humble in heart, and you will find rest for your souls.[30] For my yoke is easy, and my burden is light" (Matt. 11:28–30).

When sending out the apostles to preach, Jesus encourages them to take refuge in a different way: "Do not be anxious how you are to speak or what you are to say, for what you are to say will be given to you in that hour. For it is not you who speak, but the Spirit of your Father speaking through you" (Matt. 10:19–20). Thus God will guide and protect the devotee when in the midst of potential adversaries. The Qur'an also frequently counsels believers to take refuge in Allah from adversaries or unbelievers. The adversaries are not necessarily outward; one must also take refuge in God from one's own inner weakness or demons.

Refuge in prayer. Jesus also guides us to take refuge in prayer, and he gives explicit instructions for how to pray: "Go into your inner room (*tameion*), close the door, and pray to God who is in secret, and God who sees in secret will reward you" (Matt. 6:6). This verse is the scriptural foundation for silent contemplative prayer in the Christian tradition, and is often cited by Father Thomas Keating and the other pioneers of Centering Prayer. The Greek word *tameion* here means "private chamber" or "secret inner room." Closing this door therefore implies not mere external solitude, but more importantly, inner solitude: We close the door on the innumerable thoughts and distractions that normally consume our attention, and pray from the silent spaciousness of the heart.

We find similar counsel in the Qur'an, "Call on your Lord humbly and privately" (Q 7:55), "Remember your Lord in yourself humbly and with awe, without loudness of voice, morning and evening" (Q 7:205). Similarly in the Gita, we find the whole of chapter 6 devoted to silent meditation or prayer, with specific guidelines given: "Select a clean spot, neither too high nor too low, and seat yourself firmly on a cloth.... Once seated, strive to still your thoughts. Make your mind one-pointed in meditation, and your heart will be purified.... With all fears dissolved in the peace of the Self, and all desires dedicated to Brahman, ... sit in meditation with Me as your only goal" (6:11–14). Thus all three scriptures instruct us to take refuge in prayer or meditation—in private, without fanfare, alone with God.

Surrender to God. In his agony in the garden of Gethsemane, Jesus implores God in a moment of anguish, "*Abba*, Father, all things are possible for you, take away this cup from me," and without skipping a beat, he immediately surrenders: "Nevertheless, not what I will, but what thou wilt" (Mark 14:36). In any genuine spiritual test, we all waver, and here in extreme agony facing a hideous execution, Jesus demonstrates profound surrender to God. Later, in excruciating pain on the cross, Jesus prays for his murderers, "Father forgive them, for they know not what they do" (Luke 23:34).

The great Sufi saint Al Hallaj, who proclaimed oneness with God by declaring, "*An al Haqq* (I am the Supreme Reality)," received the same treatment as Jesus—he was publicly executed in Baghdad. As they dismembered his body, he too prayed for his executioners, saying, "Forgive them, Lord. Have mercy on them. Surely if Thou hadst shown them what Thou hast shown me, they would never have done what they have done.... Whatsoever Thou dost will, I praise Thee!"[31] It is hard to imagine a more extreme test of utter submission and taking refuge in the Divine than to pray for one's murderers at a time like this. The Indian yogi Paramahansa Yogananda avers that Jesus's prayer for his executioners is the greatest of all the miracles Jesus performed, and this same miracle was repeated by Al Hallaj.

"Not my will, but Thine" is the very foundation of surrender to God's will that is the command for all true devotees and seekers in every moment of life. Naturally, we waver, out of personal willfulness, laziness, inattentiveness, capriciousness, all manner of desires and distractions, and most especially when tested strongly. But the injunction is clear, and the wavering, when overcome, strengthens our resolve and capacity to surrender even more. The case of Jesus in the garden of Gethsemane or Al Hallaj being executed in Baghdad are extreme examples, but the same principle applies.

The Qur'an gives the same command: "Ye shall not will except as God wills—the Cherisher of the Worlds" (81:29), and "You will not unless God wills, surely God is ever All-knowing, All-wise" (76:30). The Bhagavad Gita culminates with Arjuna finally submitting his will utterly to God: "I will act according to Thy command" (18:73).

This total self giving of our human will to divine will is the very essence of unconditional love for God. To do God's will is precisely how we demonstrate our love for God in practice—without it, our protestations of love for God mean little. As Jesus put it bluntly, "If you love me, you will keep my commandments" (John 14:23).

Yogananda offers a beautiful interpretation or alternative translation of this verse of the Gita, by translating the word *ekam* (usually translated as "alone" or "only") as "oneness": "In My *oneness*, take refuge from the world of separation." This is the very heart of mystical union, and has essentially the same deep meaning as *tawhid* in Islam. Taking refuge in *tawhid* is the very realization of the supreme oneness—the one God that is the sole Reality. Taking refuge in this Reality entails renouncing the illusion of separate selfhood.

In the mysticism of the Bhagavad Gita, this realization takes place in stages (perhaps parallel to the seven heavens in Islam), and the final stages entail taking refuge in the *buddhi* (intuition) from the separation of *manas* (mind), taking refuge in the *Atman* (Light) from the *buddhi*, and at the very summit of spiritual realization, merging into the Godhead (*Purushottama*) by renouncing both *prakriti* and *purusha*, and taking refuge in the Supreme Godhead alone. Everything else flows out from this realization, as the resplendent waters rush down from the lofty peaks. "Seek ye first the kingdom of God ... and all these things shall be added unto you" (Matt. 6:33). Similarly for Krishna and Allah, respectively: "Those who worship me and meditate on me constantly, without any other thought, I will provide for all their needs" (Gita 9:22), and "For those who believe in Allah, He brings forth a way out, and gives them provision (*rizq*) from where they do not even imagine" (Q 2:3).

Nondual Devotional Path

One key point before moving on: When we consider Krishna's promise of union with the absolute Godhead (*Purushottama*)—which is also repeated elsewhere in the Gita[32]—together with the supreme secret of taking absolute refuge in the oneness of God, it becomes crystal clear that the path of love in the Gita is a path of nondual mystical realization. This is also true for the depths of Christian and Sufi mysticism. Nevertheless, *bhakti* or *para bhakti*, the supreme path of divine love, is sometimes mischaracterized as inherently dualistic, because God and the human devotee are deemed separate. This putative duality becomes grounds for dismissing or depreciating the path of love, especially among some contemporary seekers for whom "nondual realization" is fashionable as the most authentic form of spirituality. This view is coupled with a discernible (if unspoken) disdain for "dualistic" paths, which taints the path of divine love as somehow inferior, or appropriate only for "less evolved'" souls. This is a contemporary version of a regrettable, yet age-old, counterproductive rivalry among diverse spiritual pathways that has sometimes marred otherwise legitimate spiritual schools.

I Will Liberate Thee from All Sins: Do Not Grieve

Here we have the promise of divine forgiveness and salvation that Jesus Christ and Allah also promise. Father Bede Griffiths summarizes the essence of Krishna's message here:

> Have no fear, do not be afraid. "I will make thee free from the bondage of sin." ... It is remarkable how close to Christian revelation this comes. [33]

Remarkable indeed; all the more so because the concept of sin in Eastern religions generally has a very different ontological and theological context than in Christianity. Yet as theologian Francis X. Clooney demonstrates in his superb exegetical analysis of this verse and its larger context within the Gita, the concept of sin here is rich in nuance and comprehensive in its reference to all the obstacles, flaws, and faults that block movement toward God, and therefore it "might well include much of what Christians mean by sin." [34] Clooney concludes that this verse "offers a comforting message [that] may be taken as speaking to Christians and other theists," and that "for some at least, we may no longer be able to hear the voice of Jesus without an echo of Gita 18:66." [35]

　　Similar promises of forgiveness and salvation are found in the Qur'an. "Allah is Ever-Forgiving, Most Merciful" (24:22, repeated many times). Many other verses reveal the depth and breadth of God's forgiveness: "Allah is all-pardoning, ever forgiving (22:60). [36] It is He Who accepts repentance from His servants and pardons evil acts, and He knows all they do (42:25). Those who are steadfast and do right actions will receive forgiveness and a great reward (11:11). Allah promises you forgiveness from him and abundance. Allah is All-Encompassing, All-Knowing (2:268).

Your mistakes will be forgiven you (7:161). God saved you. He knows the secrets of the heart (8:43). Ask forgiveness of your Lord. Truly He is endlessly forgiving" (71:10).[37]

Divine forgiveness entails multiple dimensions. "The masses repent of their faults. The elect repent of their neglect," says the Sufi Dhu u Nun.[38] God promises not only to forgive our gross sins and mistakes made out of ignorance or immaturity, but also the myriad ways that we have knowingly betrayed or forgotten the Divine despite our commitment, ignored the inner impulse from the heart, trampled upon the "still small voice within" in the rush of our own desire or anger, or rationalized our way out of following divine will as it was revealed in our hearts.

This promise of divine forgiveness is an astounding blessing and is absolutely essential for human existence, because we are all constantly committing one or another form of error, betrayal, or forgetfulness of God, often willfully! We are thus in need of continual forgiveness. The Prophet Muhammad exclaimed, "By Allah! I ask for forgiveness from Allah and turn to Him in repentance more than seventy times a day."[39] Most of us would need to do this many more than seventy times a day to be fully accountable for our blunders and indiscretions of awareness, thought, and deed! Jesus counsels us to forgive others "not seven times, but seventy-seven times" (Matt. 18:22). If God held us all fully accountable for all our failings and deliberate trespasses, not a single human being would be found worthy in the eyes of God. We humans are utterly dependent on this living promise of divine forgiveness that is ever streaming toward us, yet we are so accustomed to it that we generally take it for granted (which is yet another sin for which we require forgiveness).

Krishna's final words of peace and consolation, "Do not grieve," are closely echoed by Jesus: "Peace I leave with you; my peace I give to you. Not as the world gives do I give to you. Let not your hearts be troubled, neither let them be afraid" (John 14:27). We find essentially the same promise repeated frequently in the Qur'an: "God invites [everyone] to the Home of Peace" (Q 10:25) and "God guides to the ways of peace" (Q 5:16). "Whosoever believes in God and the last day and does good deeds—they shall have no fear, nor shall they grieve" (Q 5:69). The counsel not to grieve or be fearful is repeated frequently throughout the Qur'an for all virtuous believers, not just Muslims. Hence the Qur'anic promise of universal salvation: "For those who say, 'Our Lord is God' and take the straight path toward Him, the angels come down to them and say, 'Have no fear or grief, but rejoice' in the good news of Paradise, which you have been promised … as a gift from the Most Forgiving, Most Merciful One" (41:30–32).

Krishna and Christ

Reflecting on the supreme secret in its entirety, let us focus briefly on Krishna and Christ, because both proclaim themselves as human incarnations of God, something that is deemed impossible in Islam. Krishna's fundamental teaching is perhaps most closely encapsulated and aligned with Jesus Christ in his teaching: "I AM the way, the truth, and the life. No one comes to the Father except through me" (John 14:6). This "I" that Jesus speaks of is I AM, the name that God declared to Moses. This is the I AM that *is* before Abraham *was*. This is the voice of Christ-merged-with-God speaking in the first person through and as Jesus, just as the *Purushottama* speaks through and as Krishna, who also uses the personal pronoun "I." Krishna makes virtually the identical proclamation: "I am the Way, the Supporter, the Lord. I am the Father of the Universe" (Gita 9:18–17). Both Jesus and Krishna are human incarnations of the Divine—Jesus is one with the Father and Krishna is one with *Purushottama*. Each of them, united with God, speaks in the first person with the voice and word of God. Christ and Krishna each correctly affirms, in his own time and manifestation, that he is the way and the truth and the life, and that only through him, who is one with the Supreme Divine, can others also reach the Divine.

Both Christ and Krishna proclaim themselves to be the exclusive pathway to God. Yet there is no contradiction here. How can this be? Because "Christ is the Christian symbol for the whole of Reality" and other religions use different names for this same Reality, declares Raimon Panikkar in what may be his greatest masterpiece, *Christophany*.[40] "Christians do not have a monopoly on knowledge of Christ," and "the Christian recognizes Christ *in* and *through* Jesus," continues Panikkar in his nine sutras that portend a profound renewal of Christian theology. "Jesus is Christ, but Christ cannot be identified completely with Jesus."[41]

Yogananda makes essentially the same points in speaking of the universal Christ Consciousness, or *Kuthastha Chaitanya*. "Not the body of Jesus but the consciousness within it was one with the only begotten

Son, the Christ Consciousness, the only reflection of God the Father in creation.... It is a metaphysical error to speak of the historical person of Jesus as the only savior. It is the Christ Intelligence that is the universal redeemer."[42]

This is not to deny the radically unique and profound ministry of Jesus Christ. Every divine incarnation brings an unprecedented revelation and spiritual revolution in its particular historical, cultural, and evolutionary context. Yet this supreme Love and divine Power that worked in and through Jesus, which Christians call "Christ," also operates in and through other religious and spiritual traditions, where it goes by different names. "Truth is one," says the Rig Veda. "Sages call it by different names."[43]

Krishna and Christ are living gateways to something infinitely precious, supremely intimate, profoundly dynamic, alive, and powerful beyond all imagination, which, for linguistic convenience and lack of a better alternative, we call "God" or the "Divine." The human incarnations of Krishna and Christ may have vanished long ago, but the essence of who and what they are is no less alive and vibrant today than when they were incarnated in human form on earth. Both Christ and Krishna are *here*—now. Both are infinite. "I support this entire cosmos with only a fragment of my being," says Krishna (Gita 10:42). Both are eternal. "Before Abraham was, I am," says Jesus (John 8:58). "I know all beings of the past, the present, and the future," says Krishna, "but none knows Me completely" (Gita 7:26).

Both Krishna and Christ promise eternal life to their devotees. Whoever believes in Christ will "not perish, but have eternal life" (John 3:16). "Know thou, O [Arjuna], that my devotee never perishes" (Gita 9:31). Both Christ and Krishna call us to live in profound surrender to the Supreme Divine, and if we consent to this call in total sincerity and commitment, both promise to unite us with them, and to live through us.

"The Christian religion is about transformation into Christ—nothing else," says Father Thomas Keating.[44] Likewise, the spirituality of the Bhagavad Gita is about transformation into Krishna, nothing else. "Whatever facilitates and sustains this realization of supreme spirit is true wisdom. Whatever opposes it is ignorance" (Gita 13:11). Why is this? Because "our deepest self *is* Christ," affirms Keating.[45]

Our deepest self *is* Krishna. As the transformation takes place, our personal "self," which we tenaciously believe to be ourselves, is entirely replaced by the Christ or Krishna within. Then, as St. Paul says, "I live, yet not I, but Christ liveth in me" (Gal. 2:20). Similarly in the *Srimad Bhagavada*, when Arjuna journeys with Krishna to the abode of the supreme divine *Purushottama*, the latter addresses Arjuna as a "second Krishna."[46]

When the Christ child appeared once to St. Teresa of Avila and asked who she was, she replied, "I am Teresa of Jesus," to which the child replied, "I am Jesus of Teresa." The two have become one. Arjuna dissolves and merges into Krishna, just as Teresa dissolves and merges into Christ.

We, too, are called to this selfsame transformation. We are to merge into the living Christ, the living Krishna. This is the profound teaching of the Gita and the Gospels, and of the Qur'an as well: We are called to give ourselves utterly to this mysterious, transformative process of divine love. Not only does Jesus declare, "I am the light of the world" (John 8:12), but he also proclaims, "*You* are the light of the world" (Matt. 5:14; emphasis added). Like Christ, we are here to burn brightly with the light and fire of divine love, to see all with the same eyes of Christ, the *jyothisam* of the Gita (13:8), the *nur* of the Qur'an. "The world of God takes over our world. There *is* only God, ultimately," explains Keating.[47]

The true purpose of the Bhagavad Gita and the Gospels and the Qur'an is to inspire and facilitate—in fact and not just metaphorically—this radical transformation of the human being. This is the whole point of the teaching; this is why it is "good news." As Francis D'Sa says, "It is the Christ who dwells in the deepest center of our being."[48] If this transformation into the living Krishna or living Christ or loving servant of Allah does not take place, then the deepest purpose of the scriptures remains unfulfilled, regardless of how often or how piously we may read, study, chant, or praise the scriptures.

And when this transformation is fulfilled, proclaims Meister Eckhart, "God must just become me, and I must just become God—so completely One that this 'I' and that 'God' become and are one *is*, and in this *is*-ness eternally perform one work.... You ought to sink down out of all your *your*-ness, and flow into his *His*-ness, and your 'yours' and his 'His' ought to become one 'mine,' so completely that you with him perceive forever his uncreated *is*-ness, and his nothingness, for which there is no name."[49]

Hints at a Universal Path of Divine Love

What are we to make of this remarkable spiritual synergy between the Bhagavad Gita, the Qur'an, and the Gospels? What are the implications for the path of love in contemporary spirituality?

Important bridges are being established here—between diverse religious traditions, between Christ and Krishna, between Christ and Allah, between Krishna and Allah, between West and East and Middle East—bridges across the enormous chasms of radically different cultures and historical epochs. Something universal appears to be emerging here—a kind of supreme covenant of love between God and the human soul.

Yet important differences remain between the traditions, and also perhaps a certain discomfort at these junctures, and the unknown mystery of where these bridges may lead us. In grappling with this discomfort, perhaps we can take a cue from one of the great interspiritual mystics, the Benedictine monk Henri Le Saux, who later became Swami Abhishiktananda after emigrating to India. Here is a mystic who profoundly engaged the links and the gulf between Hindu and Christian spirituality, and spent a lifetime forging, and becoming, a profound bridge between these two traditions:

> It is precisely the fact of being a bridge that makes this uncomfortable situation worthwhile. The world, at every level, needs such bridges. The danger of this life as a "bridge" is that we run the risk of not belonging to either side; whereas, however harrowing it may be, our duty is to belong wholly to both sides. This is only possible in the mystery of God.[50]

Surely it is not everyone's duty to "belong wholly to both sides" in the sense of making a full commitment to two (or more) spiritual traditions. But for those of us who are called, this is precisely the charge. A universal path of divine love is beginning to reveal itself, through the teachings of Krishna and Christ and the Islamic mystics—a call to God that is profoundly nurtured by all these traditions.

As Hadith *Qudsi* says, God is with those whose hearts are broken for the sake of God. It matters little in which manner or tradition one's heart is broken open to God. The indispensable key is the profound opening, self-giving, and surrender to the Divine that constitutes the true path of the heart to God. This is a direct path that might be called "intertraditional."

It draws upon the deep wisdom of the established traditions, yet functions at the inner mystical core of the heart—shared in common by the traditions—rather than at the outer and surface levels where religious and institutional encumbrances sometimes thwart or mislead serious aspirants and disciples.

The Sufis say there are three journeys: the journey *from* God, the journey *to* God, and the journey *in* God. The first is the ordinary worldly life. The second is what most people take to be spiritual life, though it is merely preparation for the real journey of total dynamic union *in* God. Most spiritual teachings and paths merely get us started on the journey *to* God. The majority of people on a "spiritual path" never get beyond the second journey in their lifetimes.

Scriptures tell us but little of the third journey—*in* God. It is the great mystery or secret that can only be entered into, never described. "God is humanity's secret. Humanity is God's secret. This is the secret of secrets."[51] Ultimately we must discover this secret ourselves, and take the plunge into "the dark silence in which all lovers lose themselves."[52] For in that dark silence is the Real, the Supreme Godhead, the *Purushottama*, the One without a name. And never can we rest until we merge in union with that Source.

Mystics of
Divine Love

4

Many Faiths, One Summit

Ibn Arabi, Shankara, and Meister Eckhart

W hat is the highest goal of religion? What is the nature of ultimate spiritual realization? Do different religions lead to different ultimates? Is the summit of the mystical journey one and the same across the religions, or are there multiple summits in different religions?

These are crucial questions in comparative mysticism, to which many answers are given. In this book we turn to the mystics themselves for inspiration and possible answers, for they are the most qualified to speak of these profound states of spiritual attainment, having "been there" themselves. This chapter offers a fresh approach to these questions through the mystical journeys and writing of three leading mystics, one each from Islam, Hinduism, and Christianity. The chapter summarizes recent research carried out by Dr. Reza Shah-Kazemi, an interfaith scholar at the Ismaili Institute in London. His book *Paths to Transcendence* analyzes the mysticism and writings of three of the greatest mystical sages in history: Ibn Arabi (Sufi), Shankara (Hindu), and Meister Eckhart (Christian).

Shah-Kazemi found that these three mystics provide very similar descriptions of the summit of the spiritual journey, including the attainment of transcendent spiritual realization, the transformative journey to attain it, and the existential return to mortal existence after realization. His research is so illuminating and compelling that I devote this chapter to presenting a summary of his key findings, with the hope of making this information more widely accessible to practitioners on the path of divine love.

The findings of Shah-Kazemi's research provide a powerful demonstration of the transcendent unity of the highest mystical realizations attained by these three sages. He concludes that the evidence "leaves no doubt that the sages are indeed speaking of the selfsame reality. Coming from such prominent mystical authorities within their faiths, this evidence of spiritual unanimity on the ultimate values and goal of religion is of particular importance in demonstrating the oneness of religion, not on the formal, but on the transcendent plane."[1]

Yet it might be asked: How broadly applicable are insights about the interfaith mystical journey that are based on close examination of just three specific mystics? This is a valid question, and we consider other mystics in subsequent chapters to help round out the picture. Nevertheless, in the case of Shankara, Ibn Arabi, and Eckhart, few would deny that these three are rare spiritual giants who reached the summit of mystical realization within their respective faith traditions. The fact that these three masters attained what is evidently the same mystical summit therefore carries considerable weight, and provides compelling support for the transcendent unity of Christianity, Hinduism, and Islam—despite their myriad theological, cultural, and liturgical differences.

Meister Eckhart (c. 1260–1328) was a Catholic theologian in the Dominican order whose sermons and writings are widely regarded as among the most profound in the Christian mystical tradition. He was influenced by Beguine mystic Marguerite Porete's book *The Mirror of Simple Souls*, for which she was burned at the stake in 1610.[2] Shankara (c. 788–c. 820) was a theologian and philosopher widely considered to be the principal consolidator of the nondual Advaita Vedanta path of Hinduism. He traveled throughout India, engaging in public debate with proponents of orthodox and heterodox schools of Hinduism and Buddhism. Ibn Arabi (1165–1240) was a Sufi mystic, poet, and philosopher; renowned as a saint; and considered by some Sufis as "the greatest master."[3] His writings are still highly influential in the Islamic tradition.

The degree of spiritual depth, subtlety, and precision in Reza Shah-Kazemi's work is exceptional, and what follows is considerably simplified and omits extensive detail that is beyond the scope of this chapter. Any errors or inaccuracies below due to oversimplification or inadvertent misapprehension of Reza Shah-Kazemi's work are entirely the author's responsibility. Readers inspired to learn more are referred to Reza Shah-Kazemi's original works, particularly *Paths to Transcendence*.[4]

Shah-Kazemi analyzes the transcendent spiritual journey in three stages using the classic metaphor of climbing the mystical mountain: the summit of transcendent realization, the ascent to the summit, and the existential return to ordinary consciousness. Below I attempt to gather major insights from each of these stages into a series of basic principles, upon which all three mystics agree.

At times the writing in this chapter is necessarily somewhat technical, because I draw upon specific quotations and often subtle concepts or articulations from these three sages, so as to present their ideas and insights as accurately and succinctly as possible. For the sake of clarity much detail has been omitted, and along with it much subtle insight. Yet in paying this price, I hope it is outweighed for our purposes by rendering the major elements of mystical unity in a lucid and flowing manner. To aid in this process, I encourage you, at first reading, to ignore quotation marks and footnotes (which are included for accuracy and reference to specific points), as this will help to render the reading experience smooth and graceful. Throughout this chapter, unreferenced quotations (with page numbers in parentheses) are taken from Reza Shah-Kazemi's book *Paths to Transcendence*.

Approaching the Absolute

In speaking about the Absolute, or the Real, we are embarking upon a totally infeasible endeavor. In striving to speak about something that is beyond all categories of speech and mind, words and concepts necessarily fall short. The Absolute is a "supra-conceptual referent"—something to which our highest, most refined concepts cannot reach, but can at most point toward. All mental constructs and conceptualizations are therefore inadequate, and neither account for nor represent the Real.

Nevertheless, the Real can be known, and this is the profound glory of the mystics across the faith traditions, and perhaps the greatest glory of the human being. By "known" I do not mean perceived, as a mountain or the sky is perceived and experienced through the senses. Nor do I mean conceptually perceived in human thought, or meditated through thought. Rather, the mystics testify that the Absolute, or the Real, can be entered into directly, in a radical union. This is found consistently across the three mystics examined here, despite their diverse theological perspectives.

Testimony from the great sages and mystics about higher spiritual and metaphysical realities is grounded in direct experience, and is therefore more profound and reliable than the testimony of religious scholars, pundits, or theologians (unless they have equivalent experience). Moreover, the authentic mystics and sages are more reliable on spiritual matters than the vast majority of philosophers, scientists, academics, and exoteric religious ministers, who generally confine themselves to rational thought and reason as their primary epistemological apparatus. The great mystics and sages are the true "performers of the scriptural music"; they are the living exemplary embodiments of the spiritual journey. They show us the way, and by their very lives manifest the truth of the scriptures. As Rumi said, mystics don't live by their proofs; they prove by their living. The lives of the mystics prove that it is possible for human beings to realize the Divine and the transcendent Absolute, and they beckon us to join them.

Summit of Spiritual Realization: The Absolute Godhead

Shankara, Ibn Arabi, and Eckhart all speak of a transcendent Absolute, to which they refer by different concepts or names. All three emphasize the *oneness* of this Absolute, which they describe variously as the "One" (Ibn Arabi), the "solitary One" (Eckhart), or *advaita* (nondual) for Shankara. They each emphasize that a crucial distinction must be made between the *absolute transcendence* of the Godhead, and the *relative transcendence* of a personal God, or God with form. This distinction goes beyond the conventional confines of religious thought that is characteristic of their respective theistic traditions. The transcendent Godhead, or Absolute, is beyond all attributes and categories of thought. All three mystics describe the Absolute as a transcendent Oneness that is fundamentally incommensurable with all relative or determinate forms, including the names and forms of God.

Let us begin by exploring the three mystics' descriptions and characterizations of the Absolute (which is of course beyond description!), and highlight the essential principles they have in common.

1. The absolute alone is real. It is beyond all names of God.

The three mystics assert the inadequacy of the designations of the Absolute found within their respective traditions. The Absolute can only be alluded to indirectly, and then only in terms that are metaphysical, rather than theological or dogmatic. This requires an "apophatic" dialectic in regard to the Absolute, meaning it is defined more by what it is not than by what it is. For Shankara, the Absolute transcends all "name and form," and all conceptions of the Absolute are subject to the double negation *neti neti* (not this, not that). For Ibn Arabi the Essence surpasses, even while constituting the true substance of, the name Allah, as well as the other names of God; the Essence alone is real. For Eckhart, the transcendent Godhead is "as far above the God of the three Persons as heaven is above earth" (p. 194).

Note this striking distinction made by all three mystics between the transcendent Absolute and the usual religious forms or names of God found in each of their traditions. The Absolute is beyond the Trinity for Eckhart; it is beyond the Names of God (including Allah) for Ibn Arabi, and it is beyond all names and forms for Shankara. As Lao-Tzu expresses this supreme principle: "The Tao that can be named is not the Tao." The Absolute Godhead is beyond all names and forms of God, and yet it is the hidden esoteric foundation of them all.

As we move downward (to use a crude metaphor) from this highest plane of the unmanifest Godhead, the cosmos subtly "crystallizes" into graded levels of manifestation. These levels derive from and are sustained by the Absolute; they are distinct from it yet not separate. The first and most subtle level that can be distinguished relates to the "forms of God," or the "Lord." For Shankara, this first level of distinction is *Ishvara* ("the Lord") or *Brahma Saguna* (God with attributes). For Eckhart this first level is the three Persons (Father, Son, Holy Spirit), suspended in being at the level where God works. For Ibn Arabi this first level is Divinity with its distinctive Names of God, of which there are ninety-nine in Islam.

The Absolute alone is real, says Shankara, all else is *maya* (illusion). The Absolute is without any trace of the development of manifestation (*prapancha upasama*). Nevertheless, the Absolute takes on the appearance of relativity in order to rule over it. Hence, according to Shankara, "That which we designate as Creator *is* the Absolute." Eckhart refers to this same process as the "first effusion" of God, which is "His fusion with the Son, a process that in turn reduces him to Father." Notice that the Absolute transcends God the Father, and the latter emerges simultaneously with the Son; the two cannot be separated. The Father is not prior to Son. The Absolute is prior, and transcends both Father and Son (and Holy Spirit). Similarly for Ibn Arabi, the Essence surpasses all Names of God. The Names pertain to the level of Divinity. Only the Name "the One" can be said to be a Name of the Essence (inasmuch as it includes all that is, and excludes all that is distinctively conceived as other than it). The Essence alone is real, and all the Names are reduced (in the very measure of their distinctive properties) to the nature of "imagination" (p. 194).

2. "The Name is the Named."

Although the Absolute is beyond the Name of God across the traditions, it is also true esoterically that "the Name is the Named," because the Essence takes on the appearance of the Names. As Ramakrishna puts it, "God and His name are one." This holds because "the Names of God are the ontological foundations of the cosmos, while themselves possessing no ontological substance other than that of the Essence" (p. 194). The situation is somewhat analogous to a vortex or whirlpool forming in water. The whirlpool is created from water and has a clearly delineated form and dynamic structure, yet it is nothing other than water. In like manner, the Absolute comprises within itself all levels and forms of manifestation, yet in a manner that excludes separative manifestation. There is an unbridgeable gulf between the Absolute or Essence on the one hand, and all that is relative or manifest on the other.

Shankara describes the Absolute (*Brahma Nirguna*) as "beyond being," and Eckhart likewise says that in the "ground" of existence, God is "above all being." By contrast, Ibn Arabi does not refer to the Godhead as "beyond being," and such terminology seems at first antithetical to his famous metaphysical principle of "Unity of Being," which is the counterpart to the theological principle of the oneness of God (*tawhid*). However, Shah-Kazemi shows clearly that Ibn Arabi's Unity of Being presupposes different planes or degrees of being—ranging from the physical plane to an intermediate plane of divine presence, to the highest subtle plane that transcends all relativity. Hence, Ibn Arabi's ontological distinction between absolute Essence and relative Divinity corresponds precisely to the distinction made by Shankara and Eckhart between "beyond being" and "being." Moreover, Ibn Arabi affirms the ultimately illusory nature of everything apart from the Essence, which brings him closely in line with Shankara's view that the

Absolute alone is fully real, and all else is illusion. In short, all three mystics affirm the Absolute in a similar fashion, and their characterizations are unavoidably paradoxical in conceptual or linguistic terms, which necessarily fall short of the reality. The Absolute is a higher ontological essence or Godhead that is incommensurable with or "beyond" the planes of manifest existence, yet also constitutes the one essential Reality of all that exists.

3. There is one transcendent absolute. The summit of the spiritual journey is the same for all three mystics.

The three mystics assert that the Absolute is one. The question remains, however, is there just one Absolute that is ontologically identical for all three mystics? Or are they referring to different Absolutes within their three traditions? Is there one summit, or three?

If it were only a matter of simple logic, the resolution would be straightforward: There could only be one Absolute. For if there were two or more Absolutes, then even if they overlapped to some degree, no one of these Absolutes would be all-inclusive. Therefore, something exists outside each of these Absolutes, which contradicts the claim by all three mystics that nothing exists outside the Absolute. Hence, there cannot be two or more Absolutes. In short, there can only be *one* One. If there were two or more Ones, then none of them would be *one*.

However, ordinary logic does not always apply in spirituality, and a more metaphysically subtle and nuanced stream of analysis is called for here. To address this question, Shah-Kazemi distinguishes between a "lesser Absolute" and a "higher Absolute," and it is only to the lesser Absolute that determinate conceptions apply. So we can reformulate our question as follows: To what extent can outwardly different names and designations for the lesser Absolute be regarded as converging upon a unique, indefinable higher Absolute? Or to put it in vernacular metaphor: How do we know if the three mystics' fingers are pointing to one and the same moon?

First, all three mystics assert that there is an essential disjuncture between the word/name/concept for the Absolute and the Absolute itself. If this were not the case, then one (or more) of these conceptions would have absolute status, which would preclude the validity of the others. But because the Absolute transcends all conceptions thereof, it is legitimate to posit the possibility of a unique Absolute—a unique "supra-conceptual referent"—to which all these conceptions point. To clarify this point with an analogy, the words *water* in English, *eau* in French, *Wasser* in German, and *pani* in Hindi all point to their "supra-linguistic referent": water itself. Water is one and the same substance in each case—there are not multiple waters in different cultures. Water is the same everywhere, and different languages refer to it by various names. This analogy helps us visualize the incommensurability of the Absolute with any conceptual designation thereof. Water is incommensurable with the *concept* of water, and incommensurable with the linguistic *names* for water; you can't drink the *concept* of water, nor can you shower in the various *names* for water. In like manner, the Absolute is incommensurable with all *conceptions* or *names* of the Absolute.

Second, Meister Eckhart articulates a principle of spiritual inclusivity: While all material things limit and exclude each other, all things of a spiritual or divine nature include each other. Applying this principle here: Because each conception of the Absolute points to an indefinable spiritual reality, and because the content of that reality is, by Eckhart's principle, inclusive of all spiritual things, then these spiritual realities are necessarily united inwardly; that is, each includes the others. Moreover, recall that each of these realities has been identified by the three mystics as an absolute infinitude, apart from which nothing exists.

Taking these points together, Shah-Kazemi concludes that "outwardly differing formal conceptions thus converge [pointing toward a single Absolute] insofar as their supra-conceptual referent consists in a spiritual reality that is infinite and unitive, outside or apart from which nothing exists." Finally, the very infinitude of the Absolute, together with its all-inclusivity, precludes the possibility of formulating one definitive conception that excludes the others. Hence, even if the conceptions diverge in terms of their form, they all converge in terms of their intended content. "Therefore each conception of the Absolute is assimilable to the other in the measure that it opens out onto and intends the infinite and transcendent Reality" (p. 197). In short, there is one Absolute, which is the same for all three mystics.

One summit, diverse mystical paths. Although there is just one summit, mystics and seekers who are highly advanced on the path—having climbed far up the mystic mountain—may indeed undergo very different experiences of the ascent. One pathway may entail ice and snowfields, another sheer rock; the weather may be bright sunshine on one side, shrouded in clouds on another. Only at the summit does the boundary between religions vanish altogether. Even a few feet below the summit, the mystical mountain climber can still see only her side of the mountain; she cannot see the other faces of this vast and majestic mountain, which may be radically different. The Christian still sees only a Christian mountain, the Hindu only a Hindu mountain, and not until reaching the summit can the Christian mystic gaze down another side and realize, perhaps with a shock, that this selfsame mountain has a vast and complex Hindu face, and another equally vast and intricate Islamic face, and so on—all leading to the same summit.

This could help explain why some contemplatives from different traditions, even those who have achieved a high level of realization, sometimes report different mystical experiences across the traditions. Some scholars have taken these differing accounts as evidence that there must exist multiple spiritual summits across the faith traditions, but the evidence here points to a single transcendent summit. Even so, some scholars object to this perennialist view, because they believe it entails ranking the mystical journeys of giants like Eckhart, Shankara, and Ibn Arabi above those of other mystics.[5] Yet even if we sympathize with such an objection in principle, there is an overriding point here: The great mystics themselves uphold the transcendent Absolute as a higher state of mystical realization; it is not we ordinary mortals who are asserting this hierarchical distinction.

4. There are three "characteristics" of transcendent realization.

How can the summit of the mystical journey be characterized? This is inherently challenging because the essence of the Absolute is ontologically incommensurate with all determinate and relative forms, including language. Moreover, mystics generally say that the Absolute, once realized, turns out to be nothing like they had expected. By their very human nature, mystics cannot be fully prepared in advance for the radical grace of realizing the transcendent Godhead, nor can they speak of it afterward with any degree of precision or descriptive accuracy. Nevertheless, something *can* be said about it, despite the inadequacy of language and concepts.

To the extent that transcendent realization can be spoken of or described at all, the three mystics here all speak of three fundamental characteristics, which are summarized in the well-known term *Sat Chit Ananda* associated with Shankara. *Sat* is generally translated as "Truth" or "Being" (or "Existence"), *Chit* as "Consciousness," and *Ananda* as "Bliss." In Shankara's words, the highest realization is "that beyond which there is nothing ... the inmost Self of all, free from differentiation ... the Truth-Consciousness-Bliss."[6]

Similarly, Ibn Arabi characterizes ultimate realization succinctly: "*Wujud* [Being] is the finding of the Real in ecstasy" ("finding" here corresponds to making *conscious*; the Real to *truth* and ecstasy to *bliss*). Along similar lines, Eckhart affirms that "I was bare being and the knower of myself in the enjoyment of truth," and elsewhere he speaks of three qualities: "immeasurable power, infinite wisdom, and infinite sweetness." Again, because language is inherently inadequate to the task, it is important not to push these analogies too far, but it is striking to find such close correspondence among these mystics' characterization of transcendent realization.[7]

5. The Absolute can be realized, but not "experienced."

Transcendent realization of the Absolute refers to a union of the soul with the Real, in which consciousness persists, yet individuality vanishes. To suggest that the mystic can "experience" the Real is therefore inaccurate, because the individual has ceased to exist. An experience requires an object and an experiencing subject. "To say 'experience' is to affirm duality and hence the nontranscendent, whereas to say 'transcendent realization' is to exclude dualistic experience" (p. 232). These subtleties are difficult to express in conceptual language, yet for the spiritually realized there is no confusion. As Ramana Maharshi describes it:

> The "I" casts off the illusion of "I," and yet remains as "I." Such is the paradox of Self-Realization. The realized do not see any contradiction in it.[8]

The unrealized cannot comprehend it, and if they insist on logical understanding this leads only to contradiction and confusion.

Wonderful as this sounds, there is nevertheless a price exacted for this profound union, which is one's very self. For authentic union to take place between two beings, explains Eckhart, one of the two must give up its "whole identity and being." Failing this, there may be "unitedness" but not union. God will not give up God's whole identity and being; therefore, for this union to take place, it is the human disciple who must give up her whole identity and being. This is the meaning of the saying by Christ, "Those who seek to save their life shall lose it, but those who will lose their life for My sake shall save it."[9]

The Spiritual Ascent

1. To "see God" is a relative attainment. God as "other" must be transcended by realizing the Absolute as one's inmost identity.

All three mystics maintain that seeing God or realizing God as "other," despite being a profound mystical experience, is nevertheless still a relative attainment, which must eventually be transcended to realize the Absolute as one's own inner identity.

This is evident in the Bhagavad Gita, for example. Arjuna has a full-blown mystical vision of God, both immanent and transcendent, in chapters 10 and 11, respectively. If this were the summit of the spiritual journey, the Gita would end there. But seven chapters follow, and Arjuna is called to go beyond the vision of God into a profound transmutation (which St. John of the Cross calls the "night of the spirit") that eventually leads to mergence into the transcendent form of Krishna, the *Purushottama*, through a process of radical surrender that leads to union. Krishna promises this union repeatedly in the final chapters, whereas earlier Arjuna was still separate from Krishna, seeing God as "other." This same distinction is found in Christian mysticism between the vision of God during the stage of illumination and the final radical union with God.

All three mystics enjoin the disciple to go beyond the vision of God. "If you stay with what is offered He will escape you, but if you attain Him nothing will escape you," says Ibn Arabi (p. 201). One must forsake all bestowals of God for the sake of realizing God him/her self, and persevere with the invocation of the divine name, with the intention firmly focused on the Named. Shankara says that *any* attribution of objective "otherness" to the Absolute, including any mystical vision thereof, entails the imprisonment of consciousness within the dualistically defined ego, and hence within illusion. When the ego sees the Lord/Creator, it sees nothing but the Absolute, which appears (on contact with *maya*) as the Lord (*Ishvara*) in one of its manifestations.

In like manner, Eckhart cautions that all images must be excluded for the sake of receptivity to the Word. This requires absolute stilling of all intellectual powers and functions, so that one unites with "formless essence." "Unknowing" and "silence" are most conducive to the Birth of the Word.

In his typically provocative fashion, Eckhart dismisses from the Temple not only the "merchants" of action (those who seek reward), but also the "doves" of selfless action because they still "work with attachment" and are therefore "hindered" by their action. Eckhart leaves the exact attachment and hindrance unclear, but this seems to be clarified in Shankara's distinction between "lower renunciates," who renounce selfish action and act only for the Lord, and "higher renunciates," who see "inaction in action." The doves are equivalent to Shankara's "lower renunciates," whose attachment to the status of action still constitutes a hindrance.

2. "The inmost essence of the individual is not other than the transcendent Essence of the Absolute."

This is a key principle for all three mystics, and indeed represents the Holy Grail of all mystical spirituality (p. 202). The inmost essence of the human being is the transcendent essence of the Absolute Godhead. This is the profound revelation of the divinity of every human being, and its full realization is the primary goal of all mystical traditions. It is proclaimed in different ways across the ages and scriptures, for example:

- The four *mahavakyas* (great utterances) of the Upanishads; for example, *Aham Brahmasmi* ("I am Brahman") and *Tat tvam asi* ("Thou art That")
- "I and the Father are one" (John 10:30)
- *An al haqq* ("I am the supreme reality"), proclaimed by Al Hallaj
- "Be still and know I am God" (Ps. 46:10)

3. The core mystical practice is interiorization, a concentrated withdrawal from outer awareness toward the innermost center of consciousness.

This principle follows as a natural corollary from the previous principle: Because one's innermost essence is the Absolute, the core spiritual practice is therefore to go deeply inward—to withdraw from all outward existence and concentrate on one's innermost center of awareness. That which is most inward is most exalted; depth equals height, as Eckhart puts it. The path of ever deeper interiority is the path of ascent to God, and the individual is gradually "dissolved" along the way (or, more precisely, the individual is progressively revealed not to exist). This is a key principle of contemplative practice for all three mystics.

For Shankara, this can be accomplished through *adhyatma yoga*, a superior type of meditation in which one abstains from all outward modes of sense, feeling, and thought, leading to a progressive dissolution of outward faculties. Ibn Arabi uses the same metaphor of dissolution of the composite dimensions of the person. In both cases, outward dissolution enables the disciple to dive deeply inward. Eckhart describes a similar practice of "stilling" all the powers of the intellect, so that the "silent middle" becomes receptive to nothing but the Word.

Methods to realize the Absolute. For Shankara there are several ways to accomplish this realization. One is by concentrating on the inmost source of consciousness, through the technique of abstention, as just described. Or it can be the effect of divine grace bestowed upon one who invokes the divine name *Om*. It can even be crystallized through one hearing of *Tat tvam asi*, or "hearing, cogitating over, and sustained meditation upon" the sacred texts. The only technique Eckhart explicitly mentions is concentration through abstention (stilling the mind and senses in silence).

Invoking the divine name. For Ibn Arabi, invocation of the divine name is the central, if not exclusive, practice. "The Name is the Named," as Shankara says. Shah-Kazemi explains that "the Named is immanent in the Name, even while simultaneously transcending it" (p. 203). God is in the name, yet also transcends the name. This is crucial to realize, because, as Shankara explains, "The purpose of knowing the identity of the Name and the Named is to enable oneself to dismiss Name and Named altogether and realize the Absolute which is quite different from either." Realization of the Absolute is brought about by the actualization of the grace inherent in the Name, which sacramentally represents the Absolute (p. 203).

Both Eckhart and Ibn Arabi's methods are included among Shankara's, showing they are not incompatible, and that the difference is a relative one. The function and goal of all these methods is identical:

interiorization of consciousness as a means to realize one's innermost identity (the Absolute).

4. There is a "nonreciprocal identity" between the soul and the Absolute.

The innermost "citadel" of the soul is identical with the most transcendent "solitary One" beyond the soul, says Eckhart, and only at this point of identity is the soul "divine." This affirms a subtle nonreciprocal identity between soul and God. As Ibn Arabi puts it, "The transcendent Reality *is* the relative creature, even though the creature is distinct from the Creator." Shankara expresses the same principle: The ego is nondifferent from Brahman, yet Brahman is not nondifferent from the ego. To put it perhaps more simply: The deepest essence of the soul is not different from God, yet God is different from the soul.

Eckhart urges concentration upon God not as something other, but as God is "in oneself." One must become that upon which one concentrates, affirms Shankara. Eckhart expresses this in his famous teaching of the eye gazing at a piece of wood. To "get to the bottom of everything I have ever preached about," says Eckhart, "in the point of contact between the eye and the wood, there is a single reality: 'eye-wood.'" Applying this teaching, we can say: In the point of contact between soul and God, there is a single reality: soul-God. This reflects a key stage of contemplative prayer or meditation, in which the practitioner becomes the object of his meditation—and only then does real meditation begin. Concentrating on the object "subsumes within itself that subject which had been the agent of concentration: spiritual food assimilates to itself the one who 'eats' it, in such a manner that the spiritual substance itself is revealed as one's true identity" (p. 202). To put it in simple terms, as you "eat" the spiritual food of genuine spiritual practice, God transforms you into God. Or more accurately, God replaces you with the essence of God.

Bliss and transcendence. As the summit of realization is approached, all three mystics affirm that an exalted state of bliss is experienced. Yet they all enjoin the aspirant *not* to stop and revel in this bliss; it is to be surpassed. Ibn Arabi says that, prior to extinction, the aspirant must not "stop" at the degree of blissful experience. Shankara says that approaching the state of *samadhi*, bliss is experienced but one must not "pause to savor it." Eckhart speaks of the "lesser attainment" of love over knowledge; stopping with love entails being "entangled" and "infatuated" in goodness and love, which results in getting "caught up in the gate," which is the first effusion of God (rather than the Godhead). Knowledge, on the other hand, "runs ahead" and "grasps God in His essence."

Two kinds of bliss. A question that naturally arises is this: What is the difference between these two types of bliss—the nontranscendent bliss prior to realization (which all three mystics say must be surpassed) and the transcendent bliss (*ananda*), which characterizes realization of the Absolute? This brings up the whole issue of "experience" in transcendence.

Shankara explains that the nontranscendent bliss prior to realization is a form of ordinary bliss (even if more intense), because it is still an object of awareness that is experienced by a separate subject (even if it is coming from within that subject). The ontological dualism of subject/object has not been transcended.

In strong contrast, the transcendent bliss (*ananda*) is "totally different from all objects ... [It is] uncreated because it is not produced like anything resulting from empirical perceptions." This transcendent bliss surpasses the context of ontologically differentiated experience, and is therefore indescribable. Description is impossible because transcendent Being cannot be reduced to contingent modes of thought and language. As Eckhart puts it, as long as one tries to circumscribe this reality in language and thought, one knows no more about it than the eye knows of taste. For it is not a state of bliss that defines realization; it is the conscious transcendence of duality and consequent realization of one's divine identity beyond the personal—and this necessarily brings with it the "unutterable joy," the "whole beatitude," and the "ecstasy" mentioned, respectively, by Shankara, Eckhart, and Ibn Arabi.

5. Divine grace is essential.

Divine grace is the *sine qua non* of mystical realization. Ultimately, the human aspirant can do nothing to effect this realization; it can only come from God, through God's grace. The crucial importance of divine grace is emphasized by all three mystics. The very capacity even to realize the Self is a preexisting grace, says Shankara: "Liberation of the soul can only come through knowledge proceeding from God's grace." Similarly, Eckhart emphasizes that the fact of having been created in the image of God is the preexisting grace that allows for union, which only comes about through further manifestations of grace. Grace penetrates beyond the work of grace in order to realize union with the Absolute: Eckhart's "breakthrough" to the Godhead takes place only by God's breakthrough (*Durchbruch*) to him. Finally, Ibn Arabi says that "God removed from me my contingent dimension" (p. 223), an act of sheer and unbidden grace without which he would not have realized the Essence.

Grace is stressed as instrumental in the final transcendence, and this grace is conferred through the personal God. "The Absolute that *transcends* the personal God can only be realized as a result of grace *from* the personal God" (p. 226), because nothing can proceed from the Essence without relativizing it. Hence, the vital necessity of faith and devotion—both of which are initially conceived in relation to God as "other," and which persist and deepen even after transcendent realization.

The Existential Return

After realizing the Absolute, what is the nature of the realized aspirant?

1. Consciousness of the Absolute persists.

As mentioned earlier, there can be no experience of the transcendent. Nevertheless, the consciousness within the aspirant can realize its deepest and truest identity as the transcendent Absolute. The consciousness that "knows" its true identity is none other than that which is "known."

Once the Absolute is realized, this knowledge is thereafter permanent. "Consciousness of the Absolute subsists, even in the framework of those relative modes of awareness with which it has no common measure" (p. 226).

2. Spiritual poverty.

Ibn Arabi and Eckhart both stress the "poverty" of the saint. They both use this word, by which they seem to mean the same qualities, including a standpoint of absolute surrender and the utter absence of an apparent human creature or personal self. Both distinguish between two kinds of poverty—volitional, which relates to moral and affective detachment, and ontological, which is grounded in the effacement of the human ego.

Eckhart speaks provocatively of the "asses" who still have a will to serve God's will. This, he says, does not reflect true poverty. No trace of individual will is found in true poverty; such a person is "as free of his created will as he was when he did not exist."[10] This relates to the distinction between surrender and submission. In surrender, there is still an "I" that does the surrender, whereas in submission, one's very "I" is utterly given over to God. Ibn Arabi makes a similar distinction between "slavehood," which still expresses personal affirmation prior to subordination to the Absolute, and "servitude," a perfected condition with no such affirmation of self. To cling to one's existence entails bondage in proportionate measure to one's sense of selfhood, whereas clinging to the immutable nonexistence of one's own entity results in freedom. This is the meaning of Thomas Keating's statement that "the greatest glory of the human being is to cease to exist." In ceasing to exist, one becomes nothing, and for those who love God above all else, this becomes the direct path to the summit, as St. John of the Cross makes clear: "To arrive at being all, desire to be nothing."[11]

This notion of absolute poverty may seem at first to contrast sharply with Shankara's emphasis on freedom and deliverance. Shankara emphasizes "I am the Real" as the liberated condition; the fact of nonexistence as a separate individual is implicit. For Ibn Arabi and Eckhart, the nonexistence of the individual "I" is emphasized, and hence "I am the Real" is implicit. But there is complementarity here, not contradiction, because Ibn Arabi and Eckhart focus on the nature of the realized individual, whereas Shankara focuses on the content of that realization. All three mystics are thus speaking of the same fundamental process.

3. Personal self and will are transcended entirely.

Another key aspect of the realized condition is that personal self and will have been entirely transcended. Shankara speaks of a supreme indifference to the outer world; he has become the immutable Self, and sees the empirical ego as a transient aspect of the non-Self. For Ibn Arabi, the saint sits in the "house of his immutability, not his existence," gazing on the manner in which God "turns him this way and that" (p. 215). Eckhart comes to this same point of utter detachment regarding his outer destiny, accepting all that happens to him as the will of God.

Thus all three mystics share a fundamental attitude of detachment from the exigencies of the outer world. There is one apparent theological difference, however. For Ibn Arabi and Eckhart, all that happens to them is "God's will," whereas for Shankara all that happens to him is his unspent karma playing out. This difference is nil, however, for in Shankara's exegetical writings it is the Lord (*Ishvara*) who distributes the fruits of karma. Hence it comes right back to the action or will of God that does everything.

Suffering and petitionary prayer. Regarding suffering, Eckhart invokes the image of a door on its hinge. The inner person (the hinge) remains impassive, but the outer person (the door) is "moved" by the experience of suffering. For Eckhart, prayer for help in times of suffering would presumably be inappropriate, for he generally eschews petitionary prayer. As he puts it, to "pray for this and that" is evil. On the other hand, for Ibn Arabi, such personal petitionary prayer is an obligation, for it increases the soul's humble awareness of the permanent state of need of the personal self, and the finitude of human resources, compared to the infinite power of God. However, this difference between the two may have been largely contextual and circumstantial; Eckhart was preaching largely to religious nuns who were often dominated by petitionary prayer, and he likely was striving to shift them more toward the contemplative prayer of "absolute stillness in which alone, the Word can be heard." Ibn Arabi, on the other hand, refers to the class of Sufis who believed that the virtues of resignation and patience precluded any sort of personal prayer in moments of trial, and he may have wanted them to understand that outward need and petition for God's help "does not relativize inward identity with God's Essence" (p. 217).

Sri Ramakrishna eloquently expresses the difference between the transcendent Absolute and the personal God. "In the Absolute I am not, and thou art not, and God is not, for the Absolute is beyond speech and thought. But so long as anything exists outside myself, I ought to adore Brahma [God], within the limits of the mind, as something existing outside myself."[12]

4. Devotion and praise become intensified.

It might be thought that for those who have attained supreme realization, devotion and praise for God would be "outgrown" or rendered superfluous, because the duality—of devotee as subject and God as object, upon which such practice or worship is based—has been transcended altogether. On the contrary, however, all three mystics affirm, even after supreme realization, the ongoing importance of devotion to God and praise to all that surpasses them as individuals.

Shankara speaks of bowing and prostrating to Brahman, and to the knowledge of Brahman. Eckhart maintains humble adoration of the Divine, which, far from being precluded by transcendent realization (which surpasses that very Divinity), is actually strengthened thereby. Ibn Arabi says that one should praise God "accident for accident," or manifestation for manifestation. The outer contingent self is "accident" compared to the immanent substance, which is the Reality, and the Divinity is "accident" compared to the Essence. For all three, humble adoration of the Divine is strengthened, rather than weakened, by realization of the Absolute. Knowing more profoundly than ever before that their gift of realizing the Absolute was made possible only by the sheer grace of God, their gratitude, homage, praise, and devotion are therefore only intensified and deepened.

5. The Absolute is in the Relative.

Having realized the transcendent Absolute, all three mystics affirm that the same Absolute is also found immanent in the world. "All is Brahman" says Shankara, and Ibn Arabi contends that the entire cosmos is the manifestation of the divine name, the "Outward." Shankara and Ibn Arabi emphasize that the world is both illusory and real, with Shankara giving more emphasis to the illusory (*maya*) and Ibn Arabi to the real. Both mystics regard the world as real when seen as the expression of the Absolute in its relative dimension, and illusory when emphasizing the exclusive reality of the Absolute, so that all else is but "imagined." Eckhart affirms a similar dialectic between the Absolute and the relative. The created world "is not," and the creature is "pure nothing" when viewed from the Absolute Godhead. On the other hand, there is no time when creation is not occurring as the "overflow" of the divine nature.

The Absolute and the Relative are interpenetrating to some degree. "There is an element of relativity within the Absolute; the personal Divinity," which is ultimately surpassed. "And there is an element of Absoluteness within the relative: the immanent Self," which is to be realized (p. 223). All three mystics thus affirm a profound dialectic between creation and the ultimate reality of the Godhead. "The creature is both image of God (and by that very fact reducible in its essence to that of which it is an image)—and at the same time a 'pure nothing'" (p. 220).

One Summit, One Reality

Although coming from outwardly dissimilar traditions, the mystical journeys of the three sages explored here have evidently led them to the same
supreme summit of the Absolute Godhead. In each case they attained this
realization only through the power of divine grace, and by allowing their
contingent selves to be effaced. As Ibn Arabi puts it,

> All existence is an imagination within an imagination, the only
> Reality being God.... The final end and ultimate return of the gnos-
> tics ... is that the Real is identical with them, while they do not
> exist. (p. 75)

Practice of
Divine Love

5

Intimacy with the Infinite

Devotional Surrender to God

They are the chosen ones who have surrendered.
—RUMI

Prapatti, a term from Hinduism that relates to the supreme mystical secret of divine love, could be elucidated as follows: The most profound love for God is fulfilled through absolute surrender to God. A clear example of this is the saying of Jesus: "No one has greater love than this: to lay down one's life for a friend" (John 15:13). *Prapatti* can be seen as the process of laying down one's life for God. It is said to surpass all other paths to God, and in this sense the unconditional giving of self—in absolute surrender to God—can be seen as the most profound act of divine love, albeit challenging to put into practice!

Prapatti appears to be something of a universal practice of divine love, and this helps us to see why both Christ and Krishna say the greatest love is demonstrated by the greatest surrender, and why the very essence of Islam is submission to God. Such surrender or submission to God activates a remarkable divine grace, beyond all imaginable measure. This is God's great mystic secret.

In what follows, relevant Sanskrit terms are included in parentheses below for the sake of completeness, for those interested in these details. Otherwise readers need take note of just four terms that occur frequently: *prapatti* (surrender to God), *bhakti* (path of love), *angas* (prerequisites for surrender), and *caramasloka* (the supreme secret of the Bhagavad Gita, discussed in chapter 1).

Prapatti in Hindu *Vaishnavism*

Prapatti refers to a direct means to realize God or attain spiritual liberation, by absolute surrender to God. It is chiefly associated with the great Hindu sage Ramanuja (1017–1137 CE) and his followers, although it dates back several thousand years earlier to the Vedas. Ramanuja is regarded as the founder of Vishishtadvaita Vedanta, or "qualified nondualism" in Vedanta, and he is one of the three most important classical commentators on the Bhagavad Gita, the other two being Shankara (nondualistic) and Madhva (dualistic). Ramanuja's qualified nondualism holds that God, soul, and universe together form an inseparable unity that is one—without a second; this is the "nondualism" part. However, souls and matter are regarded as intrinsic attributes of Ultimate Reality; this is the "qualified" part of nondualism.

According to the Hindu Vaishnavaite tradition, *bhakti* and *prapatti* are the two principal means of realizing God. The other traditional paths of *jnana yoga* and *karma yoga* are regarded as preliminary disciplines that lead eventually to *bhakti*. This view of *bhakti* is articulated in Ramanuja's commentary on the Bhagavad Gita. A prominent treatise states that "only either by means of intense *bhakti* [love] or by means of *prapatti* [surrender] is it possible to attain God."[1] Of the two paths, *bhakti* is generally regarded as the more difficult, being a rigorous discipline appropriate only for certain individuals. *Prapatti* is considered the easier path and is suitable for any person, regardless of creed, caste, gender, and social status. Recognizing this, Ramanuja courageously defied social taboos in India by giving direct support for the spiritual liberation of people of even the lowest caste, a remarkable stance especially for his time. The followers of Ramanuja and Yamuna upheld the doctrine of *prapatti* and developed it extensively, thereby creating a vibrant sect of Vaishnavism known as Srivaishnavism that thrives in India and the Vaishnavaite diaspora to this day.

Prapatti as a direct means (*upaya*) to realize God is a distinctive feature of Vaishnavism. The etymology of *prapatti* is from *pad* (to move) and *pra* (in the best manner). The term means self-surrender to God, and connotes an active spiritual disposition in which the devotee surrenders fully to God deliberately, with complete self-awareness and conscious intention. The theology underlying *prapatti* is that the principal or (some would say) only way to achieve spiritual liberation is to seek God's grace through total self-surrender. Although *bhakti* and *prapatti* are both upheld as paths to God by Ramanuja and his prominent disciple Vedanta Desika, both masters maintain that liberation cannot be attained without observing *prapatti* in some form. Practitioners of *bhakti* must also perform *prapatti* in some way, in order to overcome the obstacles to a fully effective *bhakti* practice. This view seems consistent with the supreme secret in the Gita, where Krishna includes both *bhakti* and *prapatti* in his final, most secret teaching (18:65–66). The reverse is not necessarily true, however: *Prapatti* can be successfully performed without *bhakti* (as traditionally understood). Although *bhakti* and *prapatti* are interrelated, *prapatti* is deemed in Srivaishnavism to be an independent and fully effective means to realize God.

Origins of *Prapatti*

The doctrine of *prapatti* dates back several millennia to the Rig Veda, where it appears under the name of *saranagati*, a synonym for *prapatti*. *Saranagati* means seeking God as the only refuge.[2] Another name for it is *nasya,* which appears in the Taittiriya Narayana Upanishad and the Svetasvatara Upanishad. Before the tenth century *prapatti* was preserved as a secret doctrine and was only imparted orally by qualified preceptors to sufficiently advanced or deserving students. However, after Nathamuni (824–924) and Ramanuja, *prapatti* was explored at length in written works, including all its details, for the benefit of subsequent generations.[3]

Both Yamuna and Ramanuja espoused the importance of *prapatti* or *saranagati* as a direct means to full spiritual realization (*moksha*, or liberation), although Ramanuja articulated *saranagati* directly only in his *Sribhasya* commentary and not in his commentary on the Bhagavad Gita (*Gitabhasya*).[4] The hymns of the Alvars, a lineage of twelve Tamil poet saints, extol the virtues of *prapatti*. The *caramasloka* in the Gita (18:66) serves as a foundational scriptural support for *prapatti*, and the verse also serves as a mantra in the practice of *prapatti*.

Prapatti Is Not Widely Known

Although expounded upon extensively in the *Rahasya* (secret) literature of Vaishnavism and scripturally supported in the supreme secret at the end of the Gita, the term *prapatti* is not directly mentioned in most contemporary commentaries on the Bhagavad Gita or the Upanishads or other Hindu texts, at least in the West. Yet the historical literature on *prapatti* is remarkably vast over the past thousand years, and only in the past few decades are scholars beginning to sift through the voluminous reams of rich material. One prominent scholar, Srinivasa Chari, claims that his book *Vaishnavism*, published in 1994, is the first attempt to present in English a comprehensive account of Vaishnavism in a single volume based on original source books.[5] Innumerable treatises and commentaries have been written on *prapatti* over the centuries, one of which alone is twice the length of the *Mahabharata*, which at ninety thousand verses is the longest epic in the world. As scholar Srilata Raman observes, "We have an oceanic corpus of literature which would have to be looked at in its entirety to do justice to *prapatti* doctrinal development."[6]

Nevertheless, *prapatti* at present seems comparatively little known outside of Srivaishnavaite circles. The term *prapatti* and its Sanskrit equivalent, *saranagati*, are nowhere mentioned in Sri Aurobindo's *Essays on the Gita* or any of his collected works, or in the Gita commentaries of Eknath Easwaran, Swami Nikhilananda, or Paramhansa Yogananda, or in the collected works of Krishnaprem, or in the Gospel of Ramakrishna. Scholar Georg Feuerstein makes a passing reference to it in his comprehensive Gita translation, without providing further substance.

A notable exception to this curious dearth of information is one brief but powerful reference to *prapatti* by Ramana Maharshi, who elucidates the transformative power of *prapatti* as the highest form of devotion. Ramana casts a profound light on the essence of *prapatti*:

> Take the case of *bhakti*—I approach Ishvara [the Lord] and pray to be absorbed in Him. I then surrender myself in faith and by concentration. What remains afterward? In place of the original "I," perfect self-surrender leaves a residuum of God in which the "I" is lost. This is the highest form of devotion (*parabhakti*), *prapatti*, surrender or the height of *vairagya*. The "I" casts off the illusion of "I" and yet remains as "I." Such is the paradox of Self-Realization. The realized do not see any contradiction in it.[7]

Different Kinds of *Prapatti*

Ramanuja articulated two basic kinds of *prapatti* in his writings. The first was to be performed by the *jnanis*, the more advanced or superior devotees, as a form of contemplative awareness in humility—acknowledging their fundamental subordination (*sesa*) to God and the fact that, being mortals, they can do nothing to accomplish their own liberation or salvation. Therefore, God is the only means, as well as the goal. The second form of *prapatti* was performed by more "ordinary" devotees, as a ritualistic act of taking refuge in order to overcome obstacles or be purified of sins, to enable them to begin their practice of *bhakti yoga*. For purposes of this book, I shall call these two forms *mystical prapatti* and *soteriological prapatti*, respectively.

Prapatti as a Vehicle of Spiritual Wisdom

In Ramanuja's *stotra*, or poem of praise titled *Sanaragatigadya*, surrender to God is put forth as the paramount path to God. The poem tells of an ordinary person, a poet, who performs *prapatti* as a way to become purified of his sins and to overcome the obscuring nature of *prakriti* (manifest realm). In the process he actually becomes a *jnani* (person of wisdom), which demonstrates the remarkable potential for an ordinary person (non-*jnani*) to be graced with the gift of spiritual wisdom and insight through self-surrender. Thereafter, as a *jnani,* he engages in a devotional meditation practice in three stages as a form of *bhakti yoga*, which leads him to full union with God.

Thus through *prapatti*, an ordinary person is not only blessed with salvation or liberation, but may also be transformed into a person of spiritual insight and wisdom. An extraordinary example of this is the great Srivaishnavaite mystic poet Nammalvar, who wrote a profound mystical praise poem (*stotra*) articulating his experience of union with God in the form of Vishnu. Nammalvar was from the lowest caste (*shudra*), and he was known to have performed *prapatti* and not *bhakti yoga*, meaning that he had not undergone the formal spiritual training typical for a realized spiritual master. People of the lowest caste in his day were not eligible for formal spiritual training, or the practice of *bhakti*. There was considerable disagreement among his commentators about which form of *prapatti* he had performed (the contemplative awareness format designed for *jnanis*, or the ritualistic purification format designed for "ordinary" people). As scholar Srilata Raman observes, "The deeper issue they were addressing, implicit in this divergence, was the issue of whether saints are born or made."[8]

Prapatti is outlined briefly below in concept and practice, highlighting its importance for the practice of divine love.[9] My purpose is to outline the foundations of *prapatti* with utmost care and all due respect for this particular tradition, but not to stop there. I have come to view *prapatti* and the *angas*, taken together with the *caramasloka*, as an important example and clear articulation of a more general and indeed universal spiritual principle of surrender to God that is also found in other traditions. Surrender to God is thus revealed to be the core unifying practice on the universal path of divine love.

Dispute Between Two Schools of *Prapatti*

After Ramanuja's death, two major divisions of Srivaishnavism emerged based on slightly different interpretations presented in his writings. Both schools viewed *prapatti* as a supreme pathway to God, yet they differed in their specific practices and theological interpretations. Initially, these differences were negligible and benevolent, but over time they diverged and deepened, eventually leading to a schism and rivalry between the two schools. A brief review of this history is illuminating and instructive, both in terms of *prapatti* itself and as a wider lesson for what can happen in divisive religious sectarianism where one might have wished for greater harmony and peaceful collaboration among religious sects that are deeply aligned and united at their core. The essence of this split had largely to do with doctrines of "grace" and "works," but included several other spiritual and social dimensions as well. As one scholar observed, the dispute centered around "the doctrine of Grace, which seemed to duplicate the old split between the Roman Catholics and the Protestants."[10]

One side of this schism was the Vatakalai sect (Northern school), founded by the illustrious sage Vedanta Desika, who wrote lengthy treatises and hymns expounding eloquently on *saranagati*, and defending it skillfully against all manner of criticism. On the other side were the great sages Pillailokacarya and his predecessor Pillai, founders of the Tenkalai sect (Southern school), who also wrote extensive treatises. The thirteenth century saw the full flowering of *rahasya* literature (texts relating to esoteric matters), covering *prapatti* and the three associated mantras, and the three basic ontological categories (*tattvas*) of Vishishtadvaita, which became the subject of lengthy treatises, written by sages such as Lokacarya and Vedanta Desika. The doctrinal dispute began to emerge in the late

thirteenth century between Northern and Southern schools over the relationship between the path of devotion (*bhakti yoga*) and surrender to the
Lord (*prapatti*). This rift deepened over subsequent centuries, and led to a
major split in the seventeenth and eighteenth centuries, which only in the
last century or so has begun to heal.

Different Interpretations of Divine Grace

The two sects are rooted in different interpretations of the *caramasloka*
of the Gita ("abandon all dharmas; take refuge in God alone"). For the
Northern school, this verse does not mean to relinquish one's dharmas
(duties) altogether, but rather to be entirely unattached to the fruits of
one's actions. A person who surrenders utterly to God is still obliged
to fulfill the duties enjoined by the scriptures, and not to do so violates
the commandments of God (citing *Vishnudharma* 76:31). The Northern
school further maintains that although *prapatti* appears easier than *bhakti*
to practice, in fact it is more difficult, because the absolute faith required
is hard to achieve in practice, yet without this supreme faith the practice
is diluted and will not succeed. Moreover, the practice of *prapatti* has
to be repeated, often many times. The mystical power and efficacy of
prapatti are attributed to acts of merit from previous lives (which give
rise to good karma), and not merely the practice of *prapatti* in the present life.

The Southern school interprets the *caramasloka* of the Gita more literally, so that, apart from *prapatti*, all other yogas are to be abandoned,
and God's free and spontaneous grace is the only cause of *prapatti*. The
path of *bhakti* is deemed very difficult to follow and must be performed
repeatedly, whereas *prapatti* is much easier, and in the Southern school
it is to be performed only once. Thus *prapatti* is the easier and better
way, and its very essence is the abandonment of self-effort. The path is
open to everyone, including ordinary people, and thus *prapatti* constitutes essentially the only practical method for many to attain salvation.
The *prapanna* (one who performs *prapatti*) is exempt from performing
any further dharma. To support this position the Southern school cites
the example of Draupadi in the *Mahabharata*, when she was about to be
publicly disrobed by Dushassana in full view of the royal court. As long as
Draupadi tried to defend herself, God did not interfere, but the moment
she surrendered utterly, Krishna intervened immediately and worked a

miracle to save her. Another example is cited in the struggle between the Elephant King and the Crocodile in the *Srimad Bhavagatam* (eighth canto). The Elephant King fought for a thousand years but could not win, until finally, depleted of all strength and utterly drained of pride and vanity, the Elephant King surrendered wholeheartedly to the Lord, and Vishnu appeared and slew the crocodile.

Caramasloka: The Monkey Versus Cat Schools

The two doctrinal positions of the Northern and Southern schools of *prapatti* came to be characterized through a whimsical metaphor of different behaviors exhibited by monkeys and cats with their young. For monkeys, the mother carries the baby around, but the young monkey must constantly cling to its mother. If the baby monkey stops clinging, it falls to the ground immediately. This represents the Northern school's doctrine of "works" required on the part of the disciple, even after surrendering to God. For cats, on the other hand, the mother picks up her kitten by the scruff of the neck and carries it around. The kitten does nothing for itself; there is no need to cling, it just goes entirely limp in its mother's grip. This represents the Southern school of "grace."

Both views can be seen as essentially correct, and therefore eminently reconcilable. The Northern school's doctrine of works is strongly supported by the entire Gita prior to verse 18:66, and indeed is specifically supported in verse 18:56, which advocates the performance of "all forms of work" always, even while having attained the supreme liberation and eternal union with God. The Southern school's doctrine is also consistent with the Gita in its central doctrine that only the three *gunas* (modes of manifest nature) perform all actions, whereas the fully realized yogi has transcended the *gunas* altogether and therefore performs no action. As a literal example of this, in the cases of some of the most remarkable saints in India, such as Ramana Maharshi, Ramakrishna, and Anandamayi Ma, during their highest states of divine ecstasy of union with God, they were utterly incapable of performing any action or dharma whatsoever. They literally had to be cared for by others, hand and foot, to the point of being fed, bathed, and physically moved around—sometimes for weeks at a time. While such a condition would be unthinkable to Western sensibilities, or else pathologized as catatonic or exceedingly self-indulgent, such states of sustained spiritual ecstasy are not unknown for Indian sadhus so merged into God that identification with the body has been entirely transcended and nothing else exists for them.

Despite the potential for reconciliation between the two schools, they became fierce rivals for several hundred years. The split began to emerge in the thirteenth century and expanded during the fifteenth and sixteenth centuries, with extended periods of division and hostility. The doctrinal schism eventually became formalized into eighteen doctrinal differences between the two schools—relating to different conceptions of God, different conceptions and roles of the Goddess, and six different understandings of *prapatti*.

Traditionally, the Northern school believes in practicing the three principal yogas of the Gita (*karma*, *jnana*, and *bhakti*), along with *prapatti*, as a means to attain salvation, and *prapatti* is regarded as an act of winning God's grace. Greater emphasis is given to the role of the Goddess Lakshmi (or Sri) as an intermediary between the human *prapanna* and God, and the school tends to be more strict about Brahmanical and Sanskritic norms, often adhering to Vedic orthodoxy regarding modes of worship and fire rituals to propitiate Vishnu. It is also more concentrated around traditional and monastic establishments than places of public worship.

By contrast, the Southern school traditionally accepts *prapatti* as the only way to attain salvation, and regards *prapatti* as the practice of unconditional surrender to God. Other yogas are not necessary, and *prapatti* is something that is to be done just once. The school adopts a more liberal approach regarding caste (following Ramanuja's support and example). In fact, various weavers and artisans from the lowest caste (*sudra*) throughout south India received initiation from sages, and progressive social movements gained momentum by offering a liberal, popular form of Vaishnavism that appealed to the masses.

Critiques of *Prapatti*

Prapatti was widely propagated over its history and sparked lively debates in various contexts. Some Vaishnavaite critics argued that faith in God alone is the sole means of spiritual liberation (*moksha*) and therefore is equivalent to *prapatti*, and thus no separate act of surrender is required. Others suggested that a knowledge of the individual self in relation to the Supreme Being in itself constitutes *prapatti*, and that realization of this truth and constantly remembering it would serve the same purpose as *prapatti*, and therefore no separate act of surrender was required for liberation. Such views were roundly dismissed and rebuked by both the Northern and the Southern *prapatti* schools. For example, the celebrated sage Vedanta Desika maintained that knowledge of the relation of the soul to God is, of course, a valuable asset, but on its own is not efficacious as a means to spiritual liberation, just as a thorough knowledge of the scriptures, although important or indeed indispensable, cannot in itself lead to spiritual liberation. Spiritual practices or disciplines are required and must be scrupulously followed, affirmed Desika, and *prapatti* offered the surest, simplest, most direct, and most profound path available.

The rift between the two schools has at times been compared to the Catholic-Protestant divide in Christianity, with the Catholics seen as more closely aligned with the Northern school, emphasizing the possibility of attaining salvation through one's own works and merits, whereas the Southern school is deemed more aligned with the Protestant position of faith and grace as sufficient unto themselves for salvation. This division was thus a kind of "grace versus works" dispute. Only in the past century or so have tensions declined and intermarriages between members of the two schools finally been allowed.

Prapatti in Practice

For the actual practice of *prapatti*, there are five *angas* (accessories, limbs) that are crucial ancillary practices required of the *prapanna* (person who performs *prapatti*), in order for the *prapatti* to be effective. The five *angas* are as follows:

1. Performing only such acts as would please God.
2. Refraining from any acts that would displease God.
3. Having absolute and unshakable faith in God as the sole protector and refuge.
4. Choosing God deliberately and voluntarily as one's protector and source of liberation.
5. Totally surrendering oneself to God.[11]

Sometimes a sixth *anga* is added—exhibiting extreme humility with an absence of pride[12]—realizing one's intrinsic ignorance, impurity, and incapacity to perform the duties prescribed in scripture, coupled with the helplessness of the soul with regard to salvation.

The fourth *anga* is sometimes expressed as making a formal request to God for protection. The theology behind this is that God rules the universe according to certain universal principles, and God must also abide by these rules. For God to confer protection or salvation without being formally asked would leave God open to a charge of unfair discrimination, and this all the more so when God is asked to grant *moksha*, or liberation, which is the highest goal of human existence (*purusartha*).

The fifth *anga* is the very essence of surrender, and its sincere practice comes with a strong conviction rooted in the realization of one's ignorance. The individual, caught up in bondage due to ignorance (*avidya*), had earlier assumed that the self belonged to him, and that he was entitled to enjoy full freedom, and thereby has developed a strong sense of ego. As the individual approaches *prapatti*, a new realization dawns, which has three aspects: (1) the self is not mine but is the property of God, (2) protection of the self is the responsibility of God, and (3) the joy derived from its protection is that of God. Vedanta Desika expressed all this succinctly: "My self, the responsibility of its protection, and the fruit of its protection are not mine; they are of God. It is in this manner that a wise person should surrender himself to God."[13]

Boiled down to their essence, the *angas* are:

1. Do God's will.
2. Refrain from acts that displease God.
3. Maintain absolute faith in God.
4. Place total trust in God's protection.
5. Surrender to God absolutely.
(6. Show humility in the face of God.)

Toward a Universal *Prapatti*: Examples from Other Religions

It is instructive to compare the practice of *prapatti* with mystical approaches in other traditions. While *prapatti* is specifically a Hindu Vaishnavaite practice, we find close parallel practices in other traditions, although they are, of course, formulated in different theological frameworks and practical protocols. The key point, however, is that parallel practices strikingly similar to *prapatti* can be discerned across the faith traditions, all of which explicitly enjoin radical surrender to God as the centerpiece on the path of divine love. A few illustrative examples are given below.

"Christian *Prapatti*"

As a general example in the Christian tradition, there are several parallels between the practice of *prapatti* and the practice of the spirituality of St. Ignatius, especially in the well-known Ignatian Spiritual Exercises. These parallels include practical exercises in the preparatory stages leading up to total surrender, as well as the essence of surrender itself. The Ignatian preliminary practices include coming to total *faith* in Christ (analogous to the third *anga*), making the commitment to follow Christ's call, thereby *fulfilling God's will* (analogous to the first *anga*), knowing oneself to be fully *forgiven*, acknowledging one's spiritual poverty, and cultivating the three degrees of *humility* (analogous to the sixth *anga*). In St. Ignatius's first degree of humility (as outlined by Joseph Tetlow, SJ) the disciple comes to an inner commitment to say in earnest to Christ: "I will not do what you don't want" (analogous to the second *anga*), and in the second degree of humility: "I will do whatever you want" (analogous to the first *anga*), and in the third degree of humility: "I prefer poverty in Christ to the esteem of the world," thereby demonstrating complete trust in Christ (analogous to the fourth *anga*). The Spiritual Exercises culminate in a complete surrender to God (analogous to the fifth *anga*), as powerfully expressed in the Suscipe Prayer of Ignatius:

> Take, Lord, and receive all my liberty, my memory, my understanding, and my entire will—all that I have and call my own. You have given it all to me. To you, Lord, I return it. Everything is yours; do with it what you will. Give me only your love and your grace. That is enough for me.

Brother Lawrence

A second example might shed more light on the nature of correspondences to *prapatti*. Consider the case of the well-loved Brother Lawrence, a Carmelite friar in seventeenth-century Paris who worked as a cook in the priory kitchen. Brother Lawrence is widely known for his sixteen personal letters and four interview conversations that were published posthumously in 1691 under the title *The Practice of the Presence of God*. This book is one of the great treasures of Christian mystical literature because it illuminates in straightforward and eminently practical terms how to actually live daily life in the eternal presence of God. Although he was a simple, unlettered man outwardly, Brother Lawrence experienced a radical transformation through his practice of the presence of God, and he became highly sought after for his uncommon spiritual wisdom during his lifetime.

A strikingly close correspondence can be discerned between the details of the prayerful methodology developed by Brother Lawrence and the practice of *prapatti* with its six *angas* in Srivaishnavism. The primary elements of Brother Lawrence's methodology—presented in excerpts quoted from his letters and conversations—are organized below into the categories of the *angas* (for clarity, the closest parallels are highlighted in italics):

- First *anga* (Do God's will). Brother Lawrence: "*Our only business in this life is to please God* (ninth letter). We ought to give ourselves utterly to God, with regard both to things temporal and spiritual, and *seek our satisfaction only in fulfilling God's will*, whether He lead us by suffering or by consolation" (first conversation).

- Second *anga* (Refrain from acts that displease God). Brother Lawrence: "I apply myself diligently to *do nothing and think nothing which may displease God*" (second letter). "We must watch continually over ourselves so that *we will not do, say, or think anything that will displease God*" (fifteenth letter). "Are we not rude and do we not deserve blame if we leave God alone to busy ourselves with *trifles that do not please Him, and perhaps even offend Him?*" (sixteenth letter).

- Third *anga* (Maintain absolute faith in God). Brother Lawrence: "*We must act purely in faith*" (fourteenth letter). "*Faith alone,* which will not fail us in time of need, ought to be our support, and the foundation of our confidence, which must be all in God" (twelfth letter). "Let us *seek God often by faith*: He is within us; seek Him not elsewhere" (fifteenth letter). "What comforts me in this life is that *I now see God by faith*; and I see Him in such a manner as might make me say sometimes, I believe no more, but *I see. I feel what faith teaches us*, and, in that assurance and that practice of faith, I will live and die with Him" (eleventh letter).

- Fourth *anga* (Place total trust in God's protection). Brother Lawrence: "*Put then all your trust in God*" (eleventh letter). "We cannot escape the dangers which abound in life, without the *actual and continual help of God*; let us then pray to Him for it continually" (ninth letter). "Make the love of God the goal of all actions ... *seeking God only*, and nothing else, not even His gifts" (second conversation). "*The trust we put in God honors Him much and draws down great graces*" (third conversation).

- Fifth *anga* (Surrender to God absolutely). Brother Lawrence: "We ought, once and for all, heartily *to put our whole trust in God*, and *make a total surrender of ourselves to God*, secure that He would not deceive us" (fourth conversation). "Let us renounce, let us generously renounce, for the love of Him, all that is not himself" (ninth letter).
- Sixth *anga* (Humility, absence of pride). Brother Lawrence: "*I consider myself as the most wretched of men*, full of faults and corruption, and who has committed all sorts of crimes against his King. Touched with a sensible regret, I confess all my wickedness to Him" (second conversation).

These close parallels between the foundational tenets of Brother Lawrence's *Practice of the Presence of God* and the six *angas* of Hindu *prapatti* point to a remarkable similarity of transformative mystical praxis at the core of these two traditions. In essence, Brother Lawrence was effectively practicing the various *angas*, and through a process of total surrender that closely resembles *prapatti*, he became a man of great spiritual wisdom, what the Hindus would call a *jnani*, and his devotion and wisdom became legendary, even in his own lifetime.

In another direct parallel to Krishna's injunction to Arjuna in the *caramasloka*, Brother Lawrence expresses a radical form of abandonment of all dharmas in his own context, as he takes refuge in God alone:

> I have quitted all forms of devotion and set prayers but those to which my state obliges me. And I make it my business only to persevere in His holy presence, ... which I may call an actual presence of God; or, to speak better, an habitual, silent, and secret conversation of the soul with God, which often causes in me joys and raptures inwardly, and sometimes also outwardly, so great that I am forced to use means to moderate them and prevent their appearance to others. (third letter)

> I ask His forgiveness, I abandon myself in His hands, that He may do what He pleases with me. This King, full of mercy and goodness, very far from chastising me, embraces me with love, makes me eat at His table, serves me with His own hands, gives me the key of His treasures; He converses and delights Himself with me incessantly,

in a thousand and a thousand ways, and treats me in all respects as His favorite. It is thus I consider myself continually in His holy presence. (second letter)

The very air we breathe in our journey with God is not one of slavery and bondage but one of freedom and liberation. (third letter)

Notice here that God's response to Brother Lawrence is the same that Krishna promises in the *caramasloka*: Instead of chastisement, God forgives Brother Lawrence his sins completely, and bestows upon him the supreme gift of radical union with him. Brother Lawrence offers us scintillating hints about the joys and impact of the divine grace that is then showered upon him. This can be considered a glimpse into the real secret that dwells in the heart of God for the soul that gives itself in love to God. The alluring accounts of being given the key of God's treasures, treated as God's favorite, and the like are neither exaggeration nor hyperbole. They are apt poetic metaphors for the profound ecstasy and wisdom that the devotee basks in when fully united with God. Mystical devotees of Krishna report the same supreme intimacy and ecstatic union with Krishna, in which each one feels utterly "chosen" to be Krishna's sole and highest consort. Similar allusions abound throughout the Sufi and Hindu literature, rendered most often in exalted poetry rather than prose, for as scholar William Chittick says, "Love needs to be tasted and experienced, and poetry is far more adequate than rational disquisition for expressing experience."

In the final analysis, Brother Lawrence offers a similar assessment of his practice as did Ramanuja, Desika, and the other Srivaishnavaite masters about *prapatti*:

You will tell me that I am always saying the same thing: it is true, for this is the best and easiest method I know; and as I use no other, I advise all the world to it. We must know before we can love [*jnana* precedes *bhakti*]. In order to know God we must often think of Him; and when we come to love Him, we shall then also think of Him often, for our heart will be with our treasure. This is an argument which well deserves your consideration. (ninth letter)

"Sufi *Prapatti*"

Another example from the Islamic tradition that corresponds closely to *prapatti* is Rabi'a, the most famous female saint in Sufism. Born in Basra,

Iraq, in the early eighth century, Rabi'a was parted from her sisters after her father's death, captured by robbers, and sold as a slave girl. She was forced into hard labor, and spent her evenings in ardent prayer, sometimes the whole night. Legend has it that one night her master woke up in the middle of the night, heard her voice in prayer, and saw a luminous light surrounding her. He was awestruck, realized that she was a saint, and decided it was sacrilegious to keep her as a slave. He freed her, and Rabi'a moved into the desert and lived in solitude as an ascetic. She spent her nights in deep prayer and contemplation and outwardly lived in material poverty. As her fame grew, she had many disciples. Rabi'a never married, which was highly unusual for her time. She turned down several offers of marriage because of her sole devotion to God.

Rabi'a never had a *sheikh* (spiritual master) to guide and instruct her, which was (and still is) highly unusual, especially for a woman in her time. She received everything she knew directly from Allah (the Most High), without any human intermediary. Rabi'a exemplifies the true mystic, totally devoted to God, who is infused with God, by God, and defies all manner of social convention and religious protocol—yet "gets away with it" all because of the profundity of her spiritual realization and awakening.

A very holy person came into Rabi'a's life; some say this was Hasan al-Basri (642–728 CE). There is some doubt among scholars because at the time of Hasan al-Basri's death, Rabi'a would have been about eleven years old and most likely she had just arrived in Baghdad as a slave-girl for her master. In spite of this discrepancy of dates, Hasan al-Basri is usually referred to as being one of the closest of the Beloveds of Allah around Rabi'a in her early life.

Hasan is recorded as offering to marry Rabi'a. He asked her, "Do you desire for us to get married?" She replied, "The bond of marriage is for those who have being. But here being has disappeared, for I have become as nothing to my self. I exist only through Allah, for I belong wholly to Him, and I live in the shadow of His control. You must ask for my hand from Him and not from me."

Hasan then replied, "How did you find this secret, Rabi'a?"

She answered, "I lost all found things in Him."

Hasan then asked, "How did you come to know Him?"

She said, "You know of the how, but I know of the way beyond 'how.'"[14]

Rabi'a lived well into her eighties, and most of what we know about her comes from the writings of the great twelfth-century Sufi saint Farid ud-Din Attar. Her extensive poetry is legendary for its mystical insight and beauty.

Here are a few sayings of Rabi'a and retellings of well-known stories from her life that align closely with *prapatti*—effectively fulfilling the five *angas* as well as the *caramasloka*. Again, the most direct correspondence with the essence of *prapatti* is indicated in italics:

- First *anga* (Do God's will). Rabi'a: "You rebel against Allah, yet you appear to love Him. I swear by my faith that this is most strange. For if your love were truthful you would have obeyed Him, since *the lover obeys the one whom he loves.*"

- Second *anga* (Don't displease God). Rabi'a: "*If I will a thing and my Lord does not will it, I shall be guilty of unbelief.*" A friend went to visit Rabi'a, and saw that she had nothing but a broken water pitcher, an old reed mat, and a brick that she sometimes used for a pillow. He felt great sadness at seeing her privation, and said to her, "I have wealthy friends, please allow me to go to them and obtain a few simple furnishings for you." Rabi'a objected strongly, "That would be a grievous error! Is not my Provider and theirs one and the same?" Her friend nodded. Rabi'a continued, "And has the Provider of the poor forgotten the poor on account of their poverty? And does He remember the rich because of their riches?" Her friend replied, "No." Rabi'a concluded, "Then since God well knows of my state, why should I remind Him? *Such is His Will, and I too wish only what He wills.*"

- Third *anga* (Maintain absolute faith in God). Rabi'a:

  O God, if I worship You from fear of Hell, then burn me in
      Hell.
  And if I worship You for hope of Paradise, then bar me from
      Paradise.
  But if, *O Beloved, I worship You for Your Own sake alone,*
  Do not deny me Your everlasting Beauty.

- Fourth *anga* (Place total trust in God's protection). Rabi'a made a pilgrimage to Mecca, and she joined a caravan of other pilgrims. She had a small donkey that carried her baggage. However, in the middle of the hot desert the donkey became very weak and then died. Some of the people in the caravan offered to carry her baggage for her, but Rabi'a said to them, "Go on your way, for *I must not depend upon you for help, but I trust myself to Allah.*" Unable to persuade her otherwise, the other pilgrims continued on. Rabi'a remained behind, alone, in the vast desert. She prayed to her Lord, saying, "O my God, do kings deal thus with a woman, a stranger who is weak? You are calling me to Your House [the Ka'ba], but in the middle of my way, You have suffered my donkey to die, and You have left me alone in the desert." Hardly had she finished praying, when her donkey began to move, and finally it stood up. Rabi'a put her baggage again on it, and continued on her way.

- Fifth *anga* (Surrender to God absolutely). Rabi'a: "O God, You are aware that the sole longing of my heart is *to be totally surrendered to Your command. I have fled from the world and all that is in it.* My prayer is for Union with You; that is the goal of my desire."

- Sixth *anga* (Show humility before God). Rabi'a: "*What appears of any [good] works, I count as nothing at all.*"

Finally, in alignment with the *caramasloka* (abandon all dharmas; take refuge in God alone), the following story illustrates the radical spirit of taking refuge solely in God:

Rabi'a was once on her way to Mecca, making a pilgrimage to the Ka'ba, the very House of God on earth. When she was half-way there, she suddenly saw the Ka'ba itself—coming to meet *her!* Yet Rabi'a rebuffed the Ka'ba. "It is the Lord of the House Whom I need!" she declared. "What have I to do with the House? I need to meet with Him Who said: 'Whoso approaches Me by a span's length I will approach him by the length of a cubit.' The Ka'ba which I see is but a stone and has no power over me. What can the Ka'ba bring to me?"

Here Rabi'a is effectively renouncing the Ka'ba for God. Yet the Ka'ba is the most sacred shrine in all of Islam; it is the hallowed destination of the *hajj*, the pilgrimage that is one of the Five Pillars of Islam. The *hajj* is regarded as the most sacred journey in the life of every Muslim who is fortunate enough to make this pilgrimage. And here, the Ka'ba itself is actually making its own "pilgrimage" to meet Rabi'a. Such is the greatness of her sainthood! Yet Rabi'a will not be satisfied with the Ka'ba, or anything else whatsoever, except her Lord Allah. This is the reality for the true mystic, and it's no different in any other tradition: God alone will suffice, nothing but God.

Rabi'a was once asked, "How is it that you have attained such a profound degree of intimacy with God?" She replied, "By constantly saying to God: *I take refuge in You from everything* that has distracted me from You, and from every hindrance that has hindered me from You." Rabi'a's secret is none other than the most secret teaching that Krishna gives to Arjuna at the end of the Gita.

Rabi'a also gives hints of the divine glories she beheld in ecstatic union with God. At one point, Rabi'a was spending many hours in prayer in her small hut, and she would not come out for days at a time. Her maidservant became concerned, and one beautiful day when she was in the garden, she called out to Rabi'a, imploring her to come outdoors. "O mistress, do come outside here in the garden, so you can see all the beautiful works of God!" Rabi'a replied, "Nay, come you inside—that you may behold the unspeakable Beauty of their Creator!"

Abandonment to Divine Providence as an Example of *Prapatti*

A final illustrative example that aligns closely with *prapatti* is provided by Jean-Pierre de Caussade, in his principal work *Abandonment to Divine Providence*, from which the quotations here are taken, arranged into the categories of the *angas*.[15]

- Following the will of God (first and second *angas*)

    We can never acquire true conformity to the will of God until we are perfectly resolved to serve God according to His will and pleasure and not to please ourselves.... Pure love consists in being content with all that pleases God, and will not permit us to will anything contrary to the will of God.... Make it your chief study to conform yourself to the will of God even in the smallest things, saying in the midst of the most annoying contradictions, and with the most alarming prospects for the future: "My God, I desire with all my heart to do Your holy will.... Therefore, from henceforth, I renounce my own will to follow Yours in all things."

- Faith (third *anga*). Three sections of Caussade's book are devoted to faith, titled "Great Faith Is Necessary," "By Faith the Operation of God Is Recognized," and "The Life of Faith."

The way that leads most directly to God is the way of bare faith.... We should attach ourselves to this bare faith preserved by God always in the center of the soul.... Faith cannot be said to be real, living faith until it is tried, and has triumphed over every effort for its destruction.... In all our spiritual exercises we must approach God by pure faith. That which is wonderful in the saints is the constancy of their faith under every circumstance.... There is nothing that the eye of faith does not penetrate, nothing that the power of faith does not overcome.

- Trusting in God's protection (fourth *anga*)

Never does God fail those who put their whole trust in His protection.... God will always come to your assistance when you require His help. He will become your Master, your Guide, your Support, your Protector, your invincible Upholder. God will never abandon any who have abandoned themselves entirely to Him, and who trust completely in His infinite mercy. When you are conducted by a guide who takes you through an unknown country at night across fields where there are no tracks, ... how can you choose but abandon yourself? Of what use is it looking about to find out where you are, to ask the passers-by, or to consult maps and travelers? The plans or fancies of a guide who insists on being trusted would not allow of this.

- Surrender and abandonment (fifth *anga*)

The first great duty of souls called by God to this state is the absolute and entire surrender of themselves to Him.... A total surrender of your whole self is the most pure and most perfect way of treating with God. It is the true prayer of the heart, a quite interior prayer, the sincere prayer of spirit to spirit.... The soul should blindly abandon itself and be indifferent about everything. This total abandonment is as simple as its effects are marvelous.

Let your soul tend above all to a total abandonment to God, ... there is no better way than always to practice total abandonment....

Keep your soul in this habitual condition of total abandonment without any reserve.

- Humility (sixth *anga*). An entire section of Caussade's book is titled "Triumph of Humility."

Solid humility is the foundation of all perfection. Humility is the foundation of all good.... The history of the world from the beginning is but the history of the struggle between the powers of the world, and of hell, against the souls which are humbly devoted to the divine action. In this struggle all the advantage seems to be on the side of pride, yet the victory always remains with humility.

Let us acquiesce in advance in a spirit of humility, love, and sacrifice.

- *Caramasloka* (Abandon all dharmas; take refuge in God alone)

Our duties must be so arranged as to be commensurate with the designs of God.... To carry out our inspirations will then become a duty to which we must be faithful.

As there are souls whose whole duty is defined by exterior laws, and who should not go beyond them because restricted by the will of God; so also there are others who, besides exterior duties, are obliged to carry out faithfully that interior rule imprinted on their hearts.... [This] third kind of duty takes precedence of all law, formalities, or marked-out rules. It is what, in saints, appears singular and extraordinary.

Types of *Prapatti*

Prapatti is sometimes viewed as a soteriological path only, but this is a limited conception. It does serve this purpose, but it also has broader manifestations. Building on Ramanuja's distinction, noted earlier, we might distinguish three kinds of *prapatti*:

1. Soteriological *prapatti*, which is for the masses, who are generally seeking primarily salvation and forgiveness of sins.
2. Mystical *prapatti*, which focuses on mystical realization and union with God. This is the form of *prapatti* on which this book is focused.
3. De facto *prapatti*, which refers to the intrinsic quality of surrender that is an essential characteristic of all spiritual paths.

I have illustrated mystical *prapatti* with several examples from the lives of prominent mystics. De facto *prapatti* relates to the fact that all religions entail surrender in various forms and degrees. Religious or spiritual practice generally begins and ends in surrender. For the practitioner, religion begins with surrender to the practices and the theology; surrender of one's time and energy to study the scriptures; and surrender to do the prayer or meditation practices. As one progresses and encounters the more interior dimensions, surrender to the rigorous process of purification is generally required, and surrender of one's egoic identity. Religious practice can also be said to end with surrender in the sense that the final stage of full realization, enlightenment, or union with God generally takes place through an act of total surrender, even if it's not called that, in which the religion itself is transcended as the aspirant is "lifted out of herself" by an unseen power into the highest realization.

Thus, any form of mystical realization or spiritual enlightenment is de facto, an unbidden gift of some form of higher "grace" or blessing of wisdom or enlightenment, regardless of the religious or theological framework involved. Whether theistic or nontheistic, we cannot "force the hand" of the Absolute Godhead or the *Atman* or the *Dharmakaya* or the Tao to bestow its profound gift of transformation or grace upon us. The most we can do is to give ourselves in earnest to the various practices—meditation, prayer, *zhikr*, *japa* (repetition of the divine name), purification, and the like—and offer ourselves up to this Supreme Reality that is so much greater than us. A Tibetan Buddhist practitioner can no more force full realization of *rigpa* in Dzogchen practice than a Christian mystic can force himself into union with God. Oneness with God, or enlightenment (or *satori* or *samadhi*), is out of our hands entirely, and can only be given from Somewhere else (even though that Somewhere exists right here and now!). "The Atman reveals itself to whom the Atman chooses" (Katha Upanishad 1:2:23), and "Many are called, few are chosen" (Matt. 22:14).

Hence there is a kind of de facto *prapatti*, or self-surrender, that is essential. This is something required not only in the theistic traditions, but also in the practice of nontheistic traditions. For example, when a Buddhist meditator sits on the cushion, she does not know or realize That for which she is sitting. By definition the meditator is ignorant of the true goal of meditation, which is beyond all categories of thought and concept, and this is precisely why she is sitting in meditation—to realize that goal.

Whether she conceives of the goal as enlightenment, *rigpa*, *mahamudra*, *dzogchen*, *satori*, *shunyata*, or even just attaining peace of mind, all these are for her merely conceptual labels for higher states of spiritual realization, of which she has as yet no experience. So the practitioner has, at best, only vague ideas and concepts of what it's all about, as she sits in meditation. The practice itself does not resolve this situation; it simply creates suitable conditions and preparation for "something else" to happen that brings liberation or profound insight. This gift of spiritual awakening or realization comes unbidden as a form of "grace" in response to her "surrender" to the practice, even if neither of these terms would be utilized in her theological framework or tradition. Moreover, as fully realized mystics and sages in all the traditions have reported, their ideas about enlightenment or union with God prior to the experience always turned out to be entirely mistaken; the spiritual goal was nothing like they expected.

Considering these parallels and commonalities, we can extract the core essentials that underlie *prapatti* across the traditions. These essentials include: a conviction of faith or trust in the efficacy of the tradition that one is practicing; submitting oneself in humility to a higher spiritual authority (whether it be conceived as the will of God, the dharma practice and teachings of a Buddhist or Jain lineage, the authority of a guru, or the like); engaging in certain sustained practices; and finally—in acknowledgment of one's own humility, incapacity, and intrinsic lack of skill and experience to understand the depths and workings of the transformative process—fully *giving* oneself over to the process, which entails essentially a form of "surrender" to the process. Nothing less will suffice. And when the practice works, it is because of two basic factors: (1) the practitioner has "let go" in some form of inner surrender, and (2) an unbidden "grace" or power, operating from another level of reality, brings a gift or transformation that is far beyond the awareness or capacity of the practitioner.

Sri Aurobindo summarizes the essence of the process of *prapatti* (though he doesn't call it that), and he also articulates some of the psychological challenges that must be endured and overcome for the truly sincere aspirant:

> There are two powers that alone can effect [spiritual realization]: a fixed and unfailing aspiration that calls from below, and a supreme Grace from above that answers.

But the supreme Grace will act only in the conditions of the Light and the Truth.... There must be a total and sincere surrender [that] seizes all parts of the being.... If part of the being surrenders, but another part reserves itself, you are yourself pushing the divine Grace away from you.... If you call for the Truth, yet something in you chooses what is false ... you will be open to attack and the Grace will recede from you. Detect first what is false or obscure in you and persistently reject it, then only can you rightly call for the Divine Power to transform you....

Make your surrender true and complete, then only will all else be done for you.... The Supreme demands your surrender to her, but does not impose it.... Your surrender must be self-made and free.... An inert passivity is constantly confused with the real surrender, but out of [this] nothing true and powerful can come.... A glad and strong and helpful submission is demanded ... of the faithful servant of the Divine. This is the true attitude and only those who can take it and keep it, and preserve a faith unshaken by disappointments and difficulties, shall pass through the ordeal to the supreme victory and the great transmutation.[16]

Toward a Universal *Prapatti*

In the contemporary emergence of a possible interspiritual or interfaith path of divine love, it seems that the ancient, long hidden practice of *prapatti* warrants something of a revival in a broader context beyond Hinduism. *Prapatti* deserves to be articulated anew, in a wider interreligious context, as a foundational principle and practice on the path of divine love. Viewed through the complex lens of multiple traditions, the key preconditions of *prapatti* shine through clearly: unwavering alignment with divine will, absolute faith and trust in the Divine, and total surrender. If a person fulfills these requirements in full sincerity and humility, God will never abandon the person, regardless of whether or not she belongs formally to a religion. God will look into her heart, and grant divine grace according to what God sees.

Prapatti also sheds new light on certain mysteries of the mystics, for example, the fact that unlettered, simple souls have achieved high levels of spiritual realization and wisdom. Another example of this is St. Thérése of Liseux, the "Little Flower," who wrote: "God would never inspire me with desires which cannot be realized; so in spite of my littleness, I can hope to be a saint.... My whole strength lies in prayer and sacrifice, these are my invincible arms; they can move hearts far better than words, I know it by experience."[17]

In *prapatti*, the aspirant has been said to literally bypass the various "long lines at check out" in the supermarket of divine grace, as it were,[18] of all those seeking liberation who are on the different traditional paths of *karma yoga*, or *jnana yoga*, or *bhakti yoga*. This metaphor seems perhaps an exaggeration, but even Ramanuja insists that *prapatti* is a complete spiritual path unto itself.

By submitting themselves absolutely to God, practitioners of *prapatti* sidestep the other paths and go directly to God. But absolute faith, absolute obedience, and absolute surrender in full humility are all required, and few are truly willing to offer themselves in this way. As Ramanuja and others have said, there is a stage of spiritual development beyond which few are prepared to truly surrender.

In the highest stages of *prapatti*, the Ultimate Source is realized as a profound mystical Nothingness, beyond all manifestation. To attain this eternal supreme, nothing manifest can serve as the means. "Nor can any attain it, since, before attainment, he who would attain must cease to be."[19] "It is beyond you, because when you reach it you have lost your self. You will enter the light but you will never touch the Flame."[20] These quotations illustrate that only by the profound agency of divine grace, via mystical *prapatti* in which the self is utterly surrendered and indeed dissolved into God, can the ultimate be attained. Only divine grace can lead to this attainment, a process in which the disciple is annihilated in total union with God.

Visible and Hidden Secrets of *Prapatti*

In summary, the supreme secret of universal *prapatti* is twofold: the injunction of absolute surrender to God—the "visible secret"—and the divine response to this surrender—the "hidden secret." The first is not really secret, because all the scriptures call us explicitly to this surrender. Yet, scriptures only reveal the doorway to the secret. The real secret is what takes place beyond that door, after the devotee surrenders utterly. The real secret is not given, nor can it be given in written word or scripture. Mystics across the ages have noted this. For example, Aurobindo said, "For the soul that has passed the shining portals and stands in the blaze of the inner light, all mental and verbal description is as poor as it is superfluous, inadequate, and an impertinence."[21]

This is the "hidden secret" that Brother Lawrence makes reference to, and that Rabi'a alludes to, and indeed all the mystics refer to in the realization of God. This hidden secret is the unfathomable mystical power that is unleashed when the human soul fully surrenders to God—the unimaginably profound and expansive gifts of divine grace, wisdom, and the blessing of eternal life that are bestowed. This resplendent secret remains ever hidden outwardly, the highest hidden secret—and yet the pathway for us to go there ourselves has been graciously revealed across the faith traditions.

> The deeper secret within the secret:
> Land that is nowhere, that is the true home.
> All changes of spiritual consciousness depend upon the Heart.
> —SECRET OF THE GOLDEN FLOWER

Science of
Divine Love

6

The Inner Net of the Heart

Science and Spirituality

The secret turning in your heart is the entire universe
turning.

—Rumi

The foregoing chapters have revealed striking parallels across the scriptures, the mystics, and the core practices of divine love in three major
world religions. What are we to make of these patterns? Are there underlying principles of some kind that give rise to this common ground across
religions? How is it that the mystics—who are mere mortals, after all—
can claim oneness with the Infinite Divine? How can we apply these principles and insights, in practical terms, to our own lives?

Throughout this book I have sought to rely primarily on spiritual
"data" drawn from the scriptures and direct testimony of leading mystics
and saints, because taken together, these canonical sources point toward
a profound path of divine love that stands strongly on its own merits. In
this chapter and the next, I build upon this foundation by exploring certain
breakthroughs at the frontiers of science that help to illuminate and weave
the insights from the scriptures and mystics into a larger unifying vision of
the spirituality and science of divine love.

Science Is Slowly Discovering Nonmaterial Reality

A powerful new awakening is taking place at the cutting edge of many
scientific disciplines today. The key emerging insight is that beyond the
physical realm, invisible patterns and principles somehow organize what

we observe and experience in the physical world. Science is discovering that "something transpires behind that which appears."[1] This startling theme is emerging in field after field: biology, physics, nonlinear dynamics, brain physiology, complexity theory, transpersonal psychology, near-death experience and other consciousness phenomena, psychoneuroimmunology, and ethnobotany, to name a few. This auspicious development points Western science in a remarkable direction toward the existence of a realm beyond the observable, material, empirical world. The stage is being set for another major scientific revolution, one that will eventually weave science and spirituality—matter and spirit—together into a larger unity.

Simultaneously, a parallel awakening is taking place across the world's spiritual and religious traditions. As East meets West and North meets South, the essential unity of human spiritual consciousness is becoming increasingly recognized. The world's religious and spiritual traditions are discovering each other in new ways, fostering unprecedented convergence and collaboration among previously disparate practices and communities. We are witnessing a revolution of consciousness—the birth of a vast, unified worldview that unites and cross-fertilizes East and West, modern and indigenous, human and nonhuman, contemporary and ancient—leading us toward a deep collective realization of the seamless *oneness* of existence.

This auspicious breakthrough is coming not a moment too soon, because humanity urgently needs a comprehensive, unifying perspective to navigate through the challenging waters ahead and begin building a new civilization of love and harmony. This is not a dreamy aspiration or impractical mystic vision, though some may dismiss it as such. It is our destiny as the human family, and it is our birthright to bring this destiny into practical manifestation.

Nonlocality and Quantum Entanglement

The classical scientific worldview conditioned Western civilization to believe that the world and the cosmos are composed of distinct, isolated, material objects, each separate from the others and set into dynamic motion according to rational mechanistic laws. This view began to crumble over one hundred years ago with the advent of quantum theory and relativity theory in physics, and continued through the twentieth century with major breakthroughs in biology, complexity theory, transpersonal psychology, and many other disciplines. Atoms, once believed to be solid nuggets of matter, are revealed to be patterns of vibrating energy. Matter is composed almost entirely of empty space. These discoveries have rapidly shifted our understanding of reality.

Science is uncovering new levels of interconnection between matter and consciousness, which began with Heisenberg's discovery that nothing exists in objective isolation from the rest of existence. Experiments in quantum physics show that every particle in the universe is to varying degrees "aware" of every other particle. New principles of interconnection, known as "nonlocality" and "quantum entanglement," have been confirmed in repeated experiments. After two particles have interacted in certain ways, their "spin" properties are thereafter fundamentally interconnected. If we measure the spin state of one particle, the spin state of the other particle is determined instantaneously, even if it's located at the opposite end of the universe. The second particle somehow "knows" immediately the result of the measurement performed on the first particle, even though the distance between them precludes any possibility of a signal of any kind carrying information from one particle to the other. This immediate "nonlocal" connection between particles transcends separation in space and time, and the entire universe exhibits intricate networks of such quantum entanglement. These discoveries hint at possible physical explanations for hidden links between consciousness and matter.

Consciousness Research at the Frontiers of Science

The science of consciousness is in its infancy, and remarkable new discoveries are emerging. Cross-cultural research on meditation that bridges neuroscience and ancient contemplative practices is leading to breakthroughs in understanding the nature of mind.[2] After decades compiling the results of experiments investigating links between consciousness and matter, research psychologist Dean Radin concludes that scientific research "has resolved a century of skeptical doubts through thousands of replicated laboratory studies" that demonstrate the reality of phenomena traditionally considered impossible by today's mainstream science, such as extrasensory perception (ESP), psychokinesis, telepathy, and near-death experiences.[3] Researcher Chris Carter underscores these findings, and provides a keenly insightful refutation of skeptical criticism that regards such data as "unscientific."[4] Physician Larry Dossey has reviewed hundreds of scientific studies that, taken together, show that intercessory prayer improves healing of medical patients, and that the healing effects are independent of spatial separation between the patients and those who prayed for them.[5] For Radin, Carter, and Dossey, these developments point toward a hitherto unrecognized role of consciousness in physical reality.

Debate continues over such findings, and these unusual phenomena remain difficult for many mainstream scientists to swallow, even when well supported experimentally. Yet this may simply be the result of a widespread lack of awareness about the evidence. Radin maintains that owing to "a general uneasiness" about unusual phenomena of consciousness and the "insular nature of scientific disciplines, the vast majority of these experiments are unknown to most scientists."[6] Radin and Carter are convinced that anyone who makes an honest inquiry into this body of research would have to agree that that something real is going on that cannot be explained by today's science.

Uniting Consciousness and Science

To discern what is emerging at the frontiers of science, I examine one specific discipline more closely—physics, the "hardest" of the sciences—to witness the essential shift that is taking place across many disciplines. Rest assured that no knowledge of physics is required to follow this chapter, only an eye for beauty.

Let's begin with the work of David Bohm (1917–1992), who was a leading physicist and pioneer in science and spirituality. Bohm was a colleague of Albert Einstein's at Princeton, and the two of them shared similar views on the theoretical foundations of quantum theory. Bohm felt the true purpose of science was a quest for truth, and he was disturbed that many scientists regarded science primarily as a pragmatic means for prediction and control of nature and technology. Like Einstein, Bohm believed that science was a kind of spiritual quest, a form of *jnana yoga* that strives to know ultimate truths.

Bohm probed not only into modern physics, where he made major contributions, but he also carried his quest well beyond science into spiritual teachings and wisdom. For more than twenty years he carried on in-depth dialogues with the Indian sage Krishnamurti and other leading spiritual masters, including the Dalai Lama. He also explored art, to discover insights about the nature of order and form. Bohm eagerly embraced both scientific and spiritual forms of inquiry as a way to "triangulate," so to speak, on the true nature of reality by taking into account the broadest possible range of data and methods of inquiry.

Bohm was disturbed by the fact that the twin pillars of the new physics—relativity theory and quantum theory—are contradictory, so he sought to unify them. He began by asking what these theories had in common, and he discovered that it is wholeness, or oneness. Both theories posited that the universe is a single, integral whole, from the tiniest atoms to the largest galaxies. Building upon this foundation over forty years of rigorous scientific work, Bohm advanced the hypothesis that the essence of the universe is what he called the "holomovement." "Movement" means that the nature of existence is a process of continual change, and "holo" means that it has a kind of holographic structure, in which each part contains the whole. In Bohm's words, "The cosmos is a single, unbroken wholeness in flowing movement,"[7] in which each part of the flow contains the entire flow.

The Implicate Order: The Unseen Realm

Bohm further posited that there are two fundamental aspects to the holomovement, which he called the "explicate order" and the "implicate order." Now one might well ask, after having just said it is oneness, why are we breaking it into two? Aren't we imposing a false duality onto what is a unity? Not quite, because the explicate and implicate orders only appear to be distinct; in truth, they are unified. But they appear convincingly separate because of human perceptual limitations. We humans have five physical senses plus the thinking mind, which together perceive only a small portion of the oneness. This limited portion—that which is directly perceived by our six human faculties—constitutes what Bohm calls the explicate order. Everything else—all that we don't directly see, hear, taste, feel, touch, or think—constitutes the implicate order. In summary, the limitations of human perception necessitate a delineation between what is directly perceptible (explicate order) and what isn't (implicate order).

To illustrate the relationship between the implicate and explicate orders, Bohm gave a simple example. Imagine two concentric cylinders, one larger than the other, and suppose the annular column between them is filled with a thick, transparent liquid, like glycerin. Now place a small droplet of ink on the surface of the glycerin, and begin rotating the inner cylinder (while the outer cylinder remains fixed). As the rotation continues, the ink droplet gets stretched out and becomes longer and thinner, growing ever fainter. Eventually, it disappears altogether. At this point, the natural conclusion to draw is that the order, or organization, of the original ink drop has been lost—rendered chaotic—as the ink seems to be randomly distributed in microscopically small particles throughout the glycerin. However, if you now rotate the inner cylinder in the opposite direction, the ink structure will begin to reappear, faintly at first, and as you keep rotating the cylinder, the ink gets thicker and darker, until it finally comes all the way back; the ink droplet reconstructs itself completely. The key insight from this experiment (which has been demonstrated in the laboratory) is that the order in the original ink drop was preserved—enfolded in the glycerin—even when it was no longer visible.

Bohm used this example as a metaphor to emphasize a fundamental lesson for all of science: "A hidden order may be present in what appears to be random." This seemingly simple, almost self-evident statement has profound implications. It is a scientific version of Shakespeare's famous quip in *Hamlet*, "There are more things in Heaven and Earth, Horatio, than are dreamt of in your philosophies!" Quantum mechanics, for example, provides a statistical description of physical reality, but this does not mean that reality *itself* is merely statistical, as imputed by the standard Copenhagen interpretation. Physical reality could well (and more likely does) entail refined and subtle orders of nature and existence that are utterly beyond and invisible to present-day science. To blur these hidden levels of reality together into a statistical description of what appear to be random processes is analytically legitimate (as the best that science can offer), but to then impute randomness itself to the nature of reality is a serious, unjustified mistake.[8] It constitutes an unwarranted projection of our own ignorance *onto* reality, which is why both Bohm and Einstein felt that "God does not play dice"[9] with the universe.

Developing these insights, Bohm proposed that there exists a vast, invisible realm beyond what we perceive as the physical universe. He called this hidden realm the "implicate order," and he demonstrated that the implicate order is fully consistent with the data of modern physics.

Although it is invisible, the implicate order is every bit as real as the physical universe (or, in fact, more so), and it provides a cogent and comprehensive explanation for all the seemingly bizarre phenomena of quantum physics.

At first blush, it's natural to suppose that the implicate order is some kind of secondary, ethereal reality, floating around somewhere behind the scenes, whereas the primary reality is the solid physical universe, just as our senses perceive and our science describes. Yet for Bohm, precisely the opposite is the case. The implicate order is the fundamental reality, and the explicate order is a secondary phenomenon. The explicate order is analogous to the foam on the waves of the ocean, and the implicate order is the ocean itself. Sea foam is a "surface phenomenon," floating on top of the ocean; similarly, the explicate order—the physical universe with its 100 billion galaxies, each of which contains 100 billion stars—is a kind of ephemeral side effect or by-product of the far vaster implicate order. This does not in any way diminish the reality, beauty, or sacredness of the physical universe, but simply places it in proper relationship to the unmanifest dimension. It is reminiscent of what Krishna said to Arjuna in the Bhagavad Gita: "I run this entire cosmos with the tiniest part of my Being" (10:42). The implicate order is vast—a kind of interpenetrating field of conscious presence and intelligence that far transcends the physical universe, yet creates the universe.

What is the nature of the implicate order? It is present everywhere, but visible nowhere. It extends throughout space and time, but also far beyond space and time. This is a crucial point to understand; space is not some giant vacuum through which matter moves. Rather, matter and empty space are intimately interconnected, and both are part of the explicate order. The implicate order transcends space and time altogether, *and* infuses every point in space-time. One can think of the implicate order as a synonym for the Unseen, for that which is neither manifest nor accessible to our mind and five senses, often called the spiritual dimension. We don't directly perceive it, except through inner intuitions, contemplative practices, and spiritual experiences.

The implicate order can be viewed as the sum total of the spiritual, archetypal, and metaphysical dimensions of consciousness that extend to infinity and are not manifest in physical form.[10] What is remarkable about Bohm's implicate order, in contrast to virtually every other model of spiritual reality, is that the implicate order rests on a firm mathematical foundation that comes directly out of the central equation of quantum mechanics—the Schrödinger equation.[11] The implicate order is therefore not just a conceptual metaphor; it defines a subtle dimension of unmanifest awareness or consciousness that interpenetrates the physical universe at every point in space and time, while also transcending space and time. It also includes levels of yet deeper implication within itself, which Bohm called the super-implicate order.

The Science of Consciousness Goes Beyond $E = mc^2$

A vital aspect of Bohm's understanding is that the nature of reality has three fundamental components, whereas science has generally dealt with only two of them: matter and energy. The whole of science has focused on matter-energy interactions, and the two are equivalent in Einstein's famous equation $E = mc^2$. This equation essentially affirms that energy and matter are interchangeable, that is, different forms of the same thing. However, Bohm insists there is a third fundamental element, which he called "meaning," or consciousness (he equated the two terms). For Bohm, consciousness is as significant as matter and energy (or more so), and each of these three fundamental building blocks contains or "enfolds" the other two. Bohm reaches a powerful conclusion: "This implies, in contrast to the usual view, that consciousness is an inherent and essential part of our overall reality, and is not merely a purely abstract and ethereal quality having its existence only in the mind."[12] Consciousness is foundational, and encompasses all the intangibles and immeasurables of life—including human dynamics of purpose, yearning, intention, love, despair—which are no less real for being intangible. Bohm emphasized that scientific instruments operate only in the explicate order, and hence they register only a small fraction of reality. Conventional science therefore misses the implicate order altogether, and with it, the entire domain of consciousness.

Bohm's theories are enjoying a considerable revival today. A growing international network of scientists and philosophers are rapidly advancing the field of "Bohmian mechanics" and advocating Bohm's interpretation of quantum theory as preferable to the century-old Copenhagen interpretation.[13] Meanwhile, startling new laboratory experiments in fluid dynamics have exhibited quantum behavior in macroscopic systems, something previously believed to be impossible, which is further bolstering new interest in Bohm's theories.[14]

As Above, So Below: Fractals and Holography

Perhaps the most important characteristic of Bohm's new scientific theory of reality is its holographic structure. To illustrate what this means, let us consider an example from mathematical physics—fractal geometry.[15] There is no need to understand any physics or mathematics to follow this narrative, only an eye for beauty. Over the past thirty years, new mathematical structures, called "fractals," have been discovered, and these are powerful tools for scientific understanding of many natural phenomena. The simplest and most fundamental example of a fractal is called the Mandelbrot set, shown in figure 6.1 This figure is generated on the computer, and is named after the twentieth-century mathematician who discovered it, Benoit Mandelbrot. At first appearance, it looks quite like a bug, or, perhaps more edifying, if rotated clockwise by 90 degrees it resembles a meditating Buddha. Regardless of what it looks like, the Mandelbrot set is a purely mathematical structure that is generated by the repeated application of the iterative process $Z = Z^2 + C$ at each point of the complex plane.[16] This little formula—so simple and easy to write down—is the most basic

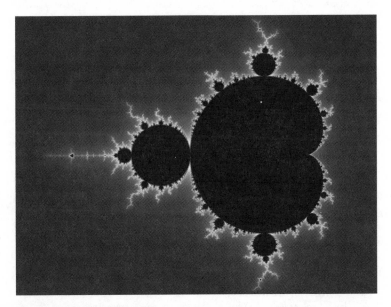

Figure 6.1. The Mandelbrot set.

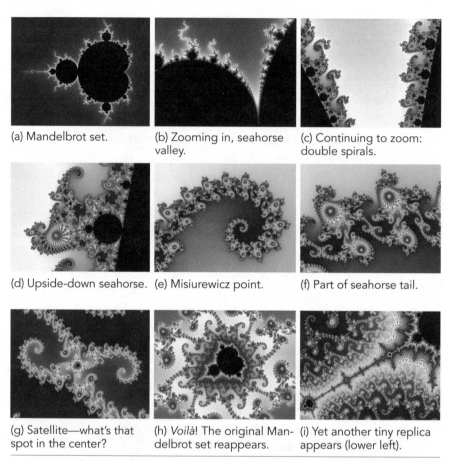

(a) Mandelbrot set.

(b) Zooming in, seahorse valley.

(c) Continuing to zoom: double spirals.

(d) Upside-down seahorse.

(e) Misiurewicz point.

(f) Part of seahorse tail.

(g) Satellite—what's that spot in the center?

(h) *Voilà!* The original Mandelbrot set reappears.

(i) Yet another tiny replica appears (lower left).

Figure 6.2. The Mandelbrot set in detail. Each image above "zooms in" on a portion of the previous image. The final image is magnified ten million times from the first.

nonlinear process in mathematics, and yet it generates one of the most amazingly complex and intricate mathematical structures ever discovered.

The structure of the Mandelbrot set is so rich and intricate that one must "zoom in" in order to perceive it. Figure 6.2 shows a series of nine sequential zooms into the interior of the Mandelbrot set. To start, the full Mandelbrot set is shown in the upper left-hand corner. The next image to its right shows a magnification of a portion of the Mandelbrot set. Each subsequent image is a further magnification of a small portion of the previous image, so in this manner we proceed step-by-step on a kind of "visual tour" into the interior of the set.[17] The last image in this series is magnified about 10 million times from the first image.

The images in figure 6.2 progressively depict the various structures within the Mandelbrot set, and are given informal names for the images they resemble, such as "seahorse valley," "satellites," "double spirals," and so on. The remarkable depth and variety of interior structure is reflected in the various images, and these images reveal just one pathway into the set, among of an infinite number of other possibilities.

Notice something remarkable in the image of figure 6.2(h): the original Mandelbrot shape reappears! The entire Mandelbrot set is replicated in miniature. It is true to form and exhibits all the rich complexity of the original, but on a smaller scale. This is the key property of all fractals: self-similarity on vastly different scales. If you keep zooming in further, many more such miniature Mandelbrot sets are revealed, such as the tiny replica that appears in the final zoomed image in figure 6.2(i). In fact, there are an infinite number of these similar replicas embedded throughout the Mandelbrot set. This is amazing enough, and even more amazing is that no two of them are exactly alike; all these replicas have the same basic "body" shape and "head," but each one is unique in terms of the details of the various nodules and fixtures around the exterior of the body and head.[18]

The remarkable mathematical structure shown in these figures gives a metaphorical representation of the holographic or fractal nature of natural systems. In science, this phenomenon is described as "nested sets of self-similar structures." Although new to science, this principle has been known to sages and mystics since ancient times, as the hermetic principle of correspondence: "As above, so below." The fractal is a modern scientific discovery of this ancient mystical principle, which can also be stated: "As within, so without." The key insight is that deeply embedded within universal structures are miniature replicas of the whole, on vastly smaller scales. The microcosm replicates the macrocosm.

Glimpsing the Unity of Science and Religion

Striking correlations emerge if we apply this fractal model metaphorically to various spiritual and religious traditions. In Hinduism, for example, the "Atman" represents the spiritual essence of the individual (or the Self), and "Brahman" is the spiritual nature of the cosmos. The enlightenment experience is the realization that Atman is Brahman—the two are identical. Imagine for a moment that Brahman is represented by the full

Mandelbrot set, and each of the miniature replicas embedded throughout the set represents a particular soul (Atman). Each individual Atman then has the identical structure of Brahman, and as the Bhagavad Gita says, we can literally "see the Atman in every creature, and all of creation in the Atman" (Gita 6:29).

Similar holographic or fractal declarations appear in the other religions, expressing a conscious identity between macrocosm and microcosm. In Judaism, "You are made in the image of God" (Gen. 1:27). In the Gospels, "The Father and I are one" (John 10:30), and "All that is mine is yours, and all that is yours is mine" (John 17:10). As the Christian mystic Julian of Norwich puts it, "We are all in God enclosed, and God is enclosed in us."[19] These declarations all express a fractal-like oneness or identity of the soul with God. Similarly, in Zen, the great master Dogen says: "We study the self to forget the self, and when we forget the self, we become one with the ten thousand things."[20] Here, the self we forget is just our physical and conditioned forms—our body, personality, ego, thoughts, family, vocation—all the attributes that characterize our manifest, temporal form. When we forget this self, we become one with the "ten thousand things," meaning we become one with that which creates all of existence, that is, the implicate order. And finally, in Tantric Buddhism, the scholar Ajit Mukerjee says unequivocally: "The entire drama of the universe is replicated in the human body. When you come to know the truth of the body, you come to know the truth of the cosmos."[21] This is meant literally, but at a consciousness level, not a physical level. If you explore the depths of consciousness, you discover in your own being everything that goes on at the cosmic scale. As transpersonal psychologist Stanislav Grof emphasizes, "Each of us is everything."[22]

The doorway to this universal consciousness is through the heart, which opens inwardly to the implicate order that links us all together. This vast inner oneness could be called the "inner net of the heart." The analogy to the Internet here is intentional, because the computerized Internet may be seen as a technological manifestation of this fractal principle. Every computer has access to the entirety of information on the Internet (apart from electronic firewalls that cordon off domains of cybersecurity). Any part of this vast cyberspace is only a few clicks away. Indeed, the very existence of the Internet is a result, in the explicate order, of a preexisting and far more refined parallel principle in the implicate order. Just as every computer can access the entire universe of cyberspace through the Internet, every human heart can access the entire cosmos of consciousness through the inner net of the heart.

Another expression of this fractal structure from Buddhist and Hindu mythology is called Indra's Net, in which the whole universe is imagined as a vast lattice of glistening jewels, each of which reflects all the others in its own facets. Fractal structures are also analogous to Aldous Huxley's concept of "holons," utilized extensively in the work of philosopher Ken Wilber and others. The same principle was articulated in the eloquent words attributed to Hermes: "God is an infinite sphere whose center is everywhere, and circumference is nowhere."[23]

The Spiritual Unity of the World's Religions

The parallels between the fractal discoveries in science and ancient insights from the world religions also reflect an emerging fundamental unity between the religions. Mystics and sages from every religious tradition articulate a version of this fractal-like identity of the individual with the Divine—each using a different symbolic metaphor to express it. Indeed, all religions reflect this unity one way or another, because they all emanate from a single luminous core of spiritual truth. The world's multiplicity of religions are thus beginning to come together in a new way, to acknowledge a kind of universal spirituality and a fundamental unity of essential teachings.

This insight is not new. Saints and sages down through the centuries have emphasized the essential unity of all religions. The Rig Veda put it succinctly thousands of years ago: "Truth is one. Sages call it by many names."[24] The Sufi saint Al Hallaj proclaimed the unity of all religions early in the tenth century CE. The revered Hindu saint Ramakrishna proclaimed it again in the late 1800s, and during this same period a whole new religion emerged in the Middle East that celebrates this essential unity (the Baha'i faith). In contemporary times, this trend is expressed in new ways, such as the "perennial philosophy" articulated by Aldous Huxley, the interspiritual dialogue initiated by Wayne Teasdale and continued by Kurt Johnson, the integral spirituality of Ken Wilber, the Snowmass Conference, the Parliament of World Religions, and growing interfaith collaboration among spiritual and religious leaders across the globe.

These auspicious developments are taking place despite ongoing conflicts across the globe along lines of religious difference. Political and fanatical elements within and beyond organized religion abuse and manipulate religious teachings to justify persecution, hatred, conflict, and war. Notwithstanding this painful reality, which will likely continue or escalate in the short term, the deeper underlying trend over the long term is in the opposite direction: a gradual but steady shift toward unification of the world religions, with a growing mutual respect and appreciation for religious diversity. Great strides forward were made in this direction during the twentieth century, and much greater strides will be made in the present century. The human spirit demands it, because the only path forward that will ever work in the long term is for the entire human community to live in harmony as one family and one species alongside billions of other species on this planet.

Relativity Theory and Universal Spirituality

Besides quantum theory, the other major revolution in physics was Einstein's relativity theory, which also bears striking metaphorical correlations with spiritual teachings in many traditions. Einstein's special theory of relativity is derived from two postulates, which are: (1) the laws of physics must be the same in all reference frames, and (2) the speed of light is the same in all reference frames. Longstanding beliefs that space and time are absolute and immutable were completely overturned by this theory. What *is* absolute is the speed of light, and this requires that space and time are rendered mutable and intertwined in a four-dimensional continuum called space-time.

In general relativity, Einstein showed that space-time does not exist independently, but only as an emergent structural quality of the gravitational field.[25] A key implication is that space and time depend for their existence on matter. Take away matter, and space and time also disappear. So what remains in that case? Nothing remains, according to Einstein. Yet this state of nothingness is not mere emptiness, for it contains latent potential for matter, space, and time to reappear, in precise alignment with David Bohm's implicate order. This nothingness, out of which time and space emerge, bears close similarity to the realms of nonbeing or nonexistence spoken of by mystics across many traditions. Referred to by different names, such as *shunyata* in Buddhism, *nada* in the mysticism of St. John of the Cross, or the "dazzling darkness," this realm of nonexistence is fundamental to the spiritual domain. Indeed, nonexistence is more fundamental than existence, just as Bohm's invisible implicate order is more real and fundamental than the explicate order that comprises the physical universe. The Sufi master Radha Mohan Lal expressed this same truth, saying, "There is nothing but nothingness."[26]

According to Einstein, "Time and space are modes by which we think, and not conditions in which we live."[27] Similarly, according to the mystics, time and space are not actually real but are part of the illusory world created by the mind. Time and space are thus free creations of the human mind, to borrow one of Einstein's own expressions. General relativity theory tells us that space and time came into being simultaneously, *as* the universe emerged, and not beforehand or independently. Saint Augustine expressed something remarkably similar in the fourth century CE. The world, he said, was made "not in time, but simultaneously with time."[28]

A major consequence of relativity theory is that matter and energy are equivalent, as expressed in Einstein's equation $E = mc^2$. Hence matter is sometimes called "frozen light." The energy contained in matter is enormous; a small paper clip contains the amount of energy released in the 1945 atomic explosion over Hiroshima. Moreover, the energy contained in every unit of mass is precisely the same; a pound of dirt contains the same energy as a pound of gold. This ontological equivalence of all created matter is again something that mystics have affirmed for millennia, as expressed, for example, in the Bhagavad Gita, which says that for those who have realized the divine Self (Atman), "a clod of dirt, a stone, and lump of gold are exactly the same" (6:18).

Toward a Universal Spirituality

Motivated by these insights, we might propose that parallel postulates mirroring relativity theory may also hold in the domain of spiritual truth. These corresponding postulates would be: (1) the "laws of spirituality" are the same in all religious frameworks, and (2) there is a universal light that functions identically in all religions. With these two postulates, we can glimpse the basis for an emerging spiritual revolution that parallels the earlier revolution in modern physics, which could one day help resolve (or more precisely, *dis*solve) the strident conflicts between divergent doctrines and dogmas that characterize what we might call today's "classical religion."

The essence of this spiritual revolution is this: there is one dynamic spiritual Truth or Reality, and there are many religions and spiritual traditions that express this one reality in different ways. Thus the world's religions are not mutually contradictory, but mutually complementary. The divine light is absolute, one and the same in every religion, though it goes by different names in different traditions, and this universal light is the glue that binds the religions together in a radiant illumination of a single ultimate spiritual reality.[29]

The disparate religions would then be seen as rays of this universal light. This is not to deny the rich and vast differences between the various religions, nor would a universal spirituality ever replace the particular religions, with all their unique teachings and specific practices. On the contrary, such a universal spirituality would uplift and celebrate the diversity of religious and spiritual faiths, while also simultaneously revealing them to be united at their core.

To put it another way, God is present within each religion, and each religion is present within God. As the divine light passes through the prism of divinity, it is refracted into a spectrum of beautiful emanations that become the different religions, each one a magnificent luminous ray of the universal divine light. Each ray is true and complete unto itself, exquisitely beautiful in its own right, and yet also takes its place within the larger spectrum of the one supreme light. No color is left out, and no ray is superior to any other ray. To posit that one religion is somehow truer than another would be tantamount to saying that blue light is better than yellow light, when both are simply emanations of one and the same universal light.

Implications of Universal Spirituality

Just as some of our everyday perceptions of physical reality have to be modified in the face of relativity, so too our ordinary perceptions of worldly and religious truths may need to be modified in the face of a universal spirituality. For example, in physics, nothing can alter the speed of light. The seeming absolutes of space and time are "altered" as necessary to preserve the constant speed of light. Similarly, in spirituality, nothing can alter the function of divine light, and seemingly absolute material and temporal laws may need to be altered to honor the absolute light of the Divine. Divine light *is*. It has no opposite, and casts no shadow. It illuminates all things from within, and enables all seeing. Darkness cannot resist or withstand it, and "comprehendeth it not" (John 1:5). All things yield to it on its own terms. Thus in both domains—physical and spiritual—light is the universal absolute, and everything else adjusts itself accordingly.

In relativity theory, as moving objects approach the speed of light, the passage of time slows down, and at the speed of light, time comes to a complete stop. Similarly, mystics have affirmed that "time stops" when the mystic's identity dissolves and merges into the divine light, and the mystic enters into eternity, beyond the flow of time altogether. Time and its seeming absoluteness are thus seen to be illusory, from the perspectives of both science and mysticism.

Just as physical light is "frozen" to become matter, so divine light is also constellated into forms and patterns of consciousness. Divine light does not merely shine upon creation; it manifests within creation and works in concert with the light inherent in creation. "In Thy Light, we see light," writes the psalmist (Ps. 36:9). The process is called *nur al nur*, "light upon light," in the Qur'an (Q 24:35), or, as described in Sri Aurobindo's integral yoga, the aspiring light in the heart of the spiritual aspirant is answered by a Supreme Grace or Light that responds from above.

God is too vast to fit inside any one religious, spiritual, or scientific framework. To be sure, the coming changes in religion will present serious challenges to dogmatic believers or orthodox missionaries of any faith who believe theirs is the one true and correct religion, just as the revolutionary implications of modern physics presented serious challenges to classical scientists. Even today, the new science remains far from fully integrated into contemporary scientific practice, which is still largely based on outdated and erroneous Newtonian and Cartesian assumptions.

Archbishop Desmond Tutu, leader of the South African Truth and Reconciliation Commission, recounts with a grin in a recent interview that he "got into a lot of trouble" when he declared that "God is not a Christian!"[30] Despite being an impeccable priest of the Christian faith, Tutu was exemplifying this broader understanding of universal spirituality. He explained that all of humanity is included within God, and therefore God cannot be confined within any one religion, but encompasses them all.

Interreligious Dialogue and the Snowmass Conference

An important practical example of the emerging unity of religious teachings is the work of the Snowmass Conference, a diverse group of spiritual leaders from the major world religions that has been meeting for more than thirty years, convened by the Cistercian monk Thomas Keating. Over the course of their meetings, the Snowmass Conference developed eight points of common agreement (presented in the Introduction; see pages xxi–xxii). In effect, these eight points constitute an articulation of a universal spiritual faith—one that is consistent with the teachings of the major world religions. In the course of articulating these universal truths common to all their traditions, the group members also developed close interpersonal bonds and friendships with one another.

While this accomplishment was inspiring in its own right, what was even more remarkable about the Snowmass Conference is that after reaching major points of agreement, the group members then began to discuss their differences in religious beliefs and practices. They embarked upon this task somewhat hesitatingly at first, aware of major differences between their religions and not wishing to disturb the sense of unity and camaraderie they had already achieved. However, to their amazement and delight, they discovered over time that they bonded even more deeply over their differences than they had over their points of commonality. The richness and intricacies of their differences turned out to be fruitful ground for deep exploration and inquiry together, and this diversity energized them and brought them even closer together as a group.

Examples like this of true collaboration and friendship across religious divisions are urgently needed in the world at this time of rampant religious conflict. Religions in conflict with each other are like branches on a tree fighting with each other, not recognizing that they're all connected to the same trunk. The branches have their very existence only through that one trunk, which represents the mystical truth at the core of every religion. And the trunk just stands there, silently supporting and nourishing each branch, as they jostle around, striving to win a trivial, unwinnable game.

The experience of the Snowmass Conference is an auspicious harbinger for future relations between the world's religions. When genuine spiritual leaders from different religious traditions come together, what emerges is rarely unbridgeable gulfs and conflicts, but rather rich and fertile ground that simultaneously unites their respective teachings in a universal wisdom and honors and celebrates the uniqueness of each tradition. The plurality of religions is something to be cherished as a profound resource and gift to humanity, something that will be increasingly realized in the coming decades and centuries.

The emerging spiritual unity of the world's religions does not mean that the different traditions will fuse or unite into a single world religion. Rather, each religion will take its proper place alongside the others, in mutual respect, to form a tapestry of traditions that together will embark upon an unprecedented level of spiritual collaboration on behalf of humanity and the earth. This process has already begun in earnest.

Toward a New Integration of Science and Religion

The oneness of all existence, long proclaimed by sages from many wisdom traditions, appears to be supported by new discoveries in science that link matter, energy, and consciousness. Theologian Thomas Berry says that the universe is not a collection of objects, but a "communion of subjects"—a beautiful phrase analogous to what we have called here the inner net of the heart. Furthermore, consciousness is observed to transcend ordinary physical laws of matter, energy, space, and time. The physical universe appears to be dwarfed by the consciousness universe.

It is every human being's birthright to discover this "inner net of the heart" within themselves, and to live from that vast interior foundation of Being. If we are connected to and guided by this larger wisdom of divine universal consciousness, then our actions and work in the world can become profoundly transformative. We can then be used as instruments of this larger Wisdom for *its* work in the world. This is what Gandhi, Mother Teresa, Martin Luther King Jr., and many other spiritual activists understood so deeply. This is not to say that one must become a Gandhi to make a difference, just as one doesn't have to be an Einstein to be a good scientist. Nevertheless, the transformative power and grace for social change and cultural evolution that Gandhi and King applied are accessible to us all, through the doorway of our own hearts.

Love is the greatest power in the universe, and divine love is the most powerful form of love. "By love has appeared everything that exists," says Persian mystic Shabestari, and "by love, that which does *not* exist, appears as existing."[31] If we give ourselves to the transforming fire of this love, with its attendant demands of radical humility and surrender, our entire lives begin to burn with passion and longing for the Divine—regardless of the path or tradition we approach it from. This leads us directly into the creative power and hidden mysteries of love, which initiates us into a profound alchemy that opens, from the inside, the inner net of the heart—the gateway to the Infinite.

> Let the drop of water that is you
> become a hundred mighty seas.
> But do not think that the drop alone
> Becomes the Ocean—
> the Ocean, too, becomes the drop!
>
> —RUMI

Infinity of Divinity

The Fractal Structure of Consciousness and Logos

"The Word which all scriptures declare" corresponds to
what the Graeco-Egyptian mystics referred to as the Logos,
the formative divine Utterance which gives pattern to the
cosmos.... This Word, or Logos, is the one central principle
around which revolves all the rich symbolism of the
scriptures.

—KRISHNAPREM (CITING KATHA UPANISHAD II:15)

W hen we see that the scriptures and mystics exhibit strong agreement
across such diverse religious traditions, the question naturally arises: Why
is this? What is going on here? In particular, how is it possible that the
mystic can actually be "one with God"? How can a Meister Eckhart proclaim, for example, that "God gives all of Himself, holding nothing back"?
How could the infinite God possibly "fit" inside the heart of a finite, mortal
human being? This seems preposterous; small wonder that Meister Eckhart
was dismissed as a heretic, like so many other mystics who were similarly
shunned or mistreated.

In the previous chapter we witnessed some of the remarkable
characteristics of fractal geometry, and here I explore them further
and propose a simple hypothesis: consciousness itself has a fractal
structure. My purpose here is to informally "extrapolate" these fractal characteristics and insights—beyond mathematics altogether—into

the realm of consciousness, suggesting that consciousness itself has some form of fractal-like structure. I do not try to "prove" this or seek to develop a fully fleshed-out theory or analysis of all the details of such a fractal model of consciousness. But an outline of some of these remarkable implications can help explain a wealth of spiritual and mystical insights. Using fractal geometry as a kind of springboard, we can discern something essential about the nature of spirituality and higher realms of consciousness.

Before proceeding further, let us briefly examine mathematical fractals more carefully. What exactly is a fractal? How does it work? There is no need to be versed in mathematics to follow this chapter, but it is important to understand at least the essence of fractal geometry before extrapolating more broadly to interfaith theology.

Mathematics of Fractals

A fractal is a type of geometric structure generated by a mathematical "seed formula." Based on repeated application of the seed formula, a complex geometric structure is generated that has the unique property of containing within it miniature "copies" of itself on smaller scales. These copies are called "self-similar" because they closely resemble the original structure, but are not identical to it. The situation is somewhat analogous to a set of Russian dolls, in which each doll contains a set of smaller similar dolls, except that, in the case of the mathematical fractal, this replication process of self-similarity goes on forever in increasingly smaller scales.

Key properties of fractals include the following:

- Fractals are defined by a simple, repeated mathematical "seed formula."
- Fractals are too irregular and complex to be easily described by traditional Euclidean geometry.
- Fractals create a nested set of self-similar structures.
- Fractals are infinitely deep; the fine structure is replicated indefinitely on ever smaller scales.

The seed formula and its resulting geometric structure are somewhat analogous to a simple algebraic equation (like $y = x^2$) and its resulting plotted graph (a parabola), as you may remember from high school algebra. The only difference is that the fractal formula entails complex

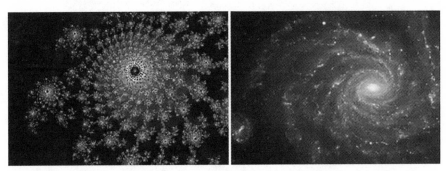

Figure 7.1. A spiral in the Mandelbrot set (left) and a photograph of the Grand Spiral Galaxy (NGC 1232) (right).

numbers, and the seed formula is applied repeatedly to each point in the plane to generate the fractal pattern.

Mathematicians were astounded to discover that plotting mathematical figures generated from repeated application of simple formulas— which only became practicable with the invention of computers—resulted in exceedingly complex and intricately beautiful geometric structures, exhibiting self-similarity replicated on multiple scales ad infinitum. Even more surprising, the resulting fractal structures in many cases powerfully model or mimic naturally occurring phenomena with uncanny precision— ranging from cosmic galaxies (see figure 7.1) to wandering coastlines, to various types of flora and fauna, to complicated mountain landscapes and cloud patterns (see figure 7.2). This was a major breakthrough, because mathematical structures frequently exhibit little or no resemblance to anything that exists in the physical world.

Fractals first became widely known in the 1980s, and they have since been used to model all manner of natural phenomena, giving rise to a rich and fruitful domain of new scientific research. The fact that fractal patterns closely mimic complex living systems suggests that fractals somehow contain something essential about the secrets of creation. One such secret is that a small number of very simple rules of order (the fractal "formula") can create vastly intricate structures that repeat themselves on multiple scales.

Fractals are the most complex mathematical structures ever discovered, yet they are precisely ordered by the simplest of principles. The uncanny beauty and complexity of fractal patterns must be seen to be appreciated, as shown in the figures throughout this chapter.[1]

Figure 7.2. A mountain landscape generated from a simple fractal transformation rule, applied repeatedly (top), and a "fractal mountain range," created from similar fractal algorithms (bottom)—this is a fractal image, not a photograph, despite the uncanny resemblance.

The Mandelbrot Set

The Mandelbrot set was introduced in chapter 6. An entirely different depiction of the Mandelbrot set is shown in figure 7.3. This image is generated from the Mandelbrot set using a different graphical algorithm. Like the fractal images in the previous chapter, this image is a strictly mathematical object, yet it appears remarkably artistic or aesthetic, and bears an uncanny resemblance to certain traditional religious symbolism, particularly of deities in Tibetan Buddhism or Hinduism. We can even discern possible "eyes" and a "third eye" in the image, although all of this interpretation is, of course, our human projection. Nevertheless, the visual correlations are striking.

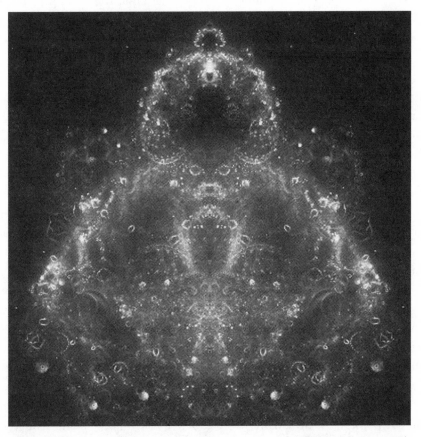

Figure 7.3. The "Buddhabrot," another representation of the Mandelbrot set. This is a purely mathematical object, yet note the startling likeness to images of Eastern deities.

Origins of Fractal Structure

Where does all this intricate beauty and complexity come from? What is the "hidden secret" of the fractal? The technical answer is that it comes from—and is somehow contained in—the fractal seed formula. The fractal pattern is simply the unveiling of this mathematical formula in the two-dimensional plane. In all the images of figures 6.1, 6.2, and 7.3, the formula is the deceptively simple $Z = Z^2 + C$.

To borrow from David Bohm's model (presented in chapter 6), this seed formula can be viewed as a specific ordering principle in the implicate order, and the fractal pattern is the resulting explicate order. The fractal pattern renders explicit what was implicate. The magic of the fractal is therefore contained within the formula itself, just as the DNA in each cell of the body contains the genetic code for the entire body. The human body contains 100,000 billion cells, all created from just one cell, the fertilized egg.

Orders of Infinity

Part of the rich complexity of fractals stems directly from the amazing properties of infinity itself, which were first set forth systematically in the nineteenth century by German mathematician Georg Cantor. He showed that there exist different orders of infinity. For example, the real numbers (all points in a straight line) constitute a much greater infinity than the whole numbers (0, 1, 2, 3, and so on). Both sets are infinite, but one is much larger than the other. Intuitively this makes sense, because there are so many more points in a continuous line than just the round whole numbers in that line. However, many of Cantor's other findings are far more startling.

For example, Cantor proved mathematically that the finite can "contain" the infinite. In particular, he showed that the number of points in a short line segment, such as this little dash—is precisely equal to the infinite number of points in a multidimensional universe.[2] That's right, even though the universe is infinitely many times bigger than the dash! This may seem patently absurd, but it is possible to set up a one-to-one correspondence between every single point throughout the universe, and a corresponding unique point in the little dash shown above. Pairing up the points from each set, one-to-one in this manner, it is thereby proven that the dash and the universe both contain precisely the same quantity of points.

Mathematically, this means that the entire universe can be "collapsed" to fit neatly inside the little dash above—with a unique position in the dash for each and every point throughout the universe. Now that is amazing! This proves that the finite can in some sense "contain" the infinite. The entire universe—not just the earth and the solar system, but the 100 billion galaxies, each of which contains 100 billion stars—can be neatly "landed" onto the mathematical "airstrip" of a short little dash. The fractal is another example of this same principle, and every tiny Mandelbrot set (embedded within the larger set) contains an infinity of smaller Mandelbrot sets embedded within itself.

Cantor contemplated deeply the larger philosophical and theological implications of his mathematical discoveries, and he identified the "Absolute Infinite" with God. Not surprisingly, he encountered strong criticism from certain mathematicians, philosophers, and theologians, but his incontrovertible proofs have stood the test of time. As his contemporary mathematician David Hilbert put it, "No one can ever expel us from the paradise that Cantor created."

Cantor also developed a "reflection principle," which states that every property of the Absolute Infinite is also held by some smaller object. This was a remarkably accurate intuition of fractal geometry, which was not well developed until more than fifty years after Cantor's death. It also suggests a mystical counterpart, that every property of God is also manifest in some smaller being.

Metaphysics of Fractal Geometry

The finite can contain the infinite. This is not a human invention, but a mathematical fact, a mysterious property of numbers themselves. Similarly, fractals are not a human invention; they are an inherent part of mathematics itself (although they were a total surprise to mathematicians—no one imagined that such incredible complexity and subtlety could be generated by such a simple iterative process). The beautiful fractal patterns on a computer screen are not created *by* the computer, nor are they the result of any special software wizardry on the part of computer graphic artists. Fractals are not generated through human ingenuity; they are generated simply by "plotting the graph" of a strictly mathematical process. Fractals are infinitely complex; they do not become simpler as one zooms into their detailed structure; the patterns repeat again and again on ever smaller scales—forever.

Fractals were not discovered until recently because our computing power has only now become refined enough to reveal them—but they have always been there, hidden in the mathematics, since before time began. "God is a simple essence," says Meister Eckhart, but witness all that God has created. Fractals are similar; a very simple formula produces exquisite beauty and infinite complexity.

Fractals predate human existence. They are inherent in numbers themselves, independent of manifest creation. Fractals are thus ordering principles of consciousness that until recently were entirely beyond human awareness. This is important to recognize, because it means that fractal structures can be regarded as inherent in the "mind of God." Their remarkable beauty and infinite complexity predates manifest existence altogether.

Fractals Abound in the Real World

Fractal patterns are found throughout the natural world. A few examples are shown in figure 7.4. In every case, if a small part of the figure is magnified, or zoomed in, it has the same or nearly identical structure to the larger

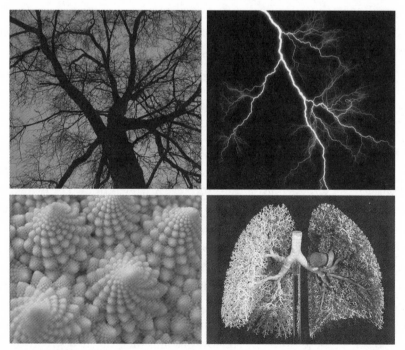

Figure 7.4. Fractals in nature: Trees, lightning, Romanesco broccoli and the respiratory system all have fractal structures.

form. The technical term for this is "scale invariance," or self-similarity. Intricate examples of fractal forms are found in the human body, including the respiratory, circulatory, and nervous systems, all of which exhibit branches that divide, and then subdivide again and again. Once the basic pattern of self-similarity or scale invariance is recognized, one can readily recognize fractal patterns in many natural phenomena.

Fractal design has been used in a plethora of practical and technological applications, ranging from antennas in cell phones to fractal art, forestry, and cardiology. In a striking example of nested sets of fractals in nature, a group of forestry researchers found that the distribution of branch lengths within a single tree closely matches the distribution of tree heights within the forest as a whole. In other words, not only is the structure of a single tree fractallic, but so is the structure of the whole forest in which that tree is found; a forest is a larger fractal made up of fractal trees.

Fractals continue to find new applications, such as in cardiology. Research has shown that healthy, robust hearts have fractal heartbeat patterns (see figure 7.5). Heartbeats that are either too uniform, or too irregular, correspond to heart problems, such as congestive heart failure or irregular heart flutters and arrhythmias. Healthy heartbeats demonstrate fractal complexity, which are associated with a healthy ability to respond and adapt

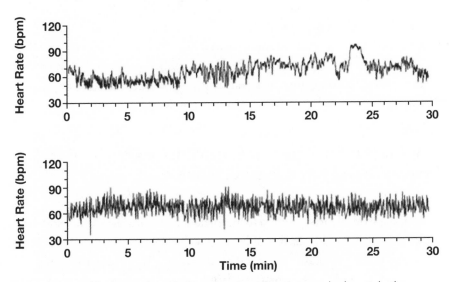

Figure 7.5. Healthy hearts beat in fractal patterns (top); irregular heart rhythms indicate atrial fibrillation (bottom).

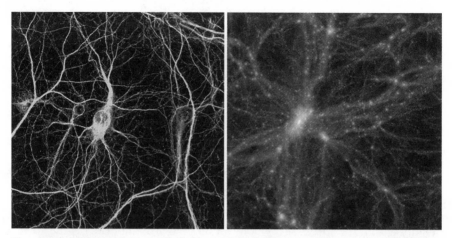

Figure 7.6. Neurons in the brain (left)—scale is a few microns wide—compared with an image of the universe constructed by astrophysicists (right)—scale is billions of light-years across.

quickly to a wide range of conditions and stressors. Physicians are beginning to use fractal analysis of heart rhythms to help diagnose heart problems.

A recent study on "network cosmology" revealed a striking fractal pattern of self-similarity in the growth of complex networks, replicated on vastly different scales, ranging from the intergalactic scale of space-times in solutions to Einstein's general relativity equations down to the "local" scale in the growth of the Internet and social and biological networks.[3] Brain cells and outer space may be linked in a common fractal structure (see figure 7.6). As one scientist summarized the emerging enthusiasm about fractals (perhaps exaggerating), "We are fractal beings moving along fractal patterns on a fractal planet in a fractal galaxy within a fractal universe."[4] Perhaps coincidentally, even the Helix Nebula appears like a cosmic eye (see figure 7.7).

The Fractal Structure of Consciousness:
Fractal Biology and Fractal Divinity

Fractals manifest not only in terms of physical form but also in terms of time and physical processes. An important example of a temporal fractal in the human body is the pulse of the heartbeat, which is replicated throughout the circulatory system in the body. The capillary bed swells and contracts with each heartbeat, bringing oxygen and nourishment to nearly every cell of the body, and removing waste products and toxins,

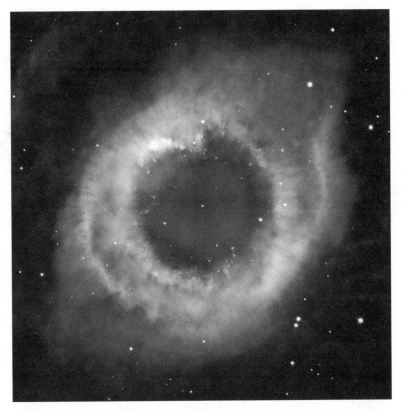

Figure 7.7. A Hubble photograph of the Helix Nebula, dubbed "Eye of God."

thereby maintaining the vibrant health of the cell. The rate of blood flow is much slower in the capillaries, which are miniscule compared to the veins and heart, but the *rhythm* of the pulse in the tiny capillaries proceeds in lockstep with the heartbeat itself.

Of course, the individual cell could never claim "identity" with the heart; the two living systems are vastly disparate in size, function, and structure. Nevertheless, the dynamic rhythm of the heart pulse is fractally replicated in the cell, and despite its tiny size the cell can be said to "contain"—or indeed, *directly* experience—the pulse of the heart. It is this pulse that gives life to the cell, and also to the heart. Were the pulse to cease, even briefly, both heart and cell would die quickly. So the cell and the heart are inextricably linked, moment to moment—to one another, and to life itself—through their shared experience of the living heartbeat.

In analogous fashion, there may exist a direct link between the human soul and the "heart of God" on the level of consciousness, in a manner that closely parallels the biological link between cell and heart. Just as the biological cell is directly linked to and utterly dependent upon the physical heart, through a life-giving pulse that is identical in both, so the human soul may be directly linked to and utterly dependent upon the "heart of God," moment by moment, through a "spiritual lifeblood" process that is also identical in both. In this way the biological fractal of the cell/heart relationship may have a fractal consciousness parallel in the soul/God relationship. Thus when the mystic claims that she experiences the living heart of God, she may not be exaggerating or speaking in metaphors. Rather, she may be speaking of her direct and dynamic experience of the *living* divine consciousness, which is fractally replicated in the depths of the human soul, and is indeed the selfsame process that takes place in the depths of the very Heart of God. In this sense, the mystic is literally one with the living God, just as the cell is one with the living heart.

Hypothesis of Fractal Consciousness

As proposed above, it is possible that consciousness itself may have a fractal structure, or, said another way, that consciousness is a fractal. The former phrasing is more precise, because ontologically consciousness is surely much "more" than just a fractal, while still preserving a fractal structure. For ease of terminology, however, I use both statements interchangeably, and refer to "fractal consciousness" for short.

What do I mean by fractal consciousness? On one level, it means that consciousness manifests, at least to some extent, in self-similar structures or patterns on different scales, analogous to a fractal. Another aspect of fractal consciousness is that there may be a seed formula or ordering process of some kind in the implicate order of consciousness. This, in turn, manifests as the content of consciousness, which is distributed fractally. (Several examples are given below.)

The ordinary fractals we have explored so far operate on the physical plane, and they link ordering principles in mathematics to geometrical structures in the physical plane. Perhaps fractal consciousness, and especially mystical consciousness, functions in an analogous way, except that it stretches "vertically" directly into the heart of God, as well as horizontally into the physical plane.

Fractal Consciousness Illuminates Mystical Oneness

The possibility that consciousness has a fractal structure sheds a unique light on some of the key findings of unity and oneness encountered in earlier chapters:

- Fractal consciousness helps us to understand and even visualize the "vertical identity" of the mystic with the Divinity or essence of God. It shows why the mystics' declarations of oneness with God (as proclaimed by Christ, Al Hallaj, and Hindu sages) could actually be true. In each case, the mystic has realized his inner essence, which is revealed to be none other than the very essence of God. By way of analogy with the mathematical fractal, the mystic contemplates his true nature and discovers that he is *not* his outer visible form (the Mandelbrot set). Rather, he is the inner creative essence, which in this analogy is symbolized by the fractal seed formula ($Z = Z^2 + C$). He further realizes that this essence is one and the same unitary source of *all* existence, on all levels from the macrocosmic to the microcosmic (because it is one grand fractal). Having realized that he *is* that very essence, the mystic thereby realizes his oneness with the essence of all of creation. The mystic is not only one with all that exists (explicate order), but also one with God (implicate order). Hence the mystic has become one with the source of everything, and can rightly say, "I and God are one."
- Fractal consciousness illuminates the "horizontal identity" of the mystics with each other, across the religions. Because consciousness is a fractal, the deeper manifestations of consciousness are the same at the divine level and the human level, regardless of which tradition the mystic belongs to, or what form her outer tradition takes. Hence we can see why the Qur'an makes the seemingly radical declaration that "we make no distinction between any of the prophets," because all the prophets have been given precisely this same realization of their true innermost identity, as one with the essence of the Godhead. Therefore the mystics *are* all one, and their respective affirmations across the traditions are ontologically equivalent:

  ▸ You are made in the image of God (Torah).
  ▸ See the Self in every creature, and all of creation in the Self (Gita).
  ▸ Everything you have is mine, and everything I have is yours (John 17:10).

These canonical statements are all direct consequences of the fractal nature of Divinity.

- Fractal consciousness sheds light on the uniformity of spiritual practice such as *prapatti*, or divine surrender. The mystic must surrender identification with form in order to realize identity as essence. Borrowing the Mandelbrot metaphor as an example, the mystic surrenders identification with her outer form (the Mandelbrot set) and realizes her true identity as the inner essence that created her: $Z = Z^2 + C$. This inner essence is the mystic "formula" that burns at the center of the heart, and indeed in every cell of every living being—from the tiniest atom to the galaxies. The hypothesis of fractal consciousness is thus consistent with the "oneness" proclaimed by all the mystics.

- Fractal consciousness is fully consonant with—and may indeed be the ontological reason *for*—one of the great axioms of spiritual consciousness down through the ages: The microcosm replicates the macrocosm. This spiritual principle is found across the traditions, for example in Indra's Net of Hinduism/Buddhism, or the correspondence principle of the ancient Greek Hermes Trismegistus. This principle finds exquisite expression in the well-known Islamic Hadith, "Heaven and Earth are too small to contain Me, but I fit easily inside the heart of my beloved devotee." Here we see that the physical space-time universe, as physicists Carl Sagan or Stephen Hawking would describe it—composed of a billion galaxies, each of which contains a billion stars—is much too small to contain God. Yet the full infinity of God fits easily inside the heart of the human disciple, because the heart is a miniature fractal of the living God. Our hearts are bigger than the universe!

The Finite Contains the Infinite

An objection might be raised here: How could the human heart be bigger than the universe? This seems preposterous. The reply is that the infinite *can* be contained within the bounds of the seemingly finite. We saw that this holds true even within the rigorous and precise realm of mathematics, such as in Cantor's work cited earlier. In the case of fractals, we find infinite complexity and profound structural beauty replicated within the finite bounds of every embedded Mandelbrot replica, no matter how small. This is an astounding discovery, and we may surmise that this same principle applies, on a more subtle level, also to consciousness.

Logically it seems absurd, of course, to suggest that the Infinity of God can be contained in the human heart, but mystics across the traditions have testified to this experience down through the ages. No doubt they were dismissed as delusional by those fully committed to rationality and reason, as they still are today, particularly in the materialistic culture of the West. Yet, if God consciousness has some type of fractal structure, then God contains miniature "replicas" of him/herself within God. The mystic realizes God through becoming or merging into one of these replicas, and because each replica contains the same infinite depth and complexity of the whole, the mystic thereby rightly claims to realize the fullness of infinite God consciousness.

Thus we can begin to glimpse what Meister Eckhart means—and how it is actually possible—when he declares emphatically that into the mystic who surrenders utterly, "God completely pours himself according to all his power; that God holds nothing back in all his life, in all his being, in all his nature, in all his divinity."[5] The smaller fractal manifestation (on the human scale) receives and reproduces in the mystic's heart the entire intricate depth and profound complexity, subtlety, and indeed the very infinity of fractal consciousness poured out from the heart of God (on the divine scale).

Thus the finite human being can "attain" and "contain" the Infinity of God. The mystic "becomes God" by realizing the God consciousness fractal as it manifests through the heart. Yet the question remains, what is the fractal seed formula for God consciousness?

Fractal Divinity: The Logos Is a Fractal

To address this question, we may posit (or, perhaps more accurately, intuit) that, corresponding to the structure of the mathematical fractal on the plane of mind and matter, there exists an analogous structure on the divine plane: a meta-fractal or "divine fractal" structure of the Logos itself, on the plane of Divinity. The ordinary mathematical fractal is then a direct consequence of this divine fractal, and the mathematical seed formula has a counterpart on the plane of Divinity, which is an ordering principle in divine consciousness. In short, we are proposing a form of fractal consciousness for the Logos itself, or divine consciousness.

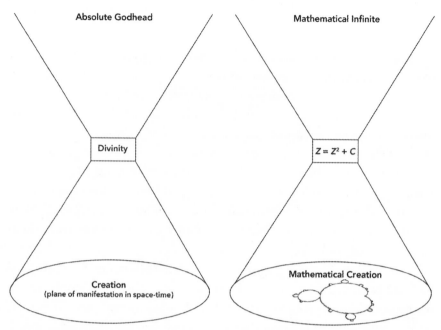

Figure 7.8. Fractal divinity: The divine Logos (or Word) "fractallates" into manifestation in space-time.

Figure 7.9. Fractal mathematics: The fractal seed formula generates a fractal geometric pattern.

The Logos (or Word) can be regarded as a fractal seed formula (on the plane of Divinity) for what is manifest here "below." This is depicted schematically in the diagram in figure 7.8, which is merely a schematic of these ontological levels, and not a literal depiction or image. The Absolute Infinite Godhead projects itself into the plane of Divinity—as Logos, or the Trinity, or Allah, or *Brahman Saguna*—each of these being on the same ontological level. This is the "first effusion" of God, or earliest phase of creation: "In the beginning was the *logos*, which was *with* God [as fractal seed or "the Word"], and *was* God [as fractal source]" (John 1:1).

The Divinity or Logos in turn "becomes flesh," or manifests, by "fractallation" on the manifest plane—thereby creating a fractal pattern of consciousness, matter, and living systems on the physical plane. The physical universe is thus a fractal pattern "down here" specified by the Logos, and the human being is a part of this pattern that is "made in the image of God," a kind of fractal miniature representation of the Logos itself. In terms of Bohm's model, the explicate order is symbolized by the circular disk at the base of the diagram (representing the physical universe), and the implicate order is the rest of the diagram that extends vertically upward.

The analogous relationship between fractal divinity and fractal mathematics is illustrated in figures 7.8 and 7.9. On the right side, the infinite set of mathematical possibilities is pared down, or "funneled through," as it were, into one particular formula (figure 7.9), which in turn manifests as a unique fractal pattern when plotted on the mathematical plane. This fractal pattern is bounded within finite limits, yet it nevertheless contains the infinite within itself. Analogously, in figure 7.8, the Infinite Godhead is funneled into a form of Divinity. This, in turn, manifests fractally as the universe in the plane of creation.

The suggestion here is that fractal divinity is the fundamental fractal consciousness; fractal geometry and other forms of fractals are reflections or corollary consequences in the mental plane, or in the realm of logic and mathematics. Fractal mathematics is thus a special case of fractal divinity. Fractal geometric forms are made explicate on the physical plane of the computer screen, but these fractal patterns are not merely mathematical, they are a consequence of the intrinsic fractal nature of consciousness itself.

The term "Divinity" (or Logos) is used here to refer to the subtle plane of God with form, and it is not limited to the Christian Logos, but applies to the Trinity, or to *Brahman Saguna*, or to Allah and the Ninety-Nine Names of God. In all these cases, the fractal structure of Divinity is the reason for the vertical identity of the mystic's soul with God.

Moreover, as Meister Eckhart emphasizes, once we have left the supreme ontological level of the one Absolute Godhead and entered the level of divine multiplicity, it makes no difference whether there are three persons (Trinity) or a hundred (as in Islam), because they are all still aspects of the One:

My Beloved is three although He is One, even as the Persons are made one Person in essence. For anyone who could grasp distinctions without number and quantity, a hundred would be as one. Even if there were a hundred Persons in the Godhead, anyone who could distinguish without number and quantity would perceive them only as one God.... [He or she] knows that three Persons are one God.[6]

Ibn Arabi describes almost the same relationship between the Absolute and the Names of God:

> In respect of His Self (i.e., His Essence), God possesses the Unity of the One, but in respect of His Names, He possesses the Unity of the many.... The Names have two connotations; the first connotation is God Himself Who is what is named, the second that by which one Name is distinguished from another.... Number does not beget multiplicity in the Divine Substance, as the Christians declare that the Three Persons of the Trinity are One God, and as the Qur'an declares: "Call upon God or call on the Merciful; however ye invoke Him, it is well, for to Him belong the most beautiful Names." (Q 17:110)

The Names are at the ontological level of Divinity, whereas the One is the Absolute Godhead. As Reza Shah-Kazemi observes, "Both Meister Eckhart and Ibn Arabi situate differentiated plurality on a plane, within the divine nature, which is below that of the Essence [and above that of Creation]; a plane which pertains to the relationship between the Creator and the created."[7] In figure 7.8, this intermediate ontological level is indicated as the plane of Divinity, between the Absolute and Creation.

In summary, the mystics have realized their inner essence, which is one and the same fractal divinity for all of them. This is why the Qur'an says, "We make no distinction between any of the prophets," for each of them *is* this fractal essence. It also explains why each of them brought the same essential message from God: "There is no god but Me, so worship Me," and through such worship, the human being can embark upon the path to also become this same essence.

Time Is a Fractal

Time is also a fractal. Jesus referenced this in his saying, "Before Abraham was, I am" (John 8:58). Here the fractal seed formula is "I am," which is the divine name God declared to Moses at the burning bush. The name and prophetic consciousness of "I am" is fractally manifest beyond—and within—both space and time. The Prophet Muhammad also refers to this same temporal fractal, in his saying, "I was a prophet when Adam was still between water and clay."[8] Krishna, too, repeatedly affirms his timeless existence across many epochs (Gita 4:1-8), and proclaims in the Gita, "I alone exist" (10:42).

So there is a supreme and subtle fractal structure of divinity or divine consciousness that is hardwired in Divinity (or the Logos) itself, even before it manifests. The fractal pattern down here on earth is a manifest reflection of this sublime fractal divinity. In the Lord's prayer, for example, "Thy will be done on earth as it is in heaven" has a deep, hidden meaning. It is not just a prayer or admonition for humans to perform certain "good" actions on earth in accord with God's wishes; it is a far grander prayer for the profound revelation of the fractal divinity of the Logos (or heaven) to be manifested in full resplendent glory here on this earthly plane. The world is intended by God to be a fractal reflection or instantiation of the Logos or Divinity itself, the infinite majesty of God. For realized mystics, the Lord's prayer is in fact answered; they *see* this heaven here on earth, because they are seeing the truth: The earth is a microcosmic reflection of the heavens. The angelic beings of the cosmos are all here, and every movement of the stars is reflected here on this earthly plane. As the Upanishads puts it, "What is There is here, and what is not here is nowhere."[9] The earth itself is a miniature heavenly cosmos; it is a smaller fractal replica of all the rich and vast infinitude of the cosmos. This is the realization that Jesus prayed for humanity to wake up to.

In summary, Divinity or Logos is a kind of fractal formula, which was *with* God and *is* God. Beyond the fractal formula is God Absolute, ever hidden. When the Logos "becomes flesh," it fractallates into manifestation, and becomes the earthly fractal structure down here, which mirrors the Divinity above. This formulation may be regarded as metaphorical in the case of the fractal, but it is literal in metaphysical terms. The mystics experience a profound revelation, in which the heavens above are literally seen and perceived here on earth.

The MandelBuddha

As noted earlier, if the Mandelbrot set is turned ninety degrees clockwise, it looks like a Buddha sitting in meditation. We might dub this the Buddhabrot or MandelBuddha (see figure 7.3 on page 159). Each of the smaller, embedded Mandelbrot sets now looks like a miniature MandelBuddha.

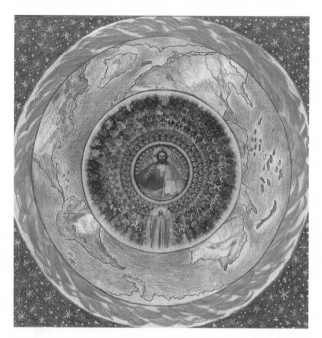

Figure 7.10. An artist's rendition of the fractal mystical body of Christ, experienced in Holotropic Breathwork.

This orientation of the Mandelbrot set may seem arbitrary, and the metaphor is admittedly cutesy, but it's worth exploring a bit. For the sake of this section, let us call the full Mandelbrot set the MandelBuddha, or we may equally think of it as MandelChrist, or MandelKrishna. The smaller embedded Mandelbrot set we will call a Mandel*bud*, to symbolize a "budding" Buddha (or a budding Christ, or budding Krishna).

Now imagine for a moment the MandelBuddha represents the actual cosmic infinite Buddha, sitting in eternal meditation. Imagine that within the MandelBuddha, there are seven billion Mandelbuds, representing the seven billion human beings on earth. Or equivalently, in Christian terms, we may imagine each of these human beings represents a particular soul within the living MandelChrist, which gives us an image of the "body of Christ." Or in Hindu terms, each soul is a particular *Atman* within the living MandelKrishna or MandelBrahman.

The mystical revelation of a multitude of human souls comprising the human embodiment of Christ, or Krishna, or Buddha is a time-honored revelation across different traditions. An artistic depiction of this is shown in figure 7.10, painted by a woman who experienced herself as a soul in the mystical body of Christ during a breathing exercise called Holotropic Breathwork. Notice the fractal-like structure in her painting of the assembly of souls, each one a miniature Christ, contained within the larger body of the mystical Christ.

As Above, So Below: Hermetic Correspondence and Indra's Net

Both fractal geometry and Cantor's reflection principle can be understood as the inevitable consequence, or modern scientific rediscovery, of an overarching and ancient principle known as the "correspondence principle" in hermeticism and alchemy. This principle is often articulated in the phrase "As above, so below"; the microcosm replicates the macrocosm. A version of this principle is found in every mystical tradition, expressed in various forms. For example, in Buddhism and Hinduism, it appears as the concept of Indra's Net, which is described in the Buddhist Avatamsaka Sutra as follows:

> Far away in the heavenly abode of the great god Indra, there is a wonderful net which has been hung by some cunning artificer in such a manner that it stretches out infinitely in all directions. In accordance with the extravagant tastes of deities, the artificer has hung a single glittering jewel in each "eye" of the net, and since the net itself is infinite in dimension, the jewels are infinite in number. There hang the jewels, glittering like stars in the first magnitude, a wonderful sight to behold. If we now arbitrarily select one of these jewels for inspection and look closely at it, we will discover that in its polished surface there are reflected all the other jewels in the net, infinite in number. Not only that, but each of the jewels reflected in this one jewel is also reflecting all the other jewels, so that there is an infinite reflecting process occurring.[10]

Indra's Net offers an exquisite image of infinite interconnectedness, characterized by self-similarity on multiple scales, just as we find in fractals. In his book *Indra's Net*, Indic scholar Rajiv Malhotra invokes the image of Indra's Net as a metaphor for the cosmology that permeates Hinduism, symbolizing the universe as a web of connections and interdependences. Plotinus describes a similar fractal-like principle of correspondence:

In our [physical plane] realm, all is part arising from part and nothing can be more than partial; but There [divine plane] each being is an eternal product of a whole and is at once a whole and an individual manifestation as part but, to the keen vision There, known for the whole it is.[11]

Another fractal metaphor comes from the story of Krishna as a child, when his mother looks in his mouth and is taken aback when she suddenly beholds the entire cosmos, blazing forth with all the heavens and whirling planets revealed in young Krishna's mouth.

For those with eyes to see, all things are linked to all other things in a magnificent, interconnected tapestry. Everything interpenetrates everything else, as David Bohm shows in his model of the holomovement and the implicate order. Krishnaprem describes this plane of Divinity beautifully:

Spanning the void, leaping from earth to heaven, gleams the great Rainbow Bridge whose substance is composed of all the Gods. The Maharishis and the Siddhas, mighty Teachers of the past, exist inscrutably within that radiant Being. Christ, Krishna, Buddha [and Allah] are all there, and whoever worships one draws near to them all.[12]

This last point is key; all divine emanations of God are in some sense ontologically equivalent. Christ and Allah and Buddha and Krishna are all distinct, and each gives rise to a unique revelation or religion on the human plane, as depicted in figure 7.11. Yet neither are they separate, and each of them contains them all. This is beautifully described by Plotinus in another description of this fractal divinity:

There everything is transparent, nothing dark, nothing resistant; every being is lucid to every other, in breadth and depth; light runs through light. And each of them contains all within itself, and at the same time sees all in every other, so that everywhere there is all, and all is all, and each is all, and infinite is the glory. Each of them is great; the small is great: stars and sun. While some manner of being is dominant in each, all are mirrored in every other.[13]

We see this (crudely) illustrated in figure 7.11, where each divine revelation is unique and gives birth to a particular revealed religion, yet the various divine emanations are also interpenetrating one another, as indicated

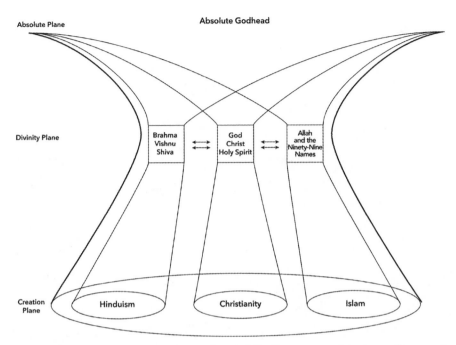

Figure 7.11. Fractal religions: the Godhead self-effuses into subtle constellations of fractal divinity, which in turn "fractallate" into manifestation as different religions.

schematically by the arrows between the Trinity and Allah and the Ninety-Nine Names and the Hindu *Trimurti* (Brahma, Vishnu, Shiva). This illustrates the principle of "homeomorphic equivalence"—between Christ, Krishna, Allah, Buddha, and so on—a term coined by the great interfaith scholar/mystic Raimon Panikkar in his pioneering work *Christophany*.[14] As depicted, each emanation of Divinity in turn fractallates into a unique religious form on the finite material plane, yet it contains within itself the Infinite Godhead. Hence each religion provides a unique and complete pathway to realizing the Absolute Godhead. Again, the illustration in figure 7.11 is an ontological schematic diagram, and should not be regarded as an actual visual representation of divine realities, which are far more profound and majestically intricate than anything that could be sketched in a two-dimensional diagram.

In another metaphorical interpretation of figure 7.11, the infinite light of God is refracted by a "fractal prism" on the plane of Divinity into the spectrum of manifest religions, each of which fractally illuminates the plane of creation. Because divine light is absolute, there is no distinction

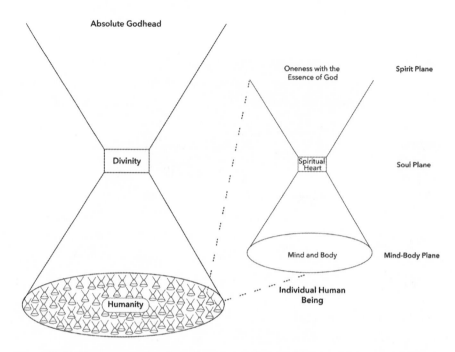

Figure 7.12. Humanity is "made in the image of God" by fractal emanation of Divinity (left). Each individual human is a "droplet of Divinity" that fractally replicates the essence, the divinity, the cosmic body, and (for mystics) the mind of God (right).

between the prophets of the religions in the sense that each of them is this light ("I am the light of the world" [John 8:12]), and they all effectively bring the same message ("You are the light of the world" [Matt. 5:14]). The unique qualities of different religions, in their particular time and space, are the beautiful "colors" of this light, which are outwardly distinct yet not contradictory because they are all ontologically equivalent as the universal light of God.

Finally, the schematic diagram in figure 7.12 offers a (crude) illustration of the fractal structure of human consciousness, and the deeper meaning of the profound teaching that we are "made in the image of God." On the left side of the figure, the entire human family is represented on the plane of creation, and each person is seen to be a miniature "droplet of God" that fractally replicates the entire structure of divine consciousness. On the right side, we zoom in on one individual human being. The created aspect of the person is the mind-body dimension, represented by the circular disk in the manifest plane. Above this is what we might call the spiritual heart, which relates to the soul of the person and transcends but also includes the physical heart. The spiritual heart is the inner gateway to spiritual consciousness, and expands upward into the deepest essence or source of the human being, which is none other than the transcendent essence of the Absolute Godhead. Thus, "I and God are one" applies to every human being, and the soul is the mediator between the Absolute Oneness, in which every human being is eternal, and the relative plane of manifest existence. Even at the created level, the mystic's mind mirrors the mind of God, and because heart and brain cells mimic galactic structure and process, then the human body can be said to fractally "replicate" the cosmic body of God (the universe).

The spiritual heart includes the unique spiritual DNA of that particular individual, if we might call it that, which relates to the person's higher self and soul's purpose for incarnation, coupled with a vast spectrum of potential destinies for the particular person. The spiritual DNA functions like a fractal seed formula in the person's life, and interacts intimately with the person's free will, psyche and personality, and the choices and decisions that person makes. The interaction among these factors determines the particular destiny that actually unfolds in the person's life.[15]

Although the sketches in figures 7.8, 7.11, and 7.12 were created as purely schematic diagrams, the visual appearance of the images is intriguing. The schematic of the individual human being in figure 7.12 happens to resemble somewhat the image of a dancer or a whirling dervish, with arms outstretched toward God. This visual resemblance is purely accidental, yet the symbolism is apt, as it represents the outstretched longing of the human heart toward God.

Science as Pattern Recognition

All of science is basically a process of pattern recognition, an attempt to infer or discern an underlying order that can explain observed data. This process applies equally in the case of the nascent science of consciousness. If the potential science of fractal consciousness is valid, it is because the deeper correspondences are already there, as a pregiven order, in the architecture of consciousness itself. These patterns are not just an anthropomorphic projection or interpretation of consciousness; the correspondences exist ontologically in consciousness itself. They are part of the design—built in by God, if you will—and the spiritual seeker merely discovers and applies them.

Fractal patterns in consciousness are thus more than just metaphor or philosophical conjecture; they are living structures of consciousness that point to something very real, a key secret to the inner science of the Divine. Fractal geometry and holography can thus be regarded as modern rediscoveries of the ancient hermetic principle of correspondence, in which "all are mirrored in every other." This inner science is far more profound than today's material science has yet recognized. It is a sacred science of consciousness, known to the ancients thousands of years ago, yet long forgotten. It contains the deep secret of faith, the faith that can move mountains, and the secret of divine fire that can transmute anything into anything else. It is a science that can also be applied in reverse: as below, so above. This means we can come to know the Above by going deeply within here below. By this method mystics across the ages have discerned the truth of larger realities of cosmic significance, by reference to their microcosmic counterparts that are observable or imaginable close at hand. This epistemological methodology is a universal key to spiritual knowledge, and its application is a skill that has been almost entirely lost in today's world.

Is God a Fractal?

Certainly not! Nor could God ever be confined to a fractal, or any other structure or concept whatsoever. Nevertheless, the emanations from God, at least those emanations that impact us humans, may have a fractal-like structure. The parallels between fractal geometry and mystical consciousness reviewed in this chapter may seem merely metaphorical or hypothetical at this stage. However, it is quite possible that in consciousness there exist ontological correlates that are fractally structured. If the hypothesis of fractal divinity is valid, then these parallels in consciousness do exist, and will likely be revealed over time as the science of consciousness continues to develop beyond its current state of infancy.

> That which is below is like that which is above, and that which
>   is above is like that which is below—to do ye miracles of
>   one only thing.
> And as all things have been and arose from one by mediation of
>   one: so all things have their birth from this one thing.
>
> —*The Emerald Tablet* (translation by Isaac Newton)

Fire of
Divine Love

8

Toward a Universal Path of Divine Love

My heart has become capable of every form:
it is a pasture for gazelles and a cloister for Christian monks,
a temple for idols and the pilgrim's Ka'ba,
and the tables of the Torah and the book of the Qur'an.

I follow the religion of Love: whatever way Love's camels
    take,
that is my religion and my faith.

> —IBN ARABI

God wants us to love our way into becoming God.

> —FATHER THOMAS KEATING

Love Is a Fire

"Whoever stands near me stands near the Fire," declares Jesus in the Gospel of Thomas.[1] The Qur'an concurs, "Blessed is the person near this Fire, and those around it" (Q 27:8).[2] Similarly in Hinduism, "The journey to the *Atman* ... begins and ends in fire."[3] Divine love is a blazing fire, and it burns alike in East or West. "God is a consuming fire" (Heb. 12:29), and the yearning for God, truth, or love is itself this same fire burning in the heart. The mystical journey is a process that transforms the human disciple into this living fire of love. "One who knows the Fire knows all that is, the secret of all being.... All the worlds are but the declension of Fire: beyond it there is Nothing."[4]

To unite with the fire of love, one must *become* this fire, on its terms. This is the secret fire of divine love, without which no true spiritual transformation can take place. In the Katha Upanishad, this fire is called the Nachiketas Fire. Mere ritual fires are of no use for spiritual transformation, but "the Nachiketas Fire is not a mere ritual fire but the secret alchemical Fire which is the means of transmutation. It therefore is the Bridge which leads ... to the Brahman.... Mere metaphysical explanations are but a painted flame, a thing as useless as a still-born child. Only the True Fire can serve as the Bridge."[5] This is the cosmic fire that Arjuna beholds in chapter 11 of the Gita.

"Thought gives off smoke to prove the existence of fire," says Rumi. "The mystic sits within the burning." This aphorism speaks to the crucial distinction between a mere theological or intellectual approach to divine love, and the direct engagement with the transformative fire itself. The same distinction is echoed in the *Cloud of Unknowing*, the fourteenth-century anonymous Christian mystical text: "By love, God can be gotten and holden; by thought, never!" As practitioners of divine love, our task is to enter into the secret fire of love, as mystics have spoken of across the ages and traditions.

St. John of the Cross describes this fire beautifully as the living flame of love:

> This flame is living because ... it makes the soul live in God spiritually and experience the life of God. In this flame the soul experiences God so vividly and tastes God with such delight and sweetness that it exclaims: *O living flame of love! that tenderly wounds my soul....* Since love is never idle, but in continual motion, it is always emitting flames everywhere like a blazing fire ... [and] dispatches tender flares of delicate love.[6]

John elaborates on the fire of divine love using the powerful metaphor of a log in a fire. The unburned log represents the untransformed human soul, which is placed in the fire and is then transformed *by* the fire *into* fire:

> The very fire of love that afterward is united with the soul, glorifying it, is what previously assailed it by purging it, just as the fire that penetrates a log of wood is the same that first makes an assault on the wood, wounding it with the flame, drying it out, and stripping

it of its unsightly qualities until it is so disposed that it can be pen-
etrated and transformed into the fire.[7]

Fractal of Divine Fire

The fire of divine love burns on every level of existence—from the heart
of the sun, to the human heart, to each tiny cell in the human body, to
the subatomic particles and the core of every star across all galaxies. It is a
grand fractal fire of love. Although physics distinguishes between chemical
fire and nuclear fire, the fundamental forces of fire—the strong and weak
nuclear interactions, and the electromagnetic interaction—are believed to
be a single unified force.[8]

Love is a transforming fire. Like all fires, it ignites, incinerates, puri-
fies, and shines with brilliant light and warmth. There is no force in the
cosmos as powerful as love, and nothing propels spiritual evolution as
swiftly as love. Ultimately the fire of love burns away everything that is
not love. "For one who can offer up all self in its flames, who can worship
it as it burns on the sacrificial altar ... it will manifest as the beneficent
divine Power, the Magic all-accomplishing creative Fire, Transmuter of all
things, giver of Immortality."[9] The flaming power "in which dwell all the
worlds" is this divine fire that "burns with an intensity not to be found in
the center of the hottest star, and yet not hot, for even the most delicate
petals of a flower are not scorched by it.... Every form we see is but the
smoke which veils its hidden Flame."[10]

Lest all this be regarded as mere fanciful mystical metaphor, Einstein's
mass-energy equivalence formula shows that the energy contained, for
example, in a delicate rose petal with a mass of only 0.075 grams is equivalent to 1,600 tons of explosive TNT. Yet this represents merely the physical dimension of the fire; its spiritual dimension contains an equally colossal
power to transform consciousness, and to unite the human soul with the
very essence of God.

"Set your life on fire," proclaims Rumi, and "seek those who fan its
flames." Why? Because in the absence of divine fire, no transformation
can take place. "How many there are who spend whole lifetimes in study
of the Vedanta and kindred philosophies," laments Krishnaprem, "and
yet who have to confess to themselves in the end that nothing has happened.... The Light that was to have shone forth has remained hidden,
and the Unitive Knowledge of which they have read and argued so much

has remained but a metaphysical theory…. All this is through ignorance of the Fire, [which is] the indispensable Bridge for those who would in very truth make the Journey."[11]

Hence the crucial need for disciplined spiritual practice that kindles the fire of divine love, and for the all-important sincerity and depth of aspiration that fuels the flames of divine love in the heart. With diligent practice, total self-giving, and surrender, this secret fire of love becomes a roaring blaze that burns away everything that stands between the devotee and the Divine.

Divine Fire Across the Traditions

The divine fire is one, yet is described differently in various traditions. As Heraclitus portrayed it, "The world order, the same for all beings, neither any of the gods hath made nor any human; but it was always, is and shall be ever-living Fire, kindled in measure and quenched in measure."[12]

In Hindu terms, the fire of love incinerates the three "knots of the heart" that keep the soul bound to material existence. These three knots are: (1) the knot of Brahma that binds us to physical form, making us believe that "I am the body"; (2) the knot of Vishnu that binds us to our desires and makes us say, "I want this" or "I am happy" or "I am sorrowful"; and (3) the knot of Shiva that binds us to the mind, making us believe "I am my mind" or "I am my thoughts and beliefs." As the three knots of the heart are removed, the soul is liberated into its original oneness with Brahman.

In Christian terms, "This flame of love … is the Holy Spirit…. And that flame, every time it flares up, bathes the soul in glory and refreshes it with the quality of divine life…. The more intense the fire of union, the more vehemently does this fire burst into flames…. As a result, all the acts of the soul are divine."[13]

In Islamic terms, Rumi's teacher Shams i Tabriz ignited the fire of divine love within him, and Rumi sums up his entire life in two lines:

> And the result is not more than these three words:
> I burnt, and burnt, and burnt.

"Shams had awakened in Rumi a fire that could only be satisfied with union, with the ecstatic loss of the self in the presence of the Beloved," says Llewellyn Vaughan-Lee.[14] Rumi became a living embodiment of this divine fire and ignited the same fire in other souls wherever he went:

It is the burning of the heart I want; this burning
    which is everything.
More precious than a worldly empire, because
    it calls God secretly, in the night.[15]

The Essence of the Mystical Journey

Where does this fire lead? What becomes of those who give themselves to it? "All that can be said ... is less than the reality," writes John of the Cross, "for transformation of the soul in God is indescribable." With that caveat, John nevertheless proceeds to summarize the essence of the entire mystical journey. "Everything can be expressed in this statement," he says:

> The soul becomes God, from God, through participation in God, and in God's divine attributes.[16]

This is the supreme gift offered to every human being. Whatever name we give to this process, whether we call it henosis or theosis or divinization, whether we conceive of it as apophatic or kataphatic, whether it takes place in a Christian or Muslim or Hindu or as a spiritual but not religious practitioner, the process is basically the same. The soul is transformed *into* the Divine, *by* the Divine, through participation *in* the Divine.

We cannot understand the process; we cannot master it; we cannot force it; we cannot co-opt it any way for our own purposes. We can only give ourselves to it, if we choose, and consent unconditionally to this process on its terms. And if we do this—or rather, *allow* it—the living truth of love empties us of ourselves and fills us with divine love. "As long as I contemplate a face of Christ that is anything other than my own face, I shall never know Christ," says Abhishiktananda. "The *real* Christ is my own self, risen again."

Many Paths, One Goal

Sri Anandamayi Ma, the remarkable female Indian saint of the twentieth century, held that religious practices are meant to acquaint the devotee with God "until such time as God becomes an ever-present reality—[so that] God, the One, is perceived behind all manifestations. Whether one calls God Rama, Krishna, Christ, or Buddha is immaterial."[17] Similarly, after a lifetime of studying religions, Wilfred Cantwell Smith, founder of the Harvard Center for the Study of Comparative Religion, came to regard the world religions as evidence of "a single, if multiform, planetary spiritual heritage."[18] "The unity of humankind's religious history is obvious, once one sees it. We have, however, been assiduously trained not to see it. Even more strongly, we have been pressured not to think it; and not to feel it. Yet today it beckons our minds"[19]—and our hearts. Leading scientist Stuart Kaufmann also affirms, in his strikingly titled book *Reinventing the Sacred*, that "the task of finding a common spiritual, ethical and moral space to span the globe could not be more urgent."[20]

Yet today many academic scholars of religion tell us that no such universal spiritual ground exists.[21] With due respect to these learned views, the evidence presented here points quite to the contrary: a unitive spiritual essence underlies the theistic religions (if not all religions). Certain universal spiritual principles do hold—not in some grand unified theology that all must subscribe to, or in an exclusive ontological doctrine that eschews the rich spectrum of religious diversity, but in the intimate depths of the heart, which unifies what the mind divides. This does not deny the unique glory and particularity of every great religious and spiritual tradition; quite the contrary, it exalts them all—as exquisite rays of one Supreme Light.

Believe in All the Prophets

Closely related to this oneness of the Eternal, the Qur'an tells us that God makes no distinction between any of the prophets. If God makes no such distinction, then who are we to do so? It seems incumbent upon us mere mortals to regard the differences between the prophets, whatever they are, to be (at most) of secondary importance. This is not to deny religious diversity, but the differences are evidently not so fundamental in God's eyes, so it seems they should not be fundamental in our eyes either. Indeed, rather than a source of division and strife, religious differences can be embraced as a source of rich insight and inspiring diversity, thereby supporting constructive dialogue and mutual collaboration among fellow practitioners across the faith traditions, as was beautifully modeled by the religious leaders of the Snowmass Conference convened by the Cistercian monk Father Thomas Keating.

The Qur'an says further that it is not right to believe in only some of the prophets and not others; we are enjoined to believe in all of them. Well, how can this be done in practice? Two strategies seem to be essential. First and foremost—given that the prophets and divine messengers do teach quite different relative teachings—it seems of paramount importance to discern what are the profound similarities of the teachings across all the prophets and their respective traditions, and to follow this essential teaching that is common to all the traditions. Second, in those areas where there are apparent contradictions, it seems essential to relegate these areas to a status of secondary importance (which is evidently how God also regards them), so they do not interfere with the deeper universal teachings. In this way we can honor the injunction to believe in all the prophets.

And so we ask: What is this common teaching among the prophets and avatars and messengers, and their traditions? We have held and explored this question throughout this book, and we found a remarkable commonality among the scriptures as well as the mystics. Weaving these various strands together, a potentially universal path of divine love begins to emerge. The essence of this path is to *give*—give up our self-centered identity, and give our heart unconditionally to our Beloved, the supreme mystery we call God. Another way to describe it is that we die to our human self, and allow a larger divine Self to replace us. This is the essence of the path.

Spiritual Transformation and Theological Disparity

The fact that the theologies and cosmologies of different religions don't agree in seemingly important ways cannot be taken as concrete evidence that those theologies are necessarily describing different ultimate realities. Spiritual truth, whatever it is, lies beyond the realm of concepts and words, and any attempt to express it in conceptual frameworks is inherently fraught with peril. Most human thought systems seek to express something that is not inherently beyond the capacity of the mind, and therefore can be properly articulated within thought. Not so theology, which is intrinsically inadequate to perform the task we ask of it.

The process of mystical transformation cannot be fully understood, because the mind can neither understand nor facilitate that which leads far beyond the mind. As Radha Mohan Lal, a spiritual master from north India, puts it, "What can be understood by the mind is not a high state."[22] Therefore, the attempt to fully explain mysticism in theological terms is an obstacle to realization. For this reason, John of the Cross emphasizes that the mystical journey is impossible to understand, and as he wisely counsels, we "advance by *not* understanding."[23]

Bearing this in mind when encountering seemingly disparate theologies, we must allow for the possibility that they may be describing precisely the selfsame transformative journey and Reality. Their apparent differences might be due to any number of confounding factors. Among them are: uncovering partial or fragmented aspects of a larger yet hidden integral truth (as reflected in the story of the blind men and the elephant); representing the same spiritual reality using vastly different conceptual systems or explanatory metaphors, thereby creating the illusion of disparity; focusing excessively on nonessential details or irrelevant issues of historical accident or cultural context; creating multiple names or conceptual labels for the same reality and arguing over which is the correct or chosen one; or generating intellectual artifacts in the mind derived from the inevitable clumsiness and epistemological inadequacy of the theological enterprise itself.

In view of this, when considering the path of divine love across the faith traditions, I have come to the opinion that the theological differences across religions are not of paramount importance, compared to the similarities. Yes, there are striking differences and they are to be appreciated, and many of them are very important within their religious contexts. I honor these differences and uphold them as integral to their respective traditions. Moreover, I never intend disrespect for any particular religious system of theology, belief, or practice. At the same time, when it comes to the soul's actual process of transformation and evolution on the path of divine love, I cannot take most of these theological differences too seriously. In the case of Islam and Christianity, for example, there are key contradictions regarding the incarnation, the "only begotten Son," the crucifixion, the "seal of the Prophets," and so forth. In the case of Hinduism and Christianity, there are debates about the historicity of Krishna, the putative polytheism of Hinduism, the "only begotten Son" versus a string of incarnated avatars, and the "docetic" incarnation of Krishna versus the "real" incarnation in the flesh of Christ (although this particular debate seems rendered meaningless by the modern discovery from quantum mechanics that all physical matter, including human flesh, is ontologically "docetic"; it isn't actually real material "stuff"). Hinduism and Islam have their differences as well, with debates about reincarnation, monotheism versus polytheism, the world as real versus illusion (*maya*), God as incommensurable other versus God as everything, and other issues.

When it comes to the essence of the true spiritual journey—the utter self-giving, the intensity and humility of genuine prayer, the rigors of purification and facing one's own darkness, the intimate communion with spirit, the alchemical transmutation and divinization that transpires in the depths of the sincere soul who is fully surrendered to God—the parallels across the faith traditions are remarkably deep. Against this practical background of the soul's transformative journey, theological disparities across the religions all but fall by the wayside. The mystics across diverse traditions are fundamentally united as one, on a higher plane of elevated spiritual awareness. St. Teresa of Avila's revelation that "Christ has no body on earth but yours, no mouth but yours ..." is not ontologically different from the Islamic Hadith in which Allah says, "I become the eyes with which he sees, the mouth with which he speaks."[24] The divinization of the human devotee is basically the same in both cases.

All these declarations refer to one and the same sacred process of the mystical transformation of the human being into the very essence of God. This is the profound, radical gift of these sacred traditions, and the transformational process is fundamentally similar in all cases. It is not merely an Eastern goal or perspective; the path is universal, and is equally found in the West, as Plotinus testifies: "Our concern is not merely to be sinless, but to be God."[25] The ultimate wisdom is one; the goal is the same—to become one with the essence of God—and the theological and doctrinal differences ultimately don't matter very much, and in any case they should never be allowed to get in the way of the transformational process itself.

My personal conviction is that God does not judge by a person's religious affiliation or doctrinal beliefs or theological orientation, but rather by the purity of the heart and the sincerity of aspiration. The Qur'an says that those who believe in God, perform good deeds, and are accountable for their actions will have their reward with God, and will not grieve. This is a promise of universal salvation; it does not require a person to be a Muslim or to adhere to the Five Pillars of Islam or the *sharia*. In Jesus's twin commandments to love God and one's neighbor, no creed is specified that one must believe, nor is one required to take any particular stand regarding the incarnation, the virgin birth, the only begotten Son, or the resurrection. Similarly, Krishna does not demand adherence to any theology or belief; he teaches silent meditation (or contemplative prayer) with God as the only goal. Yet in the advanced stages of the path, Krishna actually enjoins abandonment of all forms of practice, so the devotee can give her unconditional love to God and take refuge in God alone—which is essentially the same as the first commandment of Jesus.

Love for—and surrender to—God is the way. All else is peripheral. This seems to be the clearest and deepest message of these three scriptures. Each tradition offers a unique, magnificent doorway that opens to this transformative path to God. Each door is exquisitely crafted, and our dilemma is that we get trapped in arguments over which door is most glorious, or else we worship the doors themselves—rather than actually going *through* the doorway to embark upon the transformative journey itself.

We Need God; God Needs Us

We humans need God, and Rumi counsels us to increase our need, because God responds to genuine need. Yet our need for God is only half the circle of divine love. God also needs us, to complete the circle. There is a kind of hole in God's divine fractal tapestry if we don't fulfill our spiritual purpose. If I betray my divine destiny, that hole in me is fractally replicated on a larger scale, and becomes a kind of gap in God, even despite God's inherent completeness. There is no being who can fulfill my divine destiny except me, and if I don't do it, it is a loss not only for my life, but for some larger cosmic purpose and destiny as well.

We need God, to be fully human. God needs humanity, to be fully God.

How Do We Surrender?

The question naturally arises: Exactly how are we to walk this path of divine love in practical terms? The scriptures answer with one voice: Surrender to the will of God. "If you love me you will keep my commandments," says Jesus. Surrender (*islam*) to God's Will and Guidance, says the Qur'an. Bow down and sacrifice to God, and take absolute refuge in God, says Krishna.[26]

Surrendering to the will of God is the key, for as Thomas Keating says, "The will of God *is* God." Surrender is how we show our love; it is how we worship in practice. Without this surrender or submission to the will of

God, our claims to love or worship God are meaningless, and worse, disingenuous. Meaningless because without a sincere and total self-giving of our entire being unto God, our love is mere empty adoration. Disingenuous because without purposeful action and humble commitment to carry out the divine will, our worship is but counterfeit prattle.

The call of the scriptures is crystal clear: Whatever our religion or theology, whether Hindu, Muslim, Christian, or Jew, we are to give our very being entirely to God, holding nothing back. "Lose your life for My sake," says Jesus. "Sacrifice to Me, hold thyself as *nothing* before Me," says Krishna. "Die before you die," says Muhammad.[27]

Surrender and die. These seem to be the two key injunctions on the path of divine love, shared by all the traditions. Sound enticing? No wonder so many eschew this path! People either abandon spiritual life altogether or else follow a different path of knowledge instead. Better to become enlightened than to just die. Better for our *Atman* to become *Brahman* than to just crumble to dust in some humiliating surrender.

Yet to surrender and die is the path. But it is not what it seems. Surrender is actually a privilege, and death a huge relief. Yes, we are called to give up our life—not only our ideas and dreams and plans, but our very identity; the "I" as a human being must go—and we allow God to trample upon us in any way the Divine chooses, and to completely replace us. This is what is required by the call of divine love, yet what comes in its place far exceeds the tribulation of surrender.

But how do we actually accomplish this surrender? By simply doing it; there is no other way. Let's be frank; most of us naturally resist all this business of bowing down and surrendering, partly because of negative associations with humiliation and defeat, and more because we don't *want* to relinquish our cherished identity and attachments. Moreover, even in the scriptures, surrender is sometimes portrayed as a final act of desperation only after all else has failed, as the psalmist notes at one point: "I am utterly bowed down and prostrate" (Ps. 38:6). Although appropriate under any circumstances, ideally the bowing down and prostration is done long before we are completely spent, desperate, or lost; we surrender freely as an act of conviction, strength, and devotion while we are still vibrant and healthy.

Admittedly, surrender is difficult. As Radha Mohan Lal says, "Surrender is the most difficult thing in the world while you're doing it, and the easiest thing once it's done."[28] We are like actors in a theater company who become so thoroughly identified with our roles that we completely forget who we really are. We believe we *are* those characters and forget that it's all just a play, in a context of stage props. In like manner, we have come to believe that we *are* these fanciful characters of our ego, and we persist in this illusion, clinging to it desperately when challenged. Hence we become unwitting impostors in our own lives. Our task is to take off the costumes and adornments, turn away from the fabricated stage drama, all of which bolster the false self, and enter back into what is real. Once we've actually taken off the costumes and stepped beyond the props, we see that this was actually fairly easy to do.

There are other, less harsh ways of characterizing the path. We could say "consent" and "let go," instead of surrender and die. This sounds more palatable, and indeed it is more accurate in some ways, for the deepest truth of who we are not only doesn't die, but in fact comes to life in a far more powerful way than ever before. What "dies" is only the *illusion* of one's identity as the false self. Nothing *real* ever dies. Nothing *unreal* ever lives. Nevertheless, the illusion that the unreal is real is extremely compelling, and if you try to dispel it you generally experience a kind of death.

Absolute surrender becomes "unconditional consent," which also sounds better. Regardless of the terminology, the process is the same, and unconditional consent or surrender is still inherently difficult at times. That's just how it is. Yet if we can do it—or rather, consent to its being done—we are "repaid a hundredfold" through God's grace.

How does the disciple ensure that her surrender is actually to God within, and not to the ego's subtle manipulation to pose as the inner truth? This is a crucial issue, and high degrees of discernment and humility are required that are often lacking or underdeveloped in many practitioners, especially in the earlier stages of the journey. This is one reason why spiritual and contemplative disciplines are so important and must be practiced consistently over many years for most aspirants; it is crucial not to "abandon all dharmas" prematurely. This is also why the mystical journey is best undertaken under the guidance of a realized master. Self-guided would-be mystics are vulnerable to going seriously astray; hence, the mystical traditions have established appropriate mentoring structures and protocols to keep disciples on track. But these safeguards are often missing outside the established faith traditions. The path is radical and uncompromising, and requires total commitment and tremendous patience. Another concern is that sometimes the mentors themselves (or gurus, sheikhs, lamas, priests) have gone astray, wreaking havoc in the lives of their students and disciples. All of these are critical practical issues that apply to all spiritual paths, and the path of divine love is no exception.

The True Purpose of Spirituality

The ultimate goal of spirituality is not self-mastery, or even compassion and serving others, although these are integral to it. The true purpose of spirituality is self-transcendence. We are called to relinquish our separate self and identity altogether, and become not just an "instrument" of divine love and will but ultimately to *be* the essence of God.

This requires us to relinquish spiritual identity altogether; the very notion of being a devoted spiritual seeker must go. Our desire for experiences—even our desire to transcend individuality in union with the Godhead—becomes an obstacle, for it is "a reassertion of the ego's congenital claim to existential autonomy, and thus a violation of the indispensable prerequisite for the operation of grace.... Without self-effacement there is no grace, and without grace there can be no transcendence."[29] This is consistent with *prapatti*, which requires absolute surrender in an act of utter humility—without expectation—from a position of strength, laying down the whole of one's very self and life, unconditionally, for God.

Yet this self-effacement is not an easy process, perhaps especially for Westerners, as Sri Krishnaprem foresaw clearly eighty years ago when the West began to take a strong interest in yoga. His observations are still highly relevant today, and worth quoting at length:

> Nowadays, especially in the West, there are many who practice Yoga [for] enhanced self-hood and well-being, of increased self-mastery with its corollary of increased mastery of the outer world. So they come to this point and then stop. Beyond this point is the "otherworldliness" of the ancient East, a thing for which the average modern person has little if any use.... Again and again this attitude can be seen in Western writers otherwise sympathetic to Yoga. Jung, for instance, says that we should do well to confess that we do

not understand this utter unworldliness ... indeed, "we do not want to understand it."

Nevertheless, to stop at this point is really to fail in the Yoga, and to reduce it to the status of one of the many modern devices for increasing comfort of the human ego.... Yoga is a sacred science which leads far beyond the realm of modern conveniences and psychological adjustments.... The one force capable of taking the human being through the bottle-neck of self into the wide-extended regions beyond is the force of love.... It is on the wings of self-giving that the further reaches of the Path must be followed up.[30]

This insight is not new; it is the deeper meaning of "take up your cross" or "die before you die." It is daunting to the human ego—to be sure!— which is why Arjuna sinks into utter despair as he is about to embark upon the true spiritual journey on the battlefield between his higher and lower natures. Meister Eckhart speaks of this same widespread reluctance to walk the true path and the meaning of mystical death:

Christ says, "Whoever wishes to follow me must take up their cross, deny themselves, and follow me" (Matt. 16:24).... Now there are many people who rather than denying themselves actually maintain themselves in their own self-esteem.... These people do not follow God ... rather, they follow the self-esteem in which they hold themselves.... The soul must abandon her own being. This is where the death that is spiritual begins.... Here the soul forsakes all things, God and all creatures. Of course, it sounds astonishing to say that the soul should forsake God, but ... the soul must exist in a free nothingness. That we should forsake God is altogether what God intends, for as long as the soul has God [in a possessive way], knows God [as a concept] and is aware of God [as an object], she is far from God. This then is God's desire—that God should reduce Himself to nothing in the soul so that the soul may lose herself.... This is how we should understand the smallest [final] death which the soul undergoes in order to become divine.[31]

Science of the Heart

There is a vast, hidden inner science of the heart, of which our contemporary science knows virtually nothing. It is this inner science of the heart that is the foundation of the esoteric spiritual traditions, and which humanity today desperately needs to reclaim. This hidden science contains its own laws and truths that are every bit as real as the laws of physics and biology.

The contemporary scientific understanding of consciousness is exceedingly inadequate and underdeveloped. Science today has no credible theory or understanding of consciousness. According to mainstream neuroscience, consciousness is produced inside the brain as an "epiphenomenon," or side effect, of neurochemistry in the brain. As psychiatrist Stanislav Grof observes, "Very few people, including most scientists, realize that we have absolutely no proof that consciousness is actually produced in the brain and by the brain." While it is true that certain interconnections between consciousness and physiological processes in the brain are well established clinically, this by no means justifies the deduction that the brain is the source of consciousness. "Such a deduction," continues Grof, "is tantamount to the conclusion that the TV program is generated *inside* the TV set, simply because there is a close correlation between functioning or malfunctioning of its components and the quality of the sound and picture."[32] Compelling clinical data from controlled studies over several decades demonstrate that "human consciousness can exist independently of a functioning brain," according to Dutch cardiologist Pim van Lommel.[33] Grof, Van Lommel, and other pioneering scientists posit that consciousness originates *beyond* the brain, rather than inside it, and that the brain functions primarily as a receiver and transmitter of nonlocal consciousness. "On this subject," says Van Lommel, "science desperately needs a paradigm shift" (addressed further in appendix 2).[34] Among the many profound implications, this raises the question: What, or where, is the true center of the human being?

The Heart Is the Center of the Human Being

The center of the human being is the heart, not the head. The ancients knew this, but we moderns and postmoderns alike have forgotten it. Apart from a few cutting-edge developments at the fringes of science, the heart is profoundly misunderstood in contemporary science. This is the natural result of centuries of scientific emphasis on the outer physical aspects of material existence, while largely ignoring the subjective inner dimensions of life. The result is a lopsided science, albeit highly successful in its limited domain. "By their fruits you shall know them," and the fruits of Western science are primarily external technological advances—airplanes, computers, and the like—coupled with a dearth of spiritual fruits, and even widespread denial that such fruits exist. Only such a one-sided science—blind to these inner realities—could produce such a patently ridiculous declaration from one of its towering icons (Stephen Hawking) that "mysticism is for those who can't do the math."[35]

Ramana Maharshi tells us that the spiritual heart of the human being is centered just to the right of the center of the chest. This is not a dreamy metaphor or mere poetic sensibility; it is an esoteric fact of the spiritual heart—again, about which contemporary science knows nothing. We are conditioned to believe that the heart is basically a kind of pump, with valves and ventricles, but the heart is so much more than this physical organ. It is the spiritual lens through which God can be seen, as Jesus said, "Blessed are the pure of heart, for they shall see God" (Matt. 5:8). The pathway to God is through the heart, the "thumb-sized" center of consciousness known as the "lotus of the heart," spoken of in the Chandogya Upanishad:

> As great as the infinite space beyond is the lotus of the heart. Both heaven and earth are contained in that inner space, both fire and air, sun and moon, lightning and stars. Whether we know it in this world or know it not, everything is contained in that inner space.... Never fear that this inner treasure of all reality will wither and decay. This knows no age when the body dies; this knows no dying when the body dies.[36]

The Heart Is Infinitely Deep

In the previous chapter, we saw that the finite can contain the infinite. Fractals are a mathematical manifestation of this principle. DNA is something of a biological application of this principle. Mysticism is an application of this principle in the realm of consciousness—within the depths of the heart. The fractal nature of consciousness helps us to understand that the human heart has infinite depth—as the mystics have always maintained—despite being "contained" within the apparently finite human being. The poet William Blake's famous eternity in an hour, and the universe in a grain of sand—albeit glorious—seems to be the tip of the iceberg. The larger mystery and astonishing glory is that the full Infinity of God is contained in the human heart.

The Infinite Godhead, larger than the vast cosmos, dwells inside *your* heart, dear reader! You need only go deeply inward to discover it. This is something more profound than all the discoveries of science, all the lyrics of the poets, all the great works of art and literature, all the musical works of the great composers. For this is the Source of them all—and beyond all—and this supreme Source is none other than Love, alive and burning within you, right now, calling you to bask in the light and warmth of its eternal Flame.

"I and the Father are one" (John 10:30) applies not only to Jesus but to every one of us—it is the deepest truth of who we are. "I was a hidden treasure and longed to be known, hence I created the world," says an Hadith. This hidden treasure is *inside* each one of us, patiently longing for you and me to discover it. And for this knowing—so that *you* could know it and live it!—the entire cosmos was created.

The Essence of Divine Love

Gathering all that has been explored in the foregoing chapters, it now seems possible to distill the essence of the path of divine love into a few key principles. I conclude this book with twelve proposed principles of divine love, which seem to be eternal and perhaps universal. These principles are found both within and beyond the theistic religions, and lead to nondual realization of God.

> The day will come when,
> after harnessing space, the winds, the tides, gravitation,
>
> we shall harness for God the energies of love.
>
> And, on that day, for the second time in the history of the
>   world,
> humanity will have discovered fire.[37]
>
> —TEILHARD DE CHARDIN

And now let us relinquish words entirely, and, as Jan van Ruysbroeck beckons, enter "the dark silence in which all lovers lose themselves."[38]

Principles of Divine Love

The following principles of divine love across the theistic traditions are not set in stone, nor offered as ultimate or definitive principles. Rather, they serve as a starting point for articulating what seems to be the essence of the path of divine love, leading to nondual realization of God.

1. There is one supreme truth or ultimate Reality, which is infinite and beyond all names, forms, and concepts. It is the one Source of all being and nonbeing. It has no name, but is designated here as the Absolute Godhead.

2. The Absolute Godhead self-effuses into subtle constellations of Divinity, which take different forms in different religions and spiritual traditions. These constellations are all ontologically equivalent, yet they entail different forms, names, and numbers of divine manifestations across the traditions. On this plane of Divinity there is no essential ontological difference between, for example, the Hindu *Trimurti*, the Christian Trinity, or Allah and the Ninety-Nine Names of God in Islam.

3. Each constellation of Divinity manifests fractally or holographically on the material space-time plane—as an emanation of divine love—into a particular religion or spiritual tradition. These religious forms differ, and they evolve over time to some degree, but the inner essence of the Godhead is identical in each, and is replicated as the innermost center of every human being.

4. Those who "know" the Absolute Godhead have dissolved their separate being and identity; hence they can neither be said to exist, nor not to exist. They have gone beyond themselves, and beyond all names and forms of God—to merge into the Essence of the Absolute Godhead. Both "I" and God disappear in this union, and fuse into one *is*ness. This may be called nondual realization of God.

5. The heart is the inner gateway to the Absolute Godhead. Interiorization is therefore the key spiritual practice. The path of divine love is pursued deep within the heart.

6. Three qualities are essential for the aspirant of divine love: absolute obedience (to divine will or impulse, as revealed from within the purified heart), absolute faith, and absolute surrender.

7. Realization of the transcendent Godhead is beyond all human powers, and becomes possible only through divine grace. This grace is activated by surrender (if God wills).

8. There is a secret fire of divine love that burns at every level of manifestation. It burns in the heart, in the depths of all forms of God, and *in* and *as* the inner essence of all beings. This inner fire is one with the divine fire in the heart of God.

9. Love of God and surrender to God are ultimately the same, and constitute the first and primary commandment from God to the human soul. ("If you love Me, you will keep My commandments.")

10. Absolute surrender—or "unconditional consent"—to God is the key to the path of divine love. Surrender activates the mystery of divine alchemy and divine grace (if God wills). Divine alchemy dissolves the false self, and utterly transforms the human being. Divine grace lifts the human soul into oneness with the essence of God.

11. The infinite blessing of divine grace far exceeds the finite price of surrender. Realization of this blessing is the highest purpose of human incarnation (whether it is called union, liberation, enlightenment, salvation, divinization, transfiguration, realization of no-self, or other conceptualizations).

12. In practice, the essence of the path of divine love is *giving*—utter giving of self to the Supreme Reality or Source that some call God, and others call by many names. "To those who give all, all is given." To give our very being, fully and unconditionally, is the supreme surrender to God. We then belong to God, not to ourselves. What is then revealed is that we always did belong to God. For God alone exists, and the separate personal self never existed at all.

Divine Love in Buddhism and Nontheistic Traditions

Touching *nirvana*, touching the ultimate dimension,
is a total and unconditional surrender to God.
—THICH NHAT HANH

In this declaration, Zen Buddhist master Thich Nhat Hanh affirms the spiritual oneness of attaining ultimate reality, whether it is realized as *nirvana* in Buddhism, or attained by "surrender to God" in the theistic traditions. This is a striking example of what Raimon Panikkar calls "homeomorphic equivalence," the recognition of certain spiritual universals or close parallels across the religions—in this case between theistic and nontheistic traditions—yet without denying or belittling the differences across traditions.

Comparison of theistic and nontheistic traditions is a complex field, rich with profound and subtle issues that are beyond the scope of this book, for which there is a vast and rich literature available. The focus in this appendix is much more modest: to highlight a few parallels that point to close alignment between Buddhism and the theistic traditions as presented in this book.

Buddhism and "God"

Scholar B. Alan Wallace observes:

> Buddhism is commonly distinguished on doctrinal grounds from monotheistic and polytheistic religions by the fact that it refutes the existence of a divine Creator, and indeed there is ample textual evidence in early Buddhist, Mahayana, and Vajrayana treatises to support this claim. However, a careful analysis of Vajrayana Buddhist cosmogony, specifically as presented in the Atiyoga tradition of Indo-Tibetan Buddhism, which presents itself as the culmination of

all Buddhist teachings, reveals a theory of a transcendent ground of being and a process of creation that bear remarkable similarities with views presented in Vedanta and Neoplatonic Western Christian theories of creation.[1]

Along similar lines, in the remarkable book *Common Ground Between Islam and Buddhism*, scholar Reza Shah-Kazemi provides a wealth of striking intertraditional correspondences to conclude that the ultimate reality affirmed in Buddhism is none other than what monotheists call "God," or the essence of God. Shah-Kazemi makes his case on multiple levels, including detailed examination of scriptural passages from the Qur'an and the Pali Canon that he says point to a single ultimate reality.[2] As one of many examples, he juxtaposes the Qur'anic sura "God is one, God the self-sufficient Besought of all, He begets not, nor is begotten, And there is none like unto Him" (112:1–4) with the Buddhist scriptural verse, "There is, monks, an unborn, not become, not made, uncompounded [reality]" (*Udana* 80–81, Pali Canon). Shah-Kazemi says it does not really matter that the Qur'anic conceptualization is theistic whereas the Buddhist is non-theistic; both point to the same ultimate reality.

In a similar vein, the Rinzai Zen Buddhist master Soyen Shaku, speaking to Americans in the early twentieth century, affirmed the equivalent of God in Buddhism: "At the outset, let me state that Buddhism is not atheistic as the term is ordinarily understood. It has certainly a God, the highest reality and truth, through which and in which this universe exists. However, the followers of Buddhism usually avoid the term God ... which characteristically belongs to Christian terminology. An equivalent most commonly used is *Dharmakaya*."[3]

Devotion in Buddhism

Devotion is crucial in Buddhism, particularly in the Pure Land school, which closely resembles theistic traditions, but also in other schools. Even in Dzogchen, considered by many to be the pinnacle of the Tibetan Buddhist meditative tradition, the Tibetan master Urgyen Rinpoche is unequivocal:

> The method of realizing Buddha nature requires devotion from the core of our hearts—not mere lip-service or platitudes, but a true and genuine devotion to the Three Jewels.... We need to have faith and devotion in order to connect with the compassionate power

of the Buddhas.... Many people come to me saying, "I've tried to meditate for years, but nothing happens; I'm not making any progress." This is because of not using the effective method, the right means.... Please keep this teaching at the very core of your heart, not at the edge or to one side of your heart, but at the very center. Please think, "That old Tibetan man said devotion and compassion are essential. I'll keep that right in the center of my heart." I have wanted to say this for a long time, but I feel that now people are more willing to listen. It's because it's extremely important ... I am telling you the truth here.[4]

In the Mahayana school as well, according to Buddhist scholar C. D. Sebastian, we find:

Mahayana Buddhism is not only intellectual, but it is also devotional.... In Mahayana, Buddha was taken as God, as Supreme Reality itself that descended on the earth in human form for the good of mankind. The concept of Buddha (as equal to God in theistic systems) was never as a creator but as Divine Love that out of compassion [*karuna*] embodied itself in human form to uplift suffering humanity. He was worshipped with fervent devotion ... He represents the Absolute [*paramartha satya*] devoid of all plurality and has no beginning, middle and end.... Buddha ... is eternal, immutable.... As such He represents *Dharmakaya*.[5]

The Three *Kayas*

Buddhist cosmology speaks of three *kayas*, which are spiritual dimensions that correspond roughly to the ontological categories articulated in chapter 7. The Buddhist doctrine says that a Buddha has three *kayas*, or bodies, as follows:

1. *Dharmakaya*, or "truth body," which embodies the very principle of enlightenment and knows no limits or boundaries. It is the embodiment of the truth itself, and it is commonly seen as transcending the forms of physical and spiritual bodies.
2. *Sambhogakaya*, or "body of mutual enjoyment," which is a body of bliss or clear light manifestation. Examples are Amitabha, Vajrasattva, and Manjushri.

3. *Nirmanakaya*, or "created body," which manifests in time and space. An example would be the physical body of Gautama Buddha.[6]

As noted above, the *Dharamakaya* is regarded by many Buddhist masters as corresponding closely to what is called God in theistic traditions. In terms of the analysis presented in chapter 7, the three *kayas* could be regarded as the "homeomorphic equivalents" of the Absolute Godhead (*Dharmakaya*), the plane of Divinity (*Sambhogakaya*), and the plane of manifestation (*Nirmanakaya*). In Christian terms, the *Dharmakaya* would correspond to the Godhead, *Sambhogakaya* to the Christ, and *Nirmanakaya* to Jesus of Nazareth. In Islamic terms, *Dharmakaya* would correspond to the Essence of God (*al-Dhat*), *Sambhogakaya* to Allah and the Ninety-Nine Names, and *Nirmanakaya* to the Prophet Muhammad and perhaps all the prophets. In Hindu terms, the three *kayas* would correspond to *Brahman Nirguna* (*Dharmakaya*), the *Trimurti* (*Sambhogakaya*), and the fully realized Hindu sages (*Nirmanakaya*). These associations are proposed not as precise or definitive correlations, but merely to suggest a possible alignment between the three *kayas* as ontological categories in Buddhism, and the ontological levels (and diagrams in figures 7.8, 7.9, 7.11, and 7.12) presented in chapter 7.

Moreover, some of the same relationships between these different levels also hold. For example, in the Vakkali Sutta, the Buddha is equated with the Dharma itself, much as Christ is one with the Father. The Buddha said, "Whoever sees the Dharma sees me; whoever sees me sees the Dharma,"[7] which is closely akin to Jesus's words, "Whoever sees me has seen the Father" (John 14:9).

Atman and *Anatta*: Contradictory Forms of the Absolute?

Over the years I have been fortunate to attend many Buddhist retreats in the Vipassana tradition, Zen sesshin, and retreats with numerous Tibetan Buddhist masters. At one retreat with Tsoknyi Rinpoche, a question was asked about the oft-debated contradiction between the *anatta* doctrine (no-self) in Buddhism and the doctrine of the *Atman* (Self) in Hinduism. Tsoknyi Rinpoche responded by invoking the example of the great twentieth-century Hindu sage Ramana Maharshi, and said that Ramana's spiritual attainment was essentially equivalent to that of highly realized Buddhist masters. In another retreat, Jetsunma Tenzin Palmo was speaking about enlightened masters and mentioned two examples: the Buddha and Ramana Maharshi. In both cases these Buddhist teachers are citing a leading Hindu sage alongside realized Buddhist masters. Why? As Tsoknyi Rinpoche went on to explain, the essence of the mystical realization attained by such masters goes far beyond what any words or concepts could possibly convey, and what is called *anatta* in the Buddha's case and *Atman* in Ramana's case both refer to the same supraconceptual spiritual reality. Hence there is no substantive contradiction at the level of spiritual truth, he said, but only a conceptual contradiction between the two linguistic concepts, both of which are inherently inadequate (yet symbolically valid) representations of a higher spiritual truth.

This example illustrates that deep parallels of mystical experience across diverse traditions are not facile similarities, but profound experiential truths that are held in common across the traditions, yet they are referred to in each religious faith by different or even paradoxical theological conceptions, which are nonetheless homeomorphically equivalent. A related example is the *anatta* doctrine, which does not mean, as it may seem at first blush, that there is nothing akin to the "soul" in Buddhism. On the contrary, "given the fact that survival after death, in heavens and hells, is clearly indicated by the Buddha, one has to conclude that something akin to a soul does in fact persist posthumously."[8] These parallels of deep spiritual experience also explain why mystics across the traditions report that they have more in common with mystics from other faith traditions than with exoteric leaders of their own religion or citizens of their same nationality. As the great Catholic contemplative Thomas Merton put it, "Thich Nhat Hanh is more my brother than many who are nearer to me in race and nationality, because he and I see things the exact same way."[9]

Many other parallels could be explored, such as "Buddha nature," which seems homeomorphically equivalent to *fitra* in Islam. Buddha nature "is not a new thing we achieve through effort or meditation; rather it is something that is primordially present as our very nature," says Urgyen Rinpoche.[10] This seems directly analogous to *fitra*, which is commonly translated as "primordial nature" or "innate disposition."[11] Many other such close parallels could be explored, such as the extinction of self (*nirvana* in

Buddhism, *fana* in Islam), or emptiness (*shunyata* in Buddhism, *nada* in the apophatic mysticism of St. John of the Cross), or the deathless (*amata*, or "the eternal") in Buddhism, *baqa* in Sufism, and eternal life in Christianity. Similarly, "Compassion is inseparable from love (*metta* in Buddhism, and *mahabba* in Islam).... Islam and Buddhism come together on the centrality of this quality of compassionate love, and for both traditions, this human quality is inseparable from the Absolute, in which it is rooted, and to which it leads."[12]

There are, of course, various apparent contradictions between Buddhism and key tenets of theology that are shared more or less equally by all theistic traditions. Reza Shah-Kazemi skillfully addresses a range of these issues. As one example, the Buddha teaches us to "be a lamp unto yourself," and indeed his enlightenment came from within himself, which might seem to orthodox theists to be something less than the equal of a genuine revelation coming from on high. No mere human insight, however profound, the argument goes, could ever be the equivalent of divine revelation. Yet as Shah-Kazemi points out, "If the Buddha's enlightenment taught him that the empirical self is an illusion (*anatta*), the source of that enlightenment cannot possibly be the empirical self," because this self is rendered nonexistent by his enlightenment. "The relative self cannot reveal the relativity of the self. The 'revelation' of this relativity must be derived from something absolute: ... the objective principle whence all consciousness, life and being flow." So the Buddha's enlightenment did not originate within himself, for he has no self. "We arrive at the inescapable conclusion that Gautama, as a human being, could only have attained his enlightenment by a principle infinitely transcending his own humanity."[13] And that principle is homeomorphically equivalent to divine revelation in the theistic traditions.

Walking the Path of Transformation

Theistic and nontheistic traditions are both pathways to ultimate realization, and consequent supreme peace. Yet on the face of it, they seem very different. Relinquishing human will to follow the will of God may be regarded as a radically different approach than the Buddhist path, as characterized for example by the Four Noble Truths. Yet in the transformative spiritual journey itself, are the two paths really that different? Consider for a moment: To do "my will" means to pursue my cherished desires and avoid my particular aversions. Yet in Buddhism, desire (*tanha*) is itself the cause of suffering (second noble truth), and hence to follow "my will" is to fall squarely into the jaws of suffering (first noble truth).[14] However, this suffering can be eradicated through cessation of desire (third noble truth), and this is to be accomplished by following an eightfold path of "right" conduct (fourth noble truth).

In Buddhism we relinquish human desire to follow a higher dharma. In theistic traditions, we relinquish human will to follow a higher divine will. Either way, we must abandon our cherished attachments, ideas, and instincts to follow a path of higher wisdom, purity, integrity, and spiritual truth. The transformative journey in practice seems broadly equivalent, regardless of whether it is conceived within a Christian understanding of "not my will but Thy will," or a Buddhist understanding of "not my desires, but the Dharma," or an Islamic conceptualization of abandoning all false gods to follow the one true God. In each case, one must take leave of one's lower human proclivities, and give oneself utterly to a higher truth, reality, or essence.

This analysis is admittedly oversimplified, but the fact remains that in the higher stages of transcendent realization, separate spiritual paths are transcended and become one. As Thich Nhat Hanh puts it, "When you are a truly happy Christian, you are also a Buddhist. And vice versa."[15] In the depths of spiritual practice, the supreme truth emerges in its resplendent oneness, and the separate theologies and paths evaporate. "Once the ultimate is touched," continues Thich Nhat Hanh, "all notions are transcended: birth, death, being, non-being, before, after, one, many, and so forth. Questions like 'Does God exist?' or 'Does nirvana exist?' are no longer valid. God and nirvana as concepts have been transcended."[16]

"Belonging to God" thus becomes perhaps "belonging to *Dharmakaya*" in Buddhism. The journey in both cases entails not belonging to one*self*, because the personal self doesn't exist. In Buddhism the personal self never exists (*anatta*); in theistic mysticism the personal self ceases to exist. The transformative process is largely the same, even if the theological description and conceptualization differ.

In closing, the Buddha's final teaching is:

> Be ye lamps unto yourselves. Be ye a refuge unto yourselves. Betake yourselves to no external refuge. Hold fast to the Truth as a lamp.

> Hold fast as a refuge to the Truth.... It is they, Ananda, who shall reach the very topmost Height.[17]

How can we be a refuge unto ourselves if we have "no self" to take refuge in? This seems paradoxical, but it is the very same teaching as the supreme secret of the Gita. The one in whom to take refuge is the Truth within, the *Purushottama* within, the Christ within. This is where all the traditions meet: Krishna gives the same counsel in saying "Abandon all dharmas; take refuge in Me [within] alone." In the Gospel of Mary, Jesus says, "Seek the Son of Humanity within yourself," and the Hindu saint Lalla says, "From without enter thou into the inmost." All these commands are given precisely because the innermost essence of the human being is none other than the transcendent essence of the Absolute. To go to that deepest source within is to go to the highest Truth and deepest Love. For as the great sage Swami Venkateshananda of Rishikesh whispered just before he passed away, "Love *is* the Truth."

Science and Mysticism Are *Not* the Same

As noted in chapters 6 and 7, striking parallels are beginning to emerge between modern scientific discoveries and ancient mystical wisdom. These parallels indicate that the worldview of modern science is slowly gravitating toward an expanded paradigm of "oneness" that is consonant with spiritual wisdom down through the ages.

Inspiring as these new developments are, care must be taken not to posit a facile equivalence between science and spirituality. Contrary to what some observers might be tempted to conclude, modern science as generally practiced today does not constitute a new form of mysticism, nor is it a substitute for spirituality. In most respects, contemporary science and spirituality remain worlds apart.

Science is fundamentally a discipline of the human mind, grounded in empirical observations of the physical universe. The human mind is the epistemic foundation of science, both classical science and the contemporary "new science." Yet within the mystical traditions, the mind is the fundamental obstacle to be overcome; hence the well-known aphorism, "The mind is the slayer of the Real." From this standpoint, because manifest reality is an illusion or projection created by the mind, any epistemology grounded in the mind (such as science) is necessarily an epistemology of illusion. Therefore, science cannot dispel spiritual ignorance; for this it is essential to go beyond the mind altogether.

The vast majority of scientists today, including the most brilliant Nobel laureates, live entirely within their minds—fully identified with their mental and conceptual frameworks. From a spiritual point of view, scientists are thus no different from the majority of humanity, who also live fully identified with the contents of their minds. This is not a criticism of science per se, but rather a recognition of its inherent limitations: Advanced scientific insight is not equivalent to advanced mystical realization. The two kinds of knowing are vastly different, because science is grounded in the relative truth of the mind, and authentic mysticism is grounded in absolute truth beyond the mind.

Mystical practice generally requires a process of emptying oneself, and stilling the mind. It entails (usually) a gradual process of purging the mind of all ideas and concepts whatsoever, leading ultimately to a complete annihilation of ordinary human consciousness, which is replaced by an infusion of a larger universal, nonconceptual truth. This is what is meant by the injunction to "die before you die," which is a foundational practice common to all mystical traditions—East and West. Even Socrates defined philosophy specifically as the practice of learning to die before we die.[1] The process does not generally entail a literal death of the physical body, but rather a total dissolution of the human psychological identity, and all associated attachments, while still living in the body. As long as there remains an "I" who has the experience, the Real has not been realized. In authentic mystical realization, there is no "I" left to experience anything. Throughout this process, the mind is generally recognized as an obstacle, rather than an aid.

By contrast, science, as usually practiced, entails a process of filling oneself and engaging the mind. It involves acquiring information (data), creating conceptual frameworks (theories), and organizing these systematically within the mind. Far from being emptied, the mind is full (if not overfull) of data and conceptual structures. In science, theory or concepts are often taken to be reality itself, except by the most sophisticated scientists, who realize this is a fundamental mistake. Physicist David Bohm explains this trap as follows: "Thought creates structures, and then pretends they exist independently of thought."[2] This subtle trap of conceptual thought applies not only to scientists but also to scholars, theologians, and thinkers in virtually any field. Thought divides and analyzes, and in so doing creates the illusion of separation where there is none. By placing our faith in the mind, we are highly vulnerable to becoming unaware of its blind spots, and we close the door on higher or deeper forms of perception. A cherished weakness of the conceptual mind is to accept its own illusions, half-truths, or one-sided perceptions as the whole truth.

Mystical traditions, East and West, teach that only by bringing the mind to a complete standstill can truth be perceived directly. The very essence of yoga, for example, is defined in the ancient Yoga Sutras of

Patanjali as "the cessation of fluctuations of the mind." Physicist Ravi Ravindra once asked the Indian mystic Jeddu Krishnamurti what he meant by "total attention." Ravindra prefaced his question by confessing, "What I notice in myself is the fluctuation of attention." Krishnamurti replied, "What fluctuates is not attention. Only *in*attention fluctuates."[3] By this measure, the majority of human beings, scientists included, have never consciously experienced total attention—the nonfluctuating awareness that is the prerequisite for perceiving spiritual truth.

Acknowledging these distinctions between science and mysticism in no way denies the value or utility of science. Indeed, if Western science has erred by becoming stuck in relative truth, then the East has often erred by becoming stuck in absolute truth, such as dismissing the manifest universe as mere unreal *maya*. Both absolute and relative aspects of truth are vital, and for the latter, scientific inquiry has proven invaluable. Yet if we want to know what *is*, and enter the domain of spirit or the Absolute, we must go beyond science as it stands today.

Very few scientists have pursued a mystical or contemplative practice that cultivates their consciousness beyond their minds, nor do the vast majority of Western scientists even acknowledge the value of such an endeavor. This is partly because "thousands of scientific studies about meditation are largely ignored by mainstream neuroscience."[4] Fortunately, exceptions to this are emerging, and a small but growing minority of Western scientists faithfully pursue an active contemplative life of the spirit. Some are beginning to bring their inner experiences forward, and directly challenge the narrow materialist worldview held by the majority of their colleagues.[5]

In many non-Western countries, scientists are often more open to mysticism. I have been privileged to meet a number of remarkable scientists in India who practice science by day, often impeccably, and earnestly pursue their spiritual or religious vocations in the mornings and evenings, and quietly throughout the day. They experience no contradiction in this whatsoever; they see right through the blind spots of the scientific worldview (as well as its strengths), and they don't allow it to interfere with their inner spiritual quest.

Jetsunma Tenzin Palmo has remarked that we humans are just as ignorant today as we were 2,500 years ago when the Buddha walked the earth. Despite our vast increase of scientific knowledge, our level of enlightened wisdom has sadly changed little. Not until a full and open exploration of consciousness and the true nature of mind and its limitations are undertaken can science begin to evolve beyond its present level to a higher stage. Only then will a true synthesis of science and spirituality slowly begin to emerge.

Science and the Discovery of the Soul

Sometime in this century, probably in the next decade or two, science will finally acknowledge that human consciousness survives physical death. This will be accepted as an experimentally and clinically validated fact beyond all reasonable doubt by the majority of scientists. As physicist Ravi Ravindra puts it, the death of the body is not the death of the person. In effect, this means that science will have discovered the existence of the "soul" in some form (although this way of conceptualizing it may not be satisfactory to a Buddhist sensibility). However conceptualized, this discovery is rapidly approaching; the empirical data in support of it are becoming overwhelmingly compelling, replicated across the globe in multiple studies and clinical databases.[6] The longstanding bias within scientific and clinical research institutions against acknowledging these remarkable data, and their full implications, is steadily eroding.[7] A recent review of the available evidence concludes that "our consciousness does not end with the demise of the body, it continues to exist in another dimension of the cosmos."[8]

From one perspective, this discovery will be a watershed breakthrough for science. Not only will it be a profound and paradigm-shattering discovery about the expansive, nonphysical foundation of human consciousness but it will also help break science out of the narrow confines of its limited materialist paradigm. It has the potential to precipitate a full-blown scientific revolution.

From another perspective, what this discovery means is that science will have finally caught up with the most basic spiritual teaching, known to mystics for millennia. This is expressed, for example, in the first teaching of the Bhagavad Gita, where Krishna explains that the person does not die when the body dies. Science will have finally arrived at the beginning of chapter 2 of the Gita, written some 2,500 years ago. And there are still another sixteen chapters beyond this, about which today's mainstream science still knows virtually nothing. So in this sense we may observe that science is about 2,500 years *behind* mysticism.

Spiritual Inquiry Goes Beyond Science

For anyone who is serious about the spiritual journey, it is therefore very important *not* to limit oneself to what contemporary science knows, sees, and understands about the nature of reality. It is crucial to set aside the orthodox scientific worldview and get on with the real work of the inner journey. Otherwise, one remains stuck in the rationalist, materialist paradigm and gets nowhere on the inner planes of reality. Science today is far too limited an ontological domain and epistemological framework to provide a proper foundation for a full and deep introspective inquiry into the nature of reality. We must learn to leave the outer physical domain behind, and discover the many rich and new forms of inner "data." We must learn how to discern and parse out the inner revelations that come in contemplative meditation, the out-of-body experiences that take place, the metaphysical insights, the subtle emanations and presences, the visionary data of the imaginal realms—and how to navigate and interpret all these data appropriately without losing our grounding or balance. Then we need to integrate the profound experiences and insights that emerge, and embrace the radical transformation of consciousness that unfolds. Of all this, contemporary science knows virtually nothing as yet.

Many of us get very excited when science makes a new discovery that somehow validates or accords with mystical wisdom. I do so myself, and I have written enthusiastically about some of these discoveries, for example, in chapters 6 and 7 of this book. While it is right to be excited about current discoveries—for example, findings in neuroscience that accord with ancient Buddhist wisdom on the nature of mind—it is also true that even the best of contemporary science has little to offer to authentic, deep spiritual practice.

Again, this is not a critique of science; I am simply taking account of its limitations. Today's science, even the cutting-edge "new science," cannot lead us skillfully into the depths of the heart, which is precisely where we need to go. We are on our own, yet not without guidance, which comes from within. The deep truths of the heart are eternal, profound beyond measure, waiting internally to be discovered—and they beckon each one of us on an inner journey that reveals "many things in Heaven and Earth undreamt of in our philosophies." May you, dear reader, and I, not fail to embark upon that inner journey!

Acknowledgments

The African principle of *Ubuntu* affirms that a person is a person through other people—which beautifully characterizes my process in writing this book. I am immensely indebted to the many people who have profoundly supported and inspired me in this work over many years. Gratitude to my spiritual teacher and superiors in the lineage is unspeakably deep, and knows no bounds. My wife and primary colleague, Cynthia Brix, has been incredibly supportive on all levels; a wonderful springboard, spiritual companion, and gracious fount of endless love and enthusiasm; and a model of patience, enduring my long periods of solitude as I completed this work. Over the past two years she generously took on the bulk of the management of our Gender Reconciliation International project to enable me to complete the final stages of this book.

Father Thomas Keating has been a profound mentor for almost two decades and has provided inspiration and guidance at every level, from spiritual inspiration and companionship to scholarly inquiry, to the intimate depths and challenges of meditation and prayer practice, to personal spiritual direction and support. His mastery and visionary leadership in convening the Snowmass Conference (and later Snowmass Interspiritual Dialogue) over the past thirty-two years has been a tremendous inspiration for me, and served as a primary motivation for writing this book, and for organizing our Satyana Institute interspiritual conferences, trainings, and retreats. His example and inspiration have been instrumental, and it was a joy and privilege to witness the impeccable care he took in writing the foreword.

Ravi Ravindra is one of my earliest mentors, and a friend for nearly three decades, who shares the depths of physics research and mystical pilgrimage, and together we have reveled in these two domains with a constant stream of insight, joy, and humor. Ravi is a rare integration of spiritual and scientific mastery, and he has been a constant support in my own evolution.

Imam Jamal Rahman has been a terrific colleague and wonderful friend for years, and encouraged me greatly throughout the process of this book. Reza Shah-Kazemi has been a tremendous inspiration, and has been very supportive in Satyana Institute's interfaith conferences.

Robert McDermott is a remarkable friend whom I cannot thank enough for his strong, inexplicably persistent support over many years. His intellectual and philosophical capacities have been of invaluable help, and his sheer love and enthusiasm for my work have provided a needed injection of energy and encouragement, especially at many challenging points of tribulation.

I am very grateful for the few days I was fortunate to spend with David Bohm more than twenty-five years ago, during which we had a deep exchange, and I had the opportunity to share with him some of the ideas in this book in their earliest form, to which his response was enthusiastic and encouraging. Richard Tarnas has been another major support, unwavering friend, and revolutionary thinker from whom I have learned a tremendous amount. Stanislav Grof is another early mentor and friend whose pioneering courage, groundbreaking contributions, and intensive transpersonal training have been a source of continual strength and an invaluable contribution in my work.

Rick Paine is a friend of the heart and unflagging supporter of my work, vision, and writings, to whom I owe a big debt of gratitude. Ross Jackson and the late Hildur Jackson have been longtime friends and supporters, and have held with me the vision of authentic integration of spirituality, science, ecology, justice, and community.

Sister Lucy Kurien has been a profound inspiration and inveterate sister on the path of radical love, for whom I could never be grateful enough. Jetsunma Tenzin Palmo is a wonderful friend, an amazing wellspring of abiding spiritual mentorship and direction, and a powerful inspiration to me. Mark Collier and the late Catharine Collier have been incredible friends, providing unceasing inspiration and heartfelt support, particularly on the esoteric levels of this work, and organized my events with Contemplative Outreach in Cape Town. Llewellyn Vaughan-Lee has been a consistent support and mentor, and I was deeply nourished by engagement with his Sufi community for a few years. Swami Ambikananda has been a constant blessing, friend, and colleague, ever aligned in the heart of this work.

My gratitude goes out to my wonderful network of interspiritual colleagues, including Carol Lee Flinders, Michael Abdo, Rory McEntee, Ed Bastian, Swami Atmarupananda, Mirabai Starr, Kurt Johnson, Ken Kitatani,

Philip Novak, Adam Bucko, Cynthia Bourgeault, Father Francis D'Sa, Matthew Wright, and many others, all of whose rich insights are impressed upon me and infused into this book. Numerous spiritual friends have been instrumental over the years in helping me build the inner momentum for this book, including Duane Elgin, Joanna Macy, the late Dave Brown, Father William Treacy, Dominie Cappadonna, Karambu Ringera, Diane Haug, Heart Phoenix, the late Angeles Arrien, Jack Kornfield, Terry Hunt, Selma Naloor, Betsy MacGregor, Charles Terry, Fritz and Vivienne Hull, John Steiner, Joel and Michelle Levey, Andrew Harvey, Jed Swift, Bernie Zaleha, Barbara Findeisen, Barbara Sargent, Bernedette Muthien, Michael Lerner, Anne Stadler, and others too numerous to name.

Special gratitude goes to the late Rev. John Oliver, founder of the Cape Town Interfaith Initiative, who was highly supportive and organized several of my retreats on the interfaith path of divine love, with skillful collaboration from Shamiema McLeod. Judy Connors generously organized these same retreats in the Johannesburg area, as did Francis Padinjakera in Lonavla and Sister Celine Payyappilly in Pune and Kodaikanal, India.

Graphic artist Kathy Lavine did a superb job creating Figures 7.8, 7.9, 7.11, and 7.12. She skillfully organized all the graphics and obtained all permissions with meticulous care and cheerful spirit throughout. I am grateful to Sarah Campbell and to Lynnaea Lumbard and Rick Paine for graciously providing their homes as tranquil spaces for intensive writing retreats. Writing coach Deborah Nedelman provided helpful assistance with the book proposal and sample chapters.

Deep gratitude and appreciation go to my magnificent colleagues in Gender Reconciliation International, who have held me with magnanimous support and patience throughout this writing project. Particular thanks go to Judy Bekker, Zanele Khumalo, Antonia Porter, Emma Oliver, Lucille Lückhoff, Laurie Gaum, and Chaya Pamula. Strong support also came from Julien Devereux, Shell Goldman, Judy Connors, Dorothea Hendricks, Jabu Mashinini, Rob McLeod, Les Thomas, Shirsten Lundblad, William and Esther Diplock, Natalia Cediel, John Tsungme Guy, Janet Coster, Jane Calbreath, Carlotta Tyler, Máire Callan, Britt Conn, Alan Strachan, Patrick Fischer, Jeremy Routledge, Diane Salters, Noegh Crombie, Biata Walsh, Keith Vermeulen, Mthunzi Funo, Thuli Mbete, Sarah Oliver, and many others. I'm grateful also to our larger circle of collaborators, including Professor Pumla Gobodo-Madikizela, Mpho Tutu, Samantha van Schalkwyk, and Nozizwe Madlala Routledge.

Numerous generous donors have supported my work over the years, without which this book and all of my work would not have been possible. Some wish to remain anonymous, but I must thank my dear friends Rick Paine, Lynnaea Lumbard, Laurie McMillan, Linda Cunningham, Lowell Brook, the late Dave Brown, Ross and Hildur Jackson, Rick Lawrence, Sarah Campbell, and many individual donors and generous foundations.

Emily Wichland and Rachel Shields at SkyLight Paths have been a sheer joy to work with, combining competence with gracious support, prompt service, and professionalism in every aspect of the publishing process. Finally, thanks go to my family for their love and support, and to many others not named here who have been supportive on this journey.

Beyond all these marvelous people, I am deeply grateful for and humbled by the continual stream of divine support and inspiration that sustained and carried me throughout this process, even if I was not always aware, and which is the sole source of whatever real value this book may impart.

Suggestions for Further Reading

Abhishiktananda (Henri Le Saux). *Saccidananda: A Christian Approach to Advaitic Experiences.* Rev. ed. Delhi, India: ISPCK, 2007.

Aurobindo. *Essays on the Gita.* Pondicherry, India: Sri Aurobindo Ashram, 2000.

———. *The Mother.* Pondicherry, India: Sri Aurobindo Ashram, 1927.

Keating, Thomas. *Open Mind, Open Heart.* 20th anniv. ed. New York: Continuum, 2006.

Krishnaprem. *The Yoga of the Bhagavad Gita.* Sandpoint, ID: Morning Light Press, 2008.

Lawrence of the Resurrection. *The Practice of the Presence of God.* Radford, VA: Wilder Publications, 2008.

Mackenzie, Don, Ted Falcon, and Jamal Rahman. *Religion Gone Astray: What We Found at the Heart of Interfaith.* Woodstock, VT: SkyLight Paths, 2011.

Mandelbrot, Benoit. *The Fractal Geometry of Nature.* New York: Freeman, 1982.

Miles-Yepez, Netanel, ed. *The Common Heart: An Experience of Interreligious Dialogue.* New York: Lantern Books, 2006.

Nichol, Lee. *The Essential David Bohm.* London: Routledge, 2003.

Panikkar, Raimon. *Christophany.* New York: Orbis Books, 2009.

Rahman, Jamal. *Spiritual Gems of Islam.* Woodstock, VT: SkyLight Paths, 2013.

Shah-Kazemi, Reza. *Paths to Transcendence.* Bloomington, IN: World Wisdom, 2006.

———. *The Spirit of Tolerance in Islam.* London: I. B. Tauris, 2012.

Yogananda. *The Second Coming of Christ.* 2 vols. Los Angeles: Self-Realization Fellowship, 2004.

Notes

Introduction

1. Swami Abhishiktananda (Henri Le Saux), *The Further Shore* (Delhi, India: ISPCK, 1975; reprint edition, 1984).

2. This story is forthcoming in a subsequent book.

3. Ibn Arabi, *Fusus al-Hikam* (Bezels of Wisdom), Abu al-Ala Afifi, editor and commentator (Cairo: Dar Ihya Al-Kutub Al-Arabiyyah, Isa Al-Halabi, 1946), 113; quoted in Toshihiko Izutsu, *Sufism and Taoism* (Los Angeles: University of California Press, 1984), 254.

4. Desmond Tutu, *God Is Not a Christian: And Other Provocations* (San Francisco: Harper-One, 2011).

5. Other "multiple religious belonging" authors include Bede Griffiths, Paul Knitter, and many others. For nondual Judaism that embraces Theravada Buddhist meditation, see Jay Michaelson, *Everything Is God: The Radical Path of Nondual Judaism* (Boston: Trumpeter, 2009).

6. Perennial philosophy writings range from Aldous Huxley's popular work to academic studies by Huston Smith, Wilfred Cantwell Smith, Ross Reat, Edmund Perry, and John Hick; to in-depth treatises of "traditionalists" such as Rene Guenon, Fritjof Schuon, and Ananda Coomaraswamy; to contemporary scholars such as Reza Shah-Kazemi, Philip Novak, and others. Metaphysical scholar Toshihiko Izutsu, author of *Sufism and Taoism* (Tokyo: Iwanami Shoten, 1983), went beyond traditional perennialism to develop a meta-philosophical approach to comparative theology, rooted in rigorous study of traditional metaphysical texts. Fluent in thirty languages and expert in Islamic, Taoist, Zen Buddhist, and Hindu philosophies, Izutsu became convinced that harmony between diverse peoples could be fostered by demonstrating that definitive beliefs of a particular community can generally be found (often in a different form) in the metaphysics of other, very different, communities. Izutsu's approach has partly inspired the methodology of the present book, and the findings here seem to validate his convictions.

7. *De perenni philosophia Book 1*, chapter 1; folio 1, quoted in Charles Schmitt, "Perennial Philosophy: From Agostino Steuco to Leibniz," *Journal of the History of Ideas* 27, no. 1 (1966): 517.

8. Wayne Teasdale, *The Mystic Heart* (Novato, CA: New World Library, 2001). Other leading contemporary "interspiritual" writers include Mirabai Starr, Kurt Johnson, Ed Bastian, Rory McEntee, Adam Bucko, Ken Wilber, Beverly Lanzetta, and Matthew Wright.

9. For readers unfamiliar with Christianity, a few references may be suggested. For an insightful overview composed of scriptural excerpts, see Philip Novak, *The World's Wisdom* (Edison, NJ: Castle Books, 1994), 228–279. A shorter but excellent narrative summary of key teachings is "The Christian Context of the Gospel Readings," by

Laurence Freeman in the Dalai Lama's *The Good Heart* (Boston: Wisdom Publications, 1998), 131–63. An excellent full-length book by a contemporary nondual spiritual teacher is *Resurrecting Jesus* by Adyashanti (Boulder, CO: Sounds True, 2014).

10. A recent example of the latter is Mirabai Starr, *God of Love* (Rhinebeck, NY: Monkfish, 2013).

11. R. Kendall Soulen, "The Sign of Jonah," in P. Ochs and W. S. Johnson, eds., *Crisis, Call, and Leadership in the Abrahamic Traditions* (New York: Palgrave Macmillan, 2009), 16.

12. A fascinating example of an interpretive Christian theology in relation to Islam and Judaism is proposed by R. Kendall Soulen, using the story of Jonah. Soulen is Christian, yet he graciously concludes that "Christians must guard against the assumption that when the Qur'an differs from the letter of biblical revelation, it is therefore false, for it may be congruent with the compassionate purpose of the author of scripture in a way that the letter of biblical condemnation is not" (Soulen, "The Sign of Jonah," 27).

13. Nor is there proof that God does *not* exist. Absence of proof does not constitute proof of absence. Hence the widespread notion of "scientific atheism" is a contradiction in terms; an orthodox scientist (who accepts only what has been proven) can legitimately be agnostic, but not atheist.

14. Netanel Miles-Yepez, ed., *The Common Heart: An Experience of Interreligious Dialogue* (New York: Lantern Books, 2006).

15. Ibid.

16. For a committed atheist who believes the sole agency of creation is nothing more than random chance, "God" could perhaps serve as an acronym for the Generalized Operating Dice that are "rolled" in each moment of the cosmic evolutionary process. This would permit even avowed atheists to concede that they belong to GOD (thus conceived) because were it not for random chance they would not exist.

17. This subtle insight is addressed in chapter 8.

18. B. Alan Wallace, "Is Buddhism Really Nontheistic?," presented at American Academy of Religion, Boston, November 1999, available online at www.alanwallace.org/Is%20Buddhism%20Really%20Nontheistic_.pdf.

19. B. Alan Wallace, *The Ultimate Common Ground*, http://c-c-n.org/the-ultimate-common-ground-by-b-alan-wallace; Paul Knitter, *Without Buddha I Could Not Be a Christian* (London: Oneworld, 2013).

20. Thich Nhat Hanh, *Living Buddha, Living Christ*, 10th anniv. ed. (New York: Riverhead, 2007), 154.

21. Reza Shah-Kazemi, *Common Ground between Islam and Buddhism* (Louisville, KY: Fons Vitae, 2010), 5.

22. Don Mackenzie, Ted Falcon, and Jamal Rahman, *Religion Gone Astray: What We Found at the Heart of Interfaith* (Woodstock, VT: SkyLight Paths, 2011).

23. Thomas Keating and Ken Wilber, *The Future of Christianity*, DVD (Boulder, CO: Integral Life, 2008).

24. Reinhold Niebuhr, *Moral Man, Immoral Society* (Louisville, KY: Westminster John Knox, 2001; first ed., New York: C. Scribner's Sons, 1932).

25. Martin Luther King Jr., "My Pilgrimage to Nonviolence," in *Stride Toward Freedom* (Boston: Beacon Press, 2010).

26. Aurobindo, *The Yoga of Love and Devotion: Bhakti Yoga* (Pondicherry, India: Sri Aurobindo Ashram Trust, 1986), 6.

27. I am grateful to Sa'ddiya Shaikh for suggesting this phrase "hermeneutics of the heart" (personal communication, June 2015).

28. Jetsunma Tenzin Palmo, personal communication, December 1, 2015.

29. For example, certain esoteric *tummo* breathing practices in Tibetan Buddhism are more readily mastered by nuns than monks, owing to physiological differences (personal communication, Jetsunma Tenzin Palmo, February 2016).

30. Elizabeth A. Johnson, *She Who Is* (New York: Crossroad, 2002).

31. William Keepin, Cynthia Brix, and Molly Dwyer, *Divine Duality: The Power of Reconciliation Between Women and Men* (Chino Valley, AZ: Hohm Press, 2007).

32. Carol Kuruvilla, "Religious Denominations That Ordain Women," *Huffington Post* (September 26, 2014), www.huffingtonpost.com/2014/09/26/religion-ordain-women_n_5826422.html.

33. Feelex Lobo, "India's Female Hindu Priests Challenge Age-Old Tradition," *UCA News*, August 8, 2014, www.ucanews.com/news/indias-female-hindu-priests-challenge-age-old-tradition/71626.

34. William Keepin and Cynthia Brix, *Women Healing Women* (Chino Valley, AZ: Hohm Press, 2009).

35. Aysha A. Hidayatullah, *Feminist Edges of the Qur'an* (New York: Oxford University Press, 2014).

36. Beverly Lanzetta, *Radical Wisdom: A Feminist Mystical Theology* (Minneapolis: Fortress Press, 2005).

37. Quoted in Philip Yancey, *The Jesus I Never Knew* (Grand Rapids, MI: Zondervan, 2002), 154.

38. See Sadiyya Shaikh, *Sufi Narratives of Intimacy* (Chapel Hill: University of North Carolina Press, 2015).

39. Ibn Arabi, *Fusus al-Hikam* (*La Sagesse des Prophetes* [Wisdom of the Prophets], trans. T. Burckhardt [Paris: Editions Albin Michel, 1955]), 46; quoted in Reza Shah-Kazemi, *Paths to Transcendence* (Bloomington, IN: Wisdom, 2006), 103.

Chapter 1: The Yoga of Divine Love in the Bhagavad Gita

1. Paramhansa Yogananda, *Autobiography of a Yogi* (Los Angeles: Self-Realization Fellowship, 1993), 153.

2. One of the best and spiritually insightful contemporary commentaries is *The Yoga of the Bhagavad Gita,* by Krishnaprem (Sandpoint, ID: Morning Light Press, 2008; reprinted from 1937). Other important contemporary commentaries include *Essays on the Gita* by Sri Aurobindo (Pondicherry, India: Sri Aurobindo Ashram, 2000), Swami Nikhilananda's *Bhagavad Gita* (New York: Ramakrishna-Vivekananda Center, 1986), Paramhansa Yogananda's *God Talks with Arjuna,* 2 vols. (Encinitas, CA: Self Realization Fellowship, 2001), Eknath Easwaran's *Bhagavad Gita for Daily Living,* 3 vols. (Tomales, CA: Nilgiri Press, 1993), and Ravi Ravindra's *The Yoga of Krishna* (forthcoming from Shambhala). Ancient commentaries by Shankara and Ramanuja

and Jnaneswar are also excellent resources. Regarding translations, Eknath Easwaran has provided probably the best contemporary translation for Westerners, with an excellent introduction and cogent summaries of each chapter (Tomales, CA: Nilgiri Press, 2007). Other excellent recent translations include those by Georg Feuerstein (Boston: Shambhala, 2014) and Graham Schweig (New York: HarperOne, 2007), both of which contain excellent commentary, and Winthrop Sargent (Albany: SUNY Press, 2009) for Sanskrit word-by-word detail. Jack Hawley published a simplified, informal translation and commentary subtitled *A Walkthrough for Westerners* (Novato, CA: New World Library, 2011). Traditional translations include those by Juan Mascaro, Sir Edwin Arnold (Gandhi's favorite, though now dated), Barbara Stoler Miller, and many others.

3. *The Collected Works of Teresa of Avila*, trans. Kieran Kavanaugh and Otilio Rodriguez (Washington, DC: Institute of Carmelite Studies, 1980), 2:223; alluding to Job 7:1.

4. Mandukya Upanishad 1.2, *The Upanishads*, trans. Eknath Easwaran (Tomales, CA: Nilgiri Press, 2007).

5. Krishnaprem, *The Yoga of the Bhagavad Gita* (Sandpoint, ID: Morning Light Press, 2008; reprinted from 1937), 41.

6. For those who follow *A Course in Miracles*, this verse precisely mirrors the core summary of the entire teaching given at the outset: "Nothing real can be threatened. Nothing unreal exists."

7. Aurobindo, *Essays on the Gita* (Pondicherry, India: Sri Aurobindo Ashram, 2000), 81.

8. Krishnaprem, *Yoga of the Bhagavad Gita*, 41, 53.

9. Ibid., 41, 50.

10. This does not mean that Christianity and Hinduism agree on the nature of incarnation. In general, most Hindus regard Jesus Christ as an incarnation of Vishnu, whereas Christians regard the Hindu avatar as merely a "docetic" (apparent) incarnation.

11. Krishnaprem, *Yoga of the Bhagavad Gita*, 59.

12. Ibid., 54.

13. Ibid., 83.

14. Winthrop Sargent, *The Bhagavad Gita* (Albany: SUNY Press, 2009), 340 n.

15. In Sanskrit (transliteration): *Manmana bhava madbhakto, madyaji mam namaskuru. Mam evaishyasi satyam te, pratijane priyo si me* (Gita 18:65, equivalent to 9:34).

16. Krishnaprem, *Yoga of the Bhagavad Gita,* 113, n. 10.

17. Plotinus, *The Six Enneads*, trans. S. MacKenna and B. S. Page, fifth ennead, eighth tractate, section 4, www.sacredtexts.com.

18. Krishnaprem, *Yoga of the Bhagavad Gita,* 140–42.

19. Eknath Easwaran, *Like a Thousand Suns: The Bhagavad Gita for Daily Living*, vol. 2 (Tomales, CA: Nilgiri Press, 1993), 341.

20. For an overview of critical challenges that have arisen in the contemporary neo-Advaita path, see Timothy Conway, "Neo-Advaita or Pseudo-Advaita and *Real* Advaita-Nonduality," www.enlightened-spirituality.org/neo-advaita.html.

21. Krishnaprem, *Yoga of the Kathopanishad* (Allahbad, India: Ananda Publishing House, 1946), 80.

22. Brother Lawrence, *The Practice of the Presence of God* (Radford, VA: Wilder Publications, 2008), second letter.

23. Aurobindo, *Essays on the Gita*, 387–388.

24. Ibid., 388.

25. Krishnaprem, *Yoga of the Bhagavad Gita*, 154.

26. Verses on love and devotion to God with absolute faith are found repeatedly throughout the Gita, and are emphasized as the culmination in the final (or second to last) verse in each of the following chapters: 6, 7, 9, 11, 12, 14, 15, and 18 (final teaching). A similar culmination constitutes the last verse(s) of chapters 2, 3, and 5. Verses on taking refuge in (or surrender to) God are found throughout the Gita, including: 2:7, 4:11, 7:1, 7:14, 7:29, 9:32, 11:38, 12:11, 15:4, 18:56, 18:62, and 18:66.

27. *Manmana bhava* literally means to "become My-minded," and thus entails a form of *jnana yoga*. *Madbhakto* means to "be devoted to Me" (*bhakti yoga*), and *Madyaji* means "sacrifice to Me," or make all actions an offering to God (*karma yoga*).

28. Paul E. Szarmach, ed., *An Introduction to the Medieval Mystics of Europe* (Albany: SUNY Press, 1984), 253.

29. Bede Griffiths, *River of Compassion* (Springfield, IL: Templegate, 2001), 322.

30. Aurobindo, *Essays on the Gita*, 553.

31. I appreciate Graham Schweig's excellent translation and his beautiful commentary: *Bhagavad Gita: The Beloved Lord's Secret Love Song* (San Francisco: HarperOne, 2010). I especially value his emphasis on divine love in the Gita, and particularly the supreme secret, which I have long felt is underrecognized by most commentators, both contemporary and historical. However, I differ with Schweig's understanding of the supreme secret. He supposes the supreme secret of the Gita to be Krishna's declaration to Arjuna in verse 18:64, "You are so much loved by me!" However, most commentators, myself included, understand this verse to be the *preface* to the supreme secret, because Krishna adds, "Therefore I *shall* speak for your well-being" (18:64) (emphasis added). The supreme secret then follows in 18:65–66. This seems further validated by the fact that 18:66 is something new, taught nowhere else in the Gita.

      Schweig asks, "How are we to act in this world of conflict and suffering?" and replies, "The answer of the Gita is simply to *act out of love*.... This hidden song of the divinity calls souls to *act out of love* in all that they do, in all that they think, feel, and will." With deep respect for Schweig's erudite translation and beautiful commentary, I cannot agree that this is the essential message of the Gita. At best, it pertains only to 18:65, and does not specify that this love is to be directed to God, which is all important. Also, it omits 18:66, which calls us to go beyond our dharmas entirely, relinquishing everything we think and feel and do—in an act of total self-giving and surrender to God. Elsewhere, Schweig states that the Gita "is the secret call of the divinity for all souls to love him" (p. 4), which is closer to my understanding of 18:65, but inexplicably Schweig effectively repudiates this view in his commentary on the supreme secret.

32. *Meister Eckhart: Selected Writings*, trans. Oliver Davies (New York: Penguin, 1994), 238 (edited for gender inclusivity).

Chapter 2: The Compassion and Majesty of Islam

1. Nargis Virani, "'I Am the Nightingale of the Merciful': Rumi's Use of the Qur'an and Hadith," *Comparative Studies of South Asia, Africa and the Middle East* 22, nos. 1–2 (2002, 2003), www.cssaame.com/issues/22/virani.pdf.

2. For a solid understanding of Islam and its metaphysical relationship to other religions, see Frithjof Schuon's *Understanding Islam* (Bloomington, IN: World Wisdom, 2011), a book that both Huston Smith and Seyyed Hossein Nasr praise as the best single volume in English on Islam. For an inspirational volume on Islamic spirituality and teaching stories, see *Spiritual Gems of Islam* by Imam Jamal Rahman (Woodstock, VT: SkyLight Paths, 2013). An excellent and informed academic introduction is *The Vision of Islam* by Sachiko Murata and William Chittick. For more basic and general overviews, see Huston Smith's *Islam: A Concise Introduction* or Karen Armstrong's *Islam: A Short History*.

3. Reza Shah-Kazemi, *The Spirit of Tolerance in Islam* (London: I. B. Tauris, 2012).

4. Mackenzie, Falcon, and Rahman, *Religion Gone Astray* (Woodstock, VT: SkyLight Paths, 2011).

5. Dalai Lama, *Toward a Kinship of Faiths* (New York: Crown, 2011).

6. Rahman, *Spiritual Gems of Islam*, 11.

7. Schuon, *Understanding Islam*, 50.

8. In the aHadith of both *Al-Bukhari* and *Muslim*.

9. Hadith *At-Tirmidhi*.

10. Schuon, *Understanding Islam*, 47.

11. One of the most accessible translations of the Qur'an is *The Message of the Qur'an* by Muhammad Asad (Gibraltar, Spain: Dar Al-Andalus, 1980), which also includes many useful explanatory notes and helpful commentary in footnotes. *The Koran Interpreted* by Arthur J. Arberry (New York: Simon and Schuster, 1966) is considered by many scholars to be among the least biased English translations, and it is the translation of choice for most academics. Abdel Haleem has written another good translation (New York: Oxford University Press, 2010), apart from mistranslating *nafs* as "soul" rather than "self"—a serious mistake—and Abdullah Yusuf Ali's translation is generally well regarded (Ware, UK: Wordsworth Editions, 2000). There are other good translations, as well as numerous popularized translations that sometimes carry strong political biases and are uneven in quality. For further information, see Khaleel Mohammed, "Assessing English Translations of the Qur'an," *Middle East Quarterly* 12 no. 2 (Spring 2005): 58–71.

12. Abdal Haqq Bewley and Aisha Bewley, *The Noble Qur'an: A New Rendering of Its Meaning in English* (Norwich, UK: Bookwork, 1999).

13. Schuon, *Understanding Islam*, 47.

14. Numerous verses in the Torah and the Christian scriptures support the first *shahadah*; a few examples: "Yahweh, He is God; there is no other besides Him" (Deut. 4:35); "I am God, and there is no other" (Isaiah 46:9); "See now that I, I am He, and there is no god besides Me" (Deut. 32:39); "There is no God but one" (1 Cor. 8:4); "God indeed is one" (Rom. 3:30).

15. Reza Shah-Kazemi, "The Metaphysics of Interfaith Dialogue," in *Paths to the Heart: Sufism and the Christian East*, ed. James Cutsinger (Bloomington, IN: World Wisdom, 2002), 158.

16. Quoted in D. Gimaret, "*Tawhid*," *Encyclopedia of Islam*, 2nd ed., ed. P. Bearman, T. Bianquis, C. E. Bosworth, E. van Donzel, and W. P. Heinrichs (Brill Online, 2016), available online at www.referenceworks.brillonline.com/entries/encyclopaedia-of-islam-2/tawhid-SIM_7454.

17. Khurram Murad, *Way to the Quran* (Leicestershire, UK: Islamic Foundation, 1985). Available online at www.sunnipath.com/library/books/B0039P0000.aspx.

18. Ibid.

19. Sachiko Murata and William Chittick, *The Vision of Islam* (St. Paul, MN: Paragon House, 1994), 178.

20. I particularly recommend Reza Shah-Kazemi, *The Other in the Light of the One* (Cambridge, UK: Islamic Texts Society, 2006).

21. M. A. S. Abdel Haleem, *The Qur'an* (New York: Oxford University Press, 2010), 3.

22. Ibn alQayyim's interpretation, quoted in Muhammad Asad, *The Message of the Qur'an* (Gibraltar: Dar al-Andalus, 1980), 1.

23. Based on Muhammad Asad's interpretation in *The Message of the Qur'an*.

24. The process of self-surrender leads to the extinction of selfhood in God (*baqa*), which is the deepest meaning of *islam*. See Reza Shah-Kazemi, *The Other in the Light of the One*, 146.

25. Rashad Khalifa, trans., *Qur'an: The Final Testament* (Tucson, AZ: Islamic Productions, 1989).

26. Or "He guides therewith whomever He wills"; either translation is correct syntactically.

27. Asad, *The Message of the Qur'an*, 7, n. 19.

28. Sahih Bukhari, *Oneness, Uniqueness of Allah*, vol. 9, book 93, no. 471, available online at www.iupui.edu/~msaiupui/093.sbt.html.

29. Shah-Kazemi, "The Metaphysics of Interfaith Dialogue," 175.

30. Some commentators have suggested this verse is abrogated by other more exclusivist verses (3:85), but Tabarsi maintains that abrogation cannot be applied to any declaration of a promise, only to legal judgments. See also the earlier commentary on verse 3:85 and Shah-Kazemi, *The Other in the Light of the One*, 168.

31. Every messenger (*rasul*) is also a prophet (*nabi*), but not all prophets are messengers. A messenger delivers a new scripture, whereas a prophet continues an earlier one.

32. Nevertheless, God favored some prophets over others (see Q 2:253, 17:55), especially the five "messengers of strong will": Abraham, Noah, Moses, Jesus, and Muhammad (Q 46:35). The lack of differentiation between prophets applies to the essential message and teaching they all brought.

33. Ibn Kathir (fourteenth century) wrote a famous commentary (*tafsir*) on the Qur'an, in thirty volumes. This quotation is from his *tafsir* on Qur'an 2:136 (available online at www.alim.org/library/quran/AlQuran-tafsir/TIK/2/136).

34. Muhammad Asad, *Message of the Qur'an*, 133, n. 162.

35. Kashani, quoted in Shah-Kazemi, "The Metaphysics of Interfaith Dialogue," 162.

36. Shah-Kazemi, *The Other in the Light of the One*, 151.

37. Quoted in William Chittick, *Sufism: A Beginner's Guide* (Oxford, UK: Oneworld, 2000), 69.

38. Lex Hixon, *The Heart of the Qur'an* (Wheaton, IL: Quest Books, 2003).

Chapter 3: Divine Love in the Gita, the Qur'an, and the Gospels

A much abbreviated version of this chapter was published in *Religion and Culture: A Multicultural Discussion, Festschrift in Honour of Francis X. D'Sa* (Pune, India: Institute for the Study of Religion, 2011).

1. *The Gospel of Sri Ramakrishna*, ed. Mahendranath Gupta, trans. Swami Nikhilananda (Madras, India: Sri Ramakrishna Math, 1942) , vol. 1, 111; vol. 2, 559.

2. A valuable compilation of the many remarkable similarities between the Bhagavad Gita and the Qur'an is presented in Pandit Sunderlal, *The Gita and the Quran* (Varanasi, India: Pilgrims Publishing, 2005; originally published in 1957).

3. Rashad Khalifa, trans., *Qur'an: The Final Testament* (Tucson, AZ: Islamic Productions, 1989).

4. Llewellyn Vaughan-Lee, *Love Is a Fire* (Point Reyes Station, CA: Golden Sufi Center, 2000), 7.

5. Martin Lings, *What Is Sufism?* (Cambridge, UK: Islamic Texts Society, 1999), 25.

6. Hindu aphorism; see, for example, www.amritapuri.org/10172/one-step.aum.

7. Hadith Qudsi (*Bukhari*), quoted in Sayyed Nasr, *Islamic Spirituality: Foundations* (New York: Routledge, 1991), 201.

8. Michael Sells and Carl Ernst, *Early Islamic Mysticism* (Mahwah, NJ: Paulist Press, 1996), 131.

9. Andrew Harvey, trans., *Light Upon Light: Inspirations from Rumi* (Berkeley, CA: North Atlantic Books, 1996).

10. *Talks with Ramana Maharshi,* talk 28 (Tiruvannamalai, India: Sri Ramanasramam, 2000), 30–31.

11. Ravi Ravindra, *Yoga of the Christ* (Dorset, UK: Element Books, 1990), 126.

12. Llewellyn Vaughan-Lee, *Uniting Heaven and Earth*, audio talk (Point Reyes Station, CA: Golden Sufi Center, 2006).

13. Meister Eckhart, sermon 25, quoted in "Giving and Receiving," *Parabola* (Summer 2011).

14. Hadith Qudsi (*Al Sarraj*), cited in Annemarie Schimmel, *Mystical Dimensions of Islam* (Chapel Hill: University of North Carolina Press, 1975), 133.

15. Widely attributed to St. Teresa of Avila, this quotation likely comes from other sources; see http://mimuspolyglottos.blogspot.com/2011/11/whose-hands-another-possible-case-of.html.

16. Arthur S. Tritton, *Islam* (Salem, NH: Ayer, 1979), 101.

17. Shah-Kazemi, *Paths to Transcendence*, 207.

18. Quoted in Rom Landau, *The Philosophy of Ibn Arabi* (New York: Routledge, 2008; originally published in 1959).

19. Reynold Nicholson, *The Mystics of Islam* (London: Forgotten Books, 2008), 60.

20. Shah-Kazemi, *Paths to Transcendence*, 202.

21. There are several types of "union with the Divine" described in the Hindu scriptures. For a good description, see Swami Nikhilananda, *The Bhagavad Gita* (New York: Ramakrishna Vivekananda Center, 1978).

22. Griffiths, *River of Compassion*, 322.

23. K. Kavanaugh and O. Rodriguez, *The Collected Works of St. John of the Cross* (Washington, DC: ICS, 1991), 111.

24. Idries Shah, *Neglected Aspects of Sufi Study* (London: Octagon Press, 2002), 59.

25. Ibid.

26. There are several accounts of this story; see, for example, Timothy Conway, "Hazrat Bayazid Bistami, The Ecstatic Sufi," available online at www.enlightened-spirituality.org/support-files/sufism_bayazid_bistami.pdf.

27. *Gospel of Mary*, dialogue 1, quoted in Cynthia Bourgeault, *The Meaning of Mary Magdalene* (Boston: Shambhala, 2010), 47.

28. Aurobindo, *The Mother* (Pondicherry, India: Sri Aurobindo Ashram, 1927).

29. Chiragh Ali, "The Proposed Political, Legal and Social Reforms," *Modernist Islam 1840–1940: A Sourcebook*, ed. Charles Kurzman (New York: Oxford University Press, 2002), 281. See also Chiragh Ali, *The Proposed Political, Legal and Social Reforms Under Moslem Rule* (Bombay: Education Society's Press, 1883), xxii.

30. Etymologically, "yoke" and "yoga" both derive from the Sanskrit root *yuj*, which means "union."

31. Eric Schroeder, *Muhammad's People: A Tale by Anthology* (Portland, ME: Bond Wheelwright, 1955), quoted in "Islam," ch. 7 in Philip Novak, *The World's Wisdom* (Edison, NJ: Castle Books, 1994), 323–24.

32. "You shall know me and enter into my being" (Gita 11:54–55), and also in 8:22, 9:34, 12:8, 18:55.

33. Griffiths, *River of Compassion*, 322.

34. Francis X. Clooney, SJ, "Surrender to God Alone: The Meaning of Bhagavad Gita 18.66 in Light of Srivaisnava and Christian Tradition," in *Song Divine: Christian Commentaries on the Bhagavad Gita*, ed. Catherine Cornille (Leuven, Belgium: Peeters, 2006), 190–207.

35. Ibid.

36. In Islam, all sins are forgivable except *shirk*, to "ascribe a partner with God," that is, any form of idolatry or polytheism. Unless they repent before they die, the Qur'an says, "idolaters will have the Fire of Hell, there to remain" (98:6).

37. This is not to deny the harsh punishments prescribed for various sins in both the Qur'an and the Bible. In the Hebrew Bible, adultery is to be punished by death (Lev. 20:10, Deut. 22:22), and stoning was the usual method. Consider the two verses: "The adulterer and the adulteress shall surely be put to death" (Lev. 20:10) and "Whoever divorces his wife and marries another commits adultery against her, and if she divorces her husband and marries another, she commits adultery" (Mark 10:11). Taken literally, this means everyone who ever divorced and remarried— tens of millions of Americans today—should have been stoned to death. This example may seem ludicrous, but there are actually prominent Calvinist Christian Reconstructionists today who advocate the reinstatement of execution by stoning for all acts deemed to be capital offenses in the Hebrew Scriptures. Contrary to widespread belief, the Qur'an is far more lenient on adultery; it is not punishable by death or stoning, but by one hundred lashes for both the man and the woman, and then only if four eyewitnesses can be produced who personally witnessed the act, something virtually impossible to achieve in practice. Death by stoning for adultery came well after the Qur'an in some versions of *sharia* law (following

Torah precedent), and has been vehemently disputed—yet is still practiced today in a few Muslim countries, although the majority have abandoned the practice (see www.religioustolerance.org/isl_adul2.htm). The majority of Muslim countries today have a mixed legal system where *sharia* law plays a nondominant role, and countries like Turkey have a secular legal system in which *sharia* plays no role at all. "Most Muslim countries do not use traditional classical Islamic punishments," says expert Ali Mazrui, in Matthew Pate and Laurie A. Gould, *Corporal Punishment Around the World* (Santa Barbara, CA: ABC-CLIO, 2012), 51.

Classical *sharia* law is strictly applied in the legal systems of only a few Muslim countries, and even then, the harshest penalties are enforced inconsistently. Interpretations of *sharia* law itself also vary widely, particularly for the harshest penalties. The purported Qur'anic penalty for theft is amputation of the hand (5:38) and/or foot, yet this is widely debated; some say the Arabic is misinterpreted (www.quran-slam.org/articles/part_4/punishment_of_theft_%28P1465%29.html), and others argue that it is intended metaphorically, not literally, which also holds for various other Qur'anic verses (Mazrui, *Corporal Punishment Around the World*). The practice still exists in a few Muslim countries.

38. M. A. Sells, *Early Islamic Mysticism: Sufi, Qur'an, Miraj, Poetic and Theological Writings* (Mahwah, NJ: Paulist Press, 1995), 200.

39. Hadith *Bukhari* (book 75, Hadith 319).

40. Raimon Panikkar, *Christophany* (New York: Orbis, 2009), 143–155.

41. Ibid., 150.

42. Paramhansa Yogananda, *The Second Coming of Christ: The Resurrection of Christ Within You*, vols. 1 and 2 (Los Angeles: Self Realization Fellowship, 2004), 273–274.

43. Rig Veda, book 1, hymn 164, verse 46. A similar message is given in Rig Veda 10:114:5.

44. Thomas Keating, *The Future of Christianity*, DVD video (Boulder, CO: Integral Life, 2008).

45. Ibid.

46. Quoted in Krishnaprem, *The Yoga of the Bhagavad Gita*, 18.

47. Keating, *The Future of Christianity*.

48. Francis D'Sa, SJ, foreword to Panikkar, *Christophany*, xv.

49. Meister Eckhart, sermon 28 (DW 83, w 86), in E. Colledge and B. McGinn, trans., *Meister Eckhart: The Essential Sermons, Commentaries, Treatises, and Defense* (Mahwah, NJ: Paulist Press, 1982), 207–208.

50. James Stuart, *Swami Abhishiktananda: His Life Told Through His Letters* (Delhi, India: ISPCK, 1989), 213.

51. Sufi saying, quoted by Llewellyn Vaughan-Lee in "Part of an Ancient Story: A Conversation with Llewellyn Vaughan-Lee," *Parabola* (Nov. 15, 2015) (edited for gender inclusivity). Available online at www.parabola.org/2015/11/15/part-of-an-ancient-story-a-conversation-with-llewellyn-vaughan-lee-full-version.

52. Jan van Ruysbroeck, *The Adornment of Spiritual Marriage* (Whitefish, MT: Kessinger Publishing, 2007), chap. 4.

Chapter 4: Many Faiths, One Summit

1. Reza Shah-Kazemi, *Paths to Transcendence* (Bloomington, IN: Wisdom, 2006), 193.

2. Marguerite Porete, *The Mirror of Simple Souls* (New York: Paulist Press, 1993); see also Bernard McGinn, *Meister Eckhart and the Beguine Mystics* (New York: Continuum, 1994).

3. "Names and Titles of Ibn Arabi," The Muhyiddin Ibn Arabi Society, available at www.ibnarabisociety.org/articles/mssnames.html.

4. The lives and work of Eckhart, Ibn Arabi, and Shankara are profound; interested readers are directed to the first three chapters of Reza Shah-Kazemi's book *Paths to Transcendence*. Another important book relevant to this chapter is Shah-Kazemi's *The Other in the Light of the One*.

5. Jorge Ferrer and J. Sherman, *The Participatory Turn* (Albany: SUNY, 2007), and Jorge Ferrer, *Revisioning Transpersonal Theory* (Albany: SUNY Press, 2001).

6. Shankara, *Vivekachudamani*, trans. Swami Madhavananda (Calcutta, India: Advaita Ashrama, 1957), quoted in Shah-Kazemi, *Paths to Transcendence*, 4.

7. An immediate objection could arise here: If this transcendent realization is ineffable, how can it be characterized by Being-Consciousness-Bliss? Aren't these "effable" qualities? The reply is that these three qualities are not distinctively encountered; rather, "their undifferentiable common essence is realized in infinite mode" (Shah-Kazemi, *Paths to Transcendence*, 225), which utterly transcends the realm of ordinary experience. The finite notions of being, awareness, and joy are offered only as crude and inadequate aids to the imagination, to convey something of this transcendent realization.

8. Ramana Maharshi, *Talks with Ramana Maharshi*, talk no. 28.

9. Matthew 16:25 (edited for gender inclusivity).

10. E. Colledge and B. McGinn, trans., *Meister Eckhart: The Essential Sermons, Commentaries, Treatises, and Defense* (Mahwah, NJ: Paulist Press, 1981), 200.

11. This is one of John's many profound statements that summarize the apophatic mystical path on his famous sketch of Mt. Carmel. See K. Kavanaugh and O. Rodriguez, eds., *The Collected Works of St. John of the Cross* (Washington, DC: ICS Publications, 1991), 110–111.

12. Quoted in Fritjof Schuon, *The Transcendent Unity of Religions* (Wheaton, IL: Quest, 1993), 119.

Chapter 5: Intimacy with the Infinite

1. Quoted in Srinivasa Chari, *Vaishnavism: Its Philosophy, Theology, and Religious Discipline* (Delhi, India: Motilal Banarsidass, 1994), 264.

2. Other terms for *prapatti* occur in the literature, each with slightly different connotations: *nyaasa*, suggesting becoming freed from one's ego identity and its burdens, and *bharanyasa* and *atmaniksepa*, suggesting placing the burden for self-protection entirely upon God.

3. Chari, *Vaishnavism*, 261–264.

4. Yamuna advocates *prapatti* in his *Stotraratna* (Hollywood, CA: Vedanta Press, 1986), as does Ramanuja in his *Saranagati-Gadya* (V. Gopalachari, "Gadya Trayam of Ramanuja,"

Vishishtadvaita Philosophy and Religion [Madras, India: 1974], 71–76). Curiously, Ramanuja does not mention *prapatti* in his Gita commentary (*Gita Bhyasa*, ed. Swami Adidevananda [Kolkata, India: Advaita Ashrama, 2009]), even in his commentary on the *caramasloka*.

5. Chari, *Vaishnavism*, xxxvii.

6. Srilata Raman, *Self-Surrender (Prapatti) to God in Shrivaishnavism: Tamil Cats or Sanskrit Monkeys* (New York: Routledge, 2007), 20.

7. *Talks with Ramana Maharshi*, talk no. 28, 30–31.

8. Raman, *Self-Surrender*, 52.

9. I do not formally belong to the Srivaishnavaite tradition, although I have worked for years with the *caramasloka* of the Gita and with the *angas*, though not by that name.

10. Raman, *Self-Surrender*, 13.

11. The Sanskrit terms for the *angas* are (1) *Anukulya-sankalpa*, (2) *Pratikulya-varjana*, (3) *Maha-visvasa*, (4) *Goptrtva-varana*, (5) *Atma-niksepa*.

12. Sanskrit: *karpanya*.

13. Chari, *Vaishnavism*, 273.

14. All quotations from Rabi'a, with sources, are taken from http://sufimaster.org/teachings/adawiyya.htm.

15. Jean-Pierre de Caussade, *Abandonment to Divine Providence*, trans. Dom Dunstan and Anscar Vonier (Grand Rapids, MI: Christian Classics Ethereal Library, 2009).

16. Aurobindo, *The Mother*.

17. Terése of Liseux, *The Story of a Soul* (1897), chapter 9.

18. This metaphor is actually used by a contemporary Hindu teacher of *prapatti*. See Bashyam, "Preliminary Concepts," www.youtube.com/watch?v=tB8hpxe3lFE.

19. Krishnaprem, *The Yoga of Kathopanishad* (Allahabad, India: Ananda Publishing House, 1946), 79.

20. Mabel Collins, *Light on the Path* (Wheaton, IL: Theosophical Publishing House, 1980), 10.

21. Aurobindo, *Synthesis of Yoga*, 4th ed. (Pondicherry, India: Sri Aurobindo Ashram, 1970), 87.

Chapter 6: The Inner Net of the Heart

1. This elegant phraseology is borrowed from Pir Vilayat Khan, *That Which Transpires Behind That Which Appears* (Amherst, MA: Omega Publications, 1994).

2. Evan Thompson, *Waking, Dreaming, Being* (New York: Columbia University Press, 2015).

3. Dean Radin, *Entangled Minds* (New York: Paraview Pocket Books, 2006), and *The Conscious Universe* (San Francisco: HarperOne, 2009), and *Supernormal* (New York: Crown, 2013).

4. Chris Carter, *Science and Psychic Phenomena: The Fall of the House of Skeptics* (Rochester, VT: Inner Traditions), 207, and *Science and the Afterlife Experience: Evidence for the Immortality of Consciousness* (Rochester, VT: Inner Traditions, 2012); Larry Dossey, *Healing Words: The Power of Prayer and the Practice of Medicine* (San Francisco: HarperOne, 1995).

5. Larry Dossey, *Healing Words*.

6. Dean Radin and Roger Nelson, "Evidence for Consciousness-Related Anomalies in Random Physical Systems," *Foundations of Physics* 19, no. 12 (1989).

7. David Bohm, *Wholeness and the Implicate Order* (London: Routledge Classics, 2002).

8. We see this same unjustified assumption in Darwinian evolution of the randomness of all genetic mutation, which is accepted as an (unproven) article of faith.

9. Quoted in William Hermanns and Albert Einstein, *Einstein and the Poet* (Wellesley, MA: Branden Press, 1983), 58.

10. The implicate order is mapped out in greater detail in various esoteric systems, often comprised of seven ontological levels (as in the seven heavens of Islam, the seven great Lights of the Gita [10:6], or the "seven rays" of theosophy). In some systems each of these levels has seven sublevels (to make forty-nine in all), as in the work of the Tibetan mystic Djwal Khul, as documented in many books by theosophical writer Alice Bailey (see her introductory book, *Initiation, Human and Solar* [London: Lucis Trust, 1922]).

11. Austrian physicist Erwin Schrödinger was one of the founders of quantum mechanics. By partitioning the Schrödinger equation into real and imaginary parts, Bohm showed that the real part replicates classical physics, and the imaginary part has the form of a "quantum potential," from which Bohm developed the implicate order.

12. David Bohm, "Meaning and Information" in *The Search for Meaning: The New Spirit in Science and Philosophy*, ed. Paavo Pylkkanen (Napa Valley, CA: Crucible, 1989), 5 (available online at www.implicity.org/Downloads/Bohm_meaning+information.pdf).

13. Bohm's model was long inexplicably ignored by the mainstream physics community, and was dismissed as "Bohm baggage" by philosopher Ken Wilber (*Eye of Sprit* [Boston: Shambhala, 2001]), but interest in Bohm's work is rapidly growing today not only in physics, but also in theology and philosophy. See www.bohmian-mechanics.net, and the Workgroup Mathematical Foundation of Physics at Ludwig-Maximillians-Universitat in Munich (www.mathematik.uni-muenchen.de/~bohmmech), which has several informative videos posted on their website.

14. See a fascinating video on quantum behavior in classical fluid dynamics, "The Pilot-Wave Dynamics of Walking Droplets," at www.youtube.com/watch?time_continue=-14&v=nmC0ygr08tE, and for technical details, see D. M. Harris, J. Moukhtar, E. Fort, Y. Couder, and J. Bush, "Wavelike Statistics from Pilotwave Dynamics in a Circular Corral," *Physical Review* 88, no. 1 (July 2013).

15. Holography is a special case or application of fractal geometry, so we explore the more general field of fractal mathematics here.

16. Mathematically, Z represents a variable in the complex plane, and C represents a complex number. For each point C in the complex plane, this formula is applied repeatedly, beginning with $Z = 0$. If the resulting trajectory stays bounded, then C is said to be in the Mandelbrot set.

17. To be precise, these intricate images show the *boundary* of the Mandelbrot set (which itself is colored black).

18. Several videos online show the Mandelbrot set in remarkable depth. See, for example, "Mandelbrot Zoom 10^227," at www.youtube.com/watch?v=PD2XgQOyCCk.

19. *Collected Works of Julian of Norwich* (Haines City, FL: Revelation Insight, 2010), 141.

20. Stephanie Kaza and Kenneth Kraft, eds., *Dharma Rain* (Boston: Shambhala, 2000), 141.

21. Ajit Mukerjee, *Kundalini: The Arousal of the Inner Energy*, 3rd ed. (Rochester, VT: Destiny Books, 1986).

22. Quoted in J. Riggio, *Towards a Theory of Transpersonal Decision Making in Human Systems* (dissertation, Berne University, 2005).

23. Hermes Trismegistus, *Liber XXIV Philosophorum, Corpus Hermeticum* vol. 3, ed. Francois Hudry (Turnhout, Belgium: Brepols, 1997).

24. Rig Veda, book 1, hymn 164, verse 46. A similar message is given in Rig Veda 10:114:5.

25. Einstein's subsequent "general theory of relativity" broadened the earlier "special theory" to include accelerated reference frames and gravitational fields.

26. Quoted in Llewellyn Vaughan-Lee, "Neither of the East nor of the West," www.goldensufi.org/article_eastwest.html.

27. Quoted in Ingrid Frederiksson, *Aspects of Consciousness* (Jefferson, NC: McFarland, 2012), 22.

28. Vernon J. Bourke, ed., *The Essential Augustine* (Indianapolis: Hackett, 1974), 109.

29. Although correlated, physical light and divine light are radically different, and different laws apply. Despite his embrace of religion and God (á la Spinoza), Einstein was wary of applications of relativity theory to religion and social fields. Nevertheless, a broad literature in theology and philosophy has emerged in relation to interpretations of relativity theory; what is presented here is just a primer. For further exploration, see Max Jammer, *Einstein and Religion* (Princeton, NJ: Princeton University Press, 2002).

30. Tutu, *God Is Not a Christian*.

31. Quoted in Andrew Harvey, *Rumi: The Way of Passion* (Berkeley, CA: North Atlantic Books, 1994).

Chapter 7: Infinity of Divinity

1. For a visual introduction to fractals, see the recent NOVA documentary, *Fractals: Hunting the Hidden Dimension*, online at www.youtube.com/watch?v=HvXbQb57lsE.

2. To be more precise, the "cardinality" (number of points) in a finite line segment is equal to the cardinality of all the points in an N-dimensional infinite hyperspace (where N represents any natural number [1, 2, 3, 4, 5 ...], no matter how large).

3. Dmitri Krioukov, Maksim Kitsak, Robert S. Sinkovits, et al., "Network Cosmology," *Nature Scientific Reports* 2 (2012).

4. Adam J. Pearson, "Fractals and the Structure of Reality," November 20, 2011, http://beforeitsnews.com/metaphysics/2011/11/fractals-and-the-structure-of-reality-1402711.html.

5. Meister Eckhart, sermon 48, quoted in Jeremiah Hackett, *A Companion to Meister Eckhart* (Boston: Brill, 2013), 350.

6. *Meister Eckhart: Sermons and Treatises*, vol. 1, trans. Maurice O'Connell Walshe (Dorset, UK: Element Books, 1979), 217.

7. Reza Shah-Kazemi, "From Religious Form to Spiritual Essence: Esoteric Perspectives on Islam and Christianity According to Ibn al-'Arabi and Meister Eckhart," lecture to Australian Centre of Sufism and Irfanic Studies, December 15, 2013.

8. Quoted in Reza Shah-Kazemi, "The Wisdom of Gratitude in Islam," in *World's Great Wisdom*, ed. Roger Walsh (Albany: SUNY Press, 2014), 80, n. 20.

9. Vishva-Sara Tantra, Katha Upanishad 4, 10.

10. Quoted in Francis H. Cook, *Hua-Yen Buddhism: The Jewel Net of Indra* (University Park, PA: Penn State Press, 1977).

11. Plotinus, *The Six Enneads*, fifth ennead, eighth tractate.

12. Krishnaprem, *The Yoga of the Bhagavad Gita* 8, 142.

13. Plotinus, *The Six Enneads*.

14. Raimon Panikkar, *Christophany*.

15. The spiritual DNA functions as a fractal seed formula, regardless of which destiny manifests for the person. As an example, the spiritual DNA might include a trait that compels the person toward transcendent consciousness. The spectrum of possible manifestations would include everything from vertical transcendence in the form of exalted spiritual mastery and deep mystical realization to expansive artistic, religious, or philosophical vocations, to more horizontal transcendence, such as celebrity status or notoriety in media or politics, all the way to more problematic possibilities, such as drug or alcohol addiction, mental disorders, and the like. All these entail transcendence of ordinary human consciousness. In this manner, the spiritual DNA specifies particular qualities or propensities, plus a corresponding broad spectrum of potential destinies—and the actual reality of the person's life is determined by several factors, most important among them the person's free will.

Chapter 8: Toward a Universal Path of Divine Love

1. *The Gospel of Thomas*, logion 82, in *The Nag Hammadi Library in English*, ed. J. Robinson (San Francisco: HarperSanFrancisco, 1990), 135.

2. According to early Qur'anic commentators on this verse, the fire (*nar*) is synonymous with the Light (*nur*) of God (see Muhammad Asad, *The Message of the Qur'an*, 577, n. 7). Although fire has several other meanings in the Qur'an, many of them destructive, fire is used symbolically by Rumi in an analogous manner to the "living flame of love" of St. John of the Cross, or the "Nachiketas Fire" of the Katha Upanishad.

3. Krishnaprem, *Yoga of the Kathopanishad*, 195.

4. Ibid., 202, 210.

5. Ibid., 127–128.

6. John of the Cross, "The Living Flame of Love," in *The Collected Works of St. John of the Cross*, ed. Kieran Kavanaugh and Otilio Rodriguez (Washington, DC: ICS Publications, 1991), 643.

7. Ibid, 648.

8. Gravity is also believed to be part of this one force.

9. Krishnaprem, *Yoga of the Kathopanishad*, 227.

10. Ibid., 239.

11. Ibid., 129.

12. Heraclitus, DK22B30, available online at www.iep.utm.edu/heraclit, or see *Heraclitus: The Cosmic Fragments*, ed. G. S. Kirk (Cambridge, UK: Cambridge University Press, 1954).

13. John of the Cross, "The Living Flame of Love," 641–642.

14. Llewellyn Vaughan-Lee, *Love Is a Fire*.

15. Quoted in ibid.

16. John of the Cross, "The Living Flame of Love," 677.

17. Joseph Fitzgerald, ed., *The Essential Anandamayi Ma* (Bloomington, IN: World Wisdom, 2007), 63.

18. Quoted in Philip Novak, "A Single Planetary Heritage? *Homo Religiousus* in Big History," inaugural conference of International Big History Association (IBHA), Grand Valley State University, Grand Rapids, MI, August 2–5, 2012, 85; available online at www.thresholds-faculty_2013-11_p84-111%20(2).pdf.

19. W. C. Smith, *Towards a World Theology* (Philadelphia: Westminster, 1985), 6.

20. Stuart Kaufmann, *Reinventing the Sacred* (New York: Basic Books, 2008), 278.

21. For example, scholar Jorge Ferrer writes, "A few marginal voices notwithstanding, the search for a common core, universal essence, or single metaphysical world behind the multiplicity of religious experiences and cosmologies can be regarded as over" (Jorge Ferrer and Jacob Sherman, eds., *The Participatory Turn* [Albany: SUNY, 2008], 29). Another example is Stephen Prothero's *God Is Not One* (San Francisco: HarperOne, 2011), a popular academic textbook on comparative religion. Prothero argues that religions are inherently different because they have different purposes; he focuses almost exclusively on exoteric doctrines and institutional structures, and pays little attention to the mystical or esoteric aspects of religion.

22. Quoted in Llewellyn Vaughan-Lee, *The Signs of God* (Inverness, CA: Golden Sufi Center), 119.

23. John of the Cross, "The Living Flame of Love," 693.

24. Hadith Qudsi (*Al Sarraj*), cited in Annemarie Schimmel, *Mystical Dimensions of Islam*, 133.

25. Plotinus, *The Six Enneads*, first ennead, second tractate, section 6.

26. John 14:15, Qur'an 3:19–20 [Pickthall], Gita 18:65–66.

27. Matt. 10:39, Gita 18:65, Hadith attributed to the Prophet, quoted in Jamal Rahman, *Spiritual Gems of Islam*, 41.

28. Quoted by Llewellyn Vaughan-Lee, *Catching the Thread: Sufism, Dreamwork, and Jungian Psychology* (Inverness, CA: Golden Sufi Center, 2012), 212.

29. Shah-Kazemi, *Paths to Transcendence*, 222.

30. Krishnaprem, *Yoga of the Kathopanishad*, 171–173.

31. Oliver Davies, ed. and trans., *Meister Eckhart: Selected Writings* (New York: Penguin, 1994), sermon 30.

32. S. Grof and C. Grof, *Holotropic Breathwork* (Albany: SUNY Press, 2010), 25.

33. Pim van Lommel, *Consciousness Beyond Life* (San Francisco: HarperOne, 2011).

34. Pim van Lommel, foreword to *Infinite Awareness: The Awakening of a Scientific Mind*, by Marjorie H. Woolacott (New York: Rowman and Littlefield, 2015), xi.

35. Quoted in W. Teasdale, *The Mystic Heart* (Novato, CA: New World Library, 1999), 3.

36. Chandogya Upanishad 8.1, in *The Upanishads: Classics of Indian Spirituality*, trans. Eknath Easwaran (Tomales, CA: Nilgiri Press, 2007), 97–98.

37. Quoted in Donald Goergen, *Fire of Love: Encountering the Holy Spirit* (Mahwah, NJ: Paulist Press, 2006), 92.

38. Jan van Ruysbroeck, *The Adornment of the Spiritual Marriage*, trans. C. A. Wynschenk (New York: Cosimo Classics, 2007), 178.

Appendix 1: Divine Love in Buddhism and Nontheistic Traditions

1. Wallace, "Is Buddhism Really Nontheistic?"

2. Reza Shah-Kazemi, *Common Ground Between Islam and Buddhism* (Louisville, KY: Fons Vitae, 2010), 29.

3. Soyen Shaku, *Sermons of a Buddhist Abbot: Addresses on Religious Subjects* (Dorset, UK: Dorset Press, 1987; originally published in 1906), 14, 18. Available online at www.terebess.hu/zen/mesterek/Sermons-of-A-Buddhist-Abbot.pdf.

4. Tulku Urgyen Rinpoche, *Rainbow Painting* (Hong Kong: Ranjung Yeshe Publications, 2009), 90–97.

5. C. D. Sebastian, *Metaphysics and Mysticism in Mahayana Buddhism: An Analytical Study of the Ratnagotravibhago-mahayanaottaratantra-sastram*, Bibliotheca Indo-Buddhica Series 238 (Delhi, India: Sri Satguru Publications, 2005), 64–66.

6. "The Three *Kayas*," Buddhism: The Path to Enlightenment, December 14, 2015, available online at www.buddhist101.info/the-three-kayas.

7. Samyutta Nikaya (22:87), quoted in *The Long Discourses of the Buddha: A Translation of the Digha Nikaya*, trans. Maurice Walshe (Boston: Wisdom Publications, 1995), 409.

8. Shah-Kazemi, *Common Ground Between Islam and Buddhism*, 95–96.

9. Quoted in Thich Nhat Hanh, *Going Home: Jesus and Buddha as Brothers* (New York: Penguin, 1999), epigraph.

10. Tulku Urgyen Rinpoche, *Rainbow Painting*, 90.

11. Sachiko Murata and William Chittick, *The Vision of Islam* (Cairo, Egypt: American University in Cairo Press, 2006), 137.

12. Shah-Kazemi, *Common Ground Between Islam and Buddhism*, 93.

13. Ibid., 22.

14. The cause of suffering is sometimes presented as desire *and* aversion, but aversion is just another form of desire (its negative form). So the second noble truth can be formulated succinctly as follows: The cause of suffering is desire (*tanha*, "thirst," in Sanskrit).

15. Thich Nhat Hanh, *Living Buddha, Living Christ* (New York: Riverhead Books, 2007), 197.

16. Ibid., 188.

17. Quoted in F. Max Müller, *The Sacred Books of the East*, vol. 11 (Oxford, UK: Oxford Clarendon Press, 1881), 38.

Appendix 2: Science and Mysticism Are *Not* the Same

1. P. Kingsley, *Reality* (Inverness, CA: Golden Sufi Center, 2007), 155.

2. David Bohm, *Thought as a System* (New York: Routledge, 1994).

3. Ravi Ravindra, *Krishnamurti: Two Birds on a Tree* (Wheaton, IL: Quest Books, 1995), 69.

4. Yet these studies actually show that "meditation has an effect on the structure and function of the brain itself, ... [including] a permanent change in brain activity induced by many years of meditation" (Pim van Lommel, foreword to *Infinite Awareness* by Marjorie H. Woolacott, viii).

5. Woolacott, *Infinite Awareness*. See also Eben Alexander, *Proof of Heaven,* (New York: Simon and Schuster, 2012).

6. For definitive clinical data, see Pim van Lommel, *Consciousness Beyond Life* (San Francisco: HarperOne, 2011).

7. See the trilogy of books by Chris Carter, especially *Science and the Afterlife Experience* (Rochester, VT: Inner Traditions, 2012).

8. Ervin Laszlo with Anthony Peake, *The Immortal Mind: Science and the Continuity of Consciousness Beyond the Brain* (Rochester, VT: Inner Traditions, 2014), 143.

Credits

"This Love sacrifices all souls ..." (page 62) from *Light upon Light: Inspirations from Rumi*, translated and adapted by Andrew Harvey, published by North Atlantic Books, copyright © 1996 by Andrew Harvey. Reprinted by permission of publisher.

Primary Translation Sources

Translations of the Bhagavad Gita

Easwaran, Eknath. *The Bhagavad Gita*. Tomales, CA: Nilgiri Press, 2007.

Feuerstein, Georg. *The Bhagavad Gita*. Boston: Shambhala, 2014.

Sargent, Winthrop. *The Bhagavad Gita*. Albany, SUNY Press, 2009.

Yogananda. *God Talks with Arjuna*. 2 vols. Encinitas, CA: Self-Realization Fellowship, 2001.

Schweig, Graham. *The Bhagavad Gita*. San Francisco: HarperOne, 2007.

Ravindra, Ravi. *The Yoga of Krishna in the Bhagavad Gita*. Boston: Shambhala, forthcoming.

Translations of the Christian Scriptures

New Revised Standard Version (Anglicized Edition). © 1989, 1995 by the Division of Christian Education of the National Council of the Churches of Christ in the United States of America. Used by permission. All rights reserved.

The Holy Bible, English Standard Version® (ESV®). © 2001 by Crossway, a publishing ministry of Good News Publishers. All rights reserved.

Translations of the Qur'an

Asad, Muhammad. *The Message of the Qur'an*. Gibraltar: Dar al-Andalus, 1980.

Pickthall, Muhammad. *The Holy Qur'an*. New Delhi: Kitab Bhavan, 1999.

Haleem, Abdel. *The Qur'an*. New York: Oxford University Press, 2010.

Ali, Abdullah Yusuf. *The Holy Qur'an*. Ware, UK: Wordsworth Editions, 2001.

Arberry, Arthur J. *The Koran Interpreted*. New York: Simon and Schuster, 1966.

Translations of Rumi

Barks, Coleman. *The Essential Rumi*. San Francisco: HarperOne, 1996.

Harvey, Andrew. *Love's Fire*. Ithaca, NY: Meeramma Publications, 1988.

Star, Jonathan. *A Garden Beyond Paradise*. New York: Bantam Books, 1993.

Image Sources

Diagrams (figures 7.8, 7.9, 7.11, and 7.12) created by Kathy Lavine.

Figures 6.1, 6.2, Mandelbrot set, Wolfgang Beyer.

Figure 7.1, spiral and galaxy, Lori Gardi. Reprinted with permission.

Figure 7.2, diagram, António Miguel de Campos; image, Stevo-88.

Figure 7.3, Buddhabrot, Melinda Green, www.superliminal.com. Reprinted with permission.

Figure 7.4, Tree, Abe Bingham, Flickr; broccoli, Paul McCoubrie, Flickr; lightning, SB-Photography-Stock; lungs, Ewald E Weibel. Reprinted with permission.

Figure 7.5, heartbeat patterns, *Proceedings of the National Academy of Sciences.* Reprinted with permission.

Figure 7.6, brain cell, Uwe Konietzko, University of Zurich; universe, Volker Springel. Reprinted with permission.

Figure 7.7, Helix Nebula, NASA.

Figure 7.10, mystical body of Christ, Katia Solani, in Stanisvlav Grof, *Holotropic Breathwork*, SUNY Press, 2010. Reprinted with permission.

Index

Jesus, *cont.*
  Krishna and, 58, 77–79
  as *Nirmanakaya*, 205
  Lord's prayer, 172–73
  Pharisees and, xxv
  Qur'an's veneration of, 38
  religious law and, 70
  two commandments, 191–192
  surrender to God's will, 31, 73
jihad, greater, 5
John of the Cross, St., 69, 184–185, 187, 189–190
Johnson, Elizabeth A., xxx
Johnson, Kurt, 147
Judaism
  relation to other Abrahamic faiths, xix,
  divine love in, xxiii
  Kabballah and Zohar, xxiii
Junayd, 62

Kashani, Abd al-Razzaq, 55
Kaufmann, Stuart, 188
kayas, Buddhist, 204–205
Keating, Thomas, xxi, xxv, 78, 152, 180, 192
King, Martin Luther, xxv, 153
Krishna. *See also* Bhagavad Gita
  Absolute and, 24, 169, 176–177
  Allah and, 61–62, 67, 176
  Arjuna's vision of, 18–20
  as avatar, 13, 59
  Christ and, 77–79, 176–177
  glory of, 18
  Jesus and, 58, 77–79
  purushottama and, 24, 77–78
  teachings of, 9–29
  universe revealed in, 175
Krishnamurti, Jeddu, 212
Krishnaprem, 8, 21–22, 155, 176, 185–186, 195–196

Lal, Radha Mohan, 189, 193–194
Lanzetta, Beverly, xxx, xxxi
Lawrence, Brother, 15, 118–121, 132
Le Saux, Henri (Abhishiktananda), 80
Light of God, 57, 152, 177
Lommel, Pim van, 197, 236 n6
Logos, 155, 169–171
love, divine. *See also* devotion
  across faith traditions, 186–187, 190–192
  in Buddhism, xxiii–xxv
  direct path vs. the path of, 21–22
  divine fire of, 183–187, 201
  as first commandment, 17
  Gita's path of, 20–27, 74–75
  Gita's supreme secret, 17
  of God, reciprocal, 60–62
  in Judaism, xxiii
  knowledge of God vs., 99
  meditation and, 14–15
  nondual path of, xxvi–xxvii, 200
  oneness with the will of, 31
  power of, 154
  principles of, 200–201
  in the *Sh'ma*, 17, 60
  universal path of, 79–81, 200–201

Mackenzie, Don, 34
Maher project (India), xxx
Malhotra, Rajiv, 175
Mandelbrot, Benoit, 143
Mandelbrot set, 143–145, 146, 157, 159
MandelBuddha, 159, 173–174
Mary Magdalene, 70
  Gospel of, 70, 209
Mathnawi, 32–33, 64
maya (illusion), 89, 103, 191, 212
meditation, xxii, 6, 73, 98, 137, 212, 214, 236 n4
  in Bhagavad Gita, 14–15, 72
Merton, Thomas, 206
microcosm and macrocosm, ix, 145, 146, 168, 175–179
mind, xxxii–xxxiii, 210–212
Mirror of Simple Souls, The, 86
Muhammad, Prophet
  as prophet before Adam, 172
  forgiveness sought by, 76
  in shahadah, 41
  nothing new revealed to, 53
  patriarchy and, xxx
  profession of faith in, 41
  on sura 112, 48
  urged to consult other scriptures, 53–54
  warning to Muslims who wrong others, 34
Mukerjee, Ajit, 146
multiple religious belonging, xvii–xviii, 80
Muslims
  meaning of the word, 46
  nearness to God by, 66
  Sunni vs. Shi'ite, 41
mystical *prapatti*, 127
mysticism, 7, 65, 74, 85–104
  apophatic, xxxi, 26, 88, 207
  Buddhist, xxiiii
  Christian, xx, 95
  kataphatic, xxx, 187
  not equivalent to science, 210–214

Names of God, the, 89–91, 97, 171–172
Nammalvar, 111
Nathamuni, 109
Nhat Hanh, Thich, 202, 206
Nirmanakaya, 205
nondual realization, 74–75, 86, 199, 200
nondual *bhakti*, xxvii, 30, 200
nondual devotion, xxvi–xxvii, 74–75, 200
nondual path of love, xxvi–xxvii, 200
nonlocality, 136–137
Nur, Sheikh, 57

Oppenheimer, Robert, 19

Panikkar, Raimon, 77, 176
Paths to Transcendence, 85, 87
patriarchy, xxii. *See also* women
  transforming in religion, xxix–xxxii
Paul, St., 68, 70, 78
physics, 138–143. *See also* quantum theory; relativity theory
  contradiction between relativity and quantum theories, 139
  matter-energy equivalence, 142, 149, 185

Inspiration

The Golden Rule and the Games People Play
The Ultimate Strategy for a Meaning-Filled Life
By Rami Shapiro
A guidebook for living a meaning-filled life—using the strategies of game theory and the wisdom of the Golden Rule.
6 x 9, 176 pp, Quality PB, 978-1-59473-598-1 **$16.99**

Deepening Engagement
Essential Wisdom for Listening and Leading with Purpose, Meaning and Joy
By Diane M. Millis, PhD; Foreword by Rob Lehman
A toolkit for community building as well as a resource for personal growth and small group enrichment.
5 x 7¼, 176 pp, Quality PB, 978-1-59473-584-4 **$14.99**

The Rebirthing of God
Christianity's Struggle for New Beginnings
By John Philip Newell
Drawing on modern prophets from East and West, and using the holy island of Iona as an icon of new beginnings, Newell dares us to imagine a new birth from deep within Christianity, a fresh stirring of the Spirit.
6 x 9, 160 pp, HC, 978-1-59473-542-4 **$19.99**

Finding God Beyond Religion: A Guide for Skeptics, Agnostics & Unorthodox Believers Inside & Outside the Church
By Tom Stella; Foreword by The Rev. Canon Marianne Wells Borg
Reinterprets traditional religious teachings central to the Christian faith for people who have outgrown the beliefs and devotional practices that once made sense to them. 6 x 9, 160 pp, Quality PB, 978-1-59473-485-4 **$16.99**

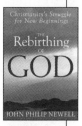

Fully Awake and Truly Alive: Spiritual Practices to Nurture Your Soul
By Rev. Jane E. Vennard; Foreword by Rami Shapiro
Illustrates the joys and frustrations of spiritual practice across religious traditions; provides exercises and meditations to help you become more fully alive.
6 x 9, 208 pp, Quality PB, 978-1-59473-473-1 **$16.99**

Perennial Wisdom for the Spiritually Independent
Sacred Teachings—Annotated & Explained
Annotation by Rami Shapiro; Foreword by Richard Rohr
Weaves sacred texts and teachings from the world's major religions into a coherent exploration of the five core questions at the heart of every religion's search.
5½ x 8½, 336 pp, Quality PB, 978-1-59473-515-8 **$16.99**

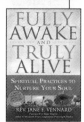

Journeys of Simplicity: Traveling Light with Thomas Merton, Bashō, Edward Abbey, Annie Dillard & Others *By Philip Harnden*
5 x 7¼, 144 pp, Quality PB, 978-1-59473-181-5 **$12.99**

Saving Civility: 52 Ways to Tame Rude, Crude & Attitude for a Polite Planet
By Sara Hacala 6 x 9, 240 pp, Quality PB, 978-1-59473-314-7 **$16.99**

Spiritually Healthy Divorce: Navigating Disruption with Insight & Hope
By Carolyne Call 6 x 9, 224 pp, Quality PB, 978-1-59473-288-1 **$16.99**

Or phone, fax, mail or email to: SKYLIGHT PATHS Publishing
Sunset Farm Offices, Route 4 • P.O. Box 237 • Woodstock, Vermont 05091
Tel: (802) 457-4000 • Fax: (802) 457-4004 • www.skylightpaths.com
Credit card orders: (800) 962-4544 (8:30AM–5:30PM EST Monday–Friday)
Generous discounts on quantity orders. SATISFACTION GUARANTEED. Prices subject to change.

Judaism / Christianity / Islam / Interfaith

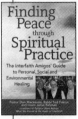

Finding Peace through Spiritual Practice
The Interfaith Amigos' Guide to Personal, Social and Environmental Healing
By Pastor Don Mackenzie, Rabbi Ted Falcon and Imam Jamal Rahman
A look at the specific issues in modern pluralistic society and the spiritual practices that can help transcend roadblocks to effective collaboration on the critical issues of today. 6 x 9, 200 pp (est), Quality PB, 978-1-59473-604-9 **$16.99**

Struggling in Good Faith
LGBTQI Inclusion from 13 American Religious Perspectives
Edited by Mychal Copeland and D'vorah Rose
Foreword by Bishop Gene Robinson; Afterword by Ani Zonneveld

A multifaceted sourcebook telling the story of reconciliation, celebration and struggle for LGBTQI inclusion across the religious landscape in America.
6 x 9, 240 pp, Quality PB, 978-1-59473-602-5 **$19.99**

Practical Interfaith: How to Find Our Common Humanity as We Celebrate Diversity
By Rev. Steven Greenebaum
Explores Interfaith as a faith—and as a positive way to move forward.
6 x 9, 176 pp, Quality PB, 978-1-59473-569-1 **$16.99**

Sacred Laughter of the Sufis: Awakening the Soul with the Mulla's Comic Teaching Stories & Other Islamic Wisdom

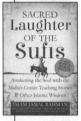

By Imam Jamal Rahman
The legendary wisdom stories of the Mulla, Islam's great comic foil, with spiritual insights for seekers of all traditions—or none.
6 x 9, 192 pp, Quality PB, 978-1-59473-547-9 **$16.99**

Religion Gone Astray: What We Found at the Heart of Interfaith
By Pastor Don Mackenzie, Rabbi Ted Falcon and Imam Jamal Rahman
Explores that which divides us personally, spiritually and institutionally.
6 x 9, 192 pp, Quality PB, 978-1-59473-317-8 **$18.99**

Blessed Relief: What Christians Can Learn from Buddhists about Suffering
By Gordon Peerman 6 x 9, 208 pp, Quality PB, 978-1-59473-252-2 **$16.99**

Christians & Jews—Faith to Faith: Tragic History, Promising Present, Fragile Future *By Rabbi James Rudin*
6 x 9, 288 pp, HC, 978-1-58023-432-0 **$24.99**; Quality PB, 978-1-58023-717-8 **$18.99***

Getting to the Heart of Interfaith: The Eye-Opening, Hope-Filled Friendship of a Pastor, a Rabbi & an Imam *By Pastor Don Mackenzie, Rabbi Ted Falcon and Imam Jamal Rahman*
6 x 9, 192 pp, Quality PB, 978-1-59473-263-8 **$16.99**

The Jewish Approach to God: A Brief Introduction for Christians
By Rabbi Neil Gillman, PhD 5½ x 8½, 192 pp, Quality PB, 978-1-58023-190-9 **$16.95***

The Jewish Approach to Repairing the World (*Tikkun Olam*)
A Brief Introduction for Christians *By Rabbi Elliot N. Dorff, PhD, with Rev. Cory Willson*
5½ x 8½, 256 pp, Quality PB, 978-1-58023-349-1 **$16.99***

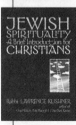

The Jewish Connection to Israel, the Promised Land: A Brief Introduction for
Christians *By Rabbi Eugene Korn, PhD*
5½ x 8½, 192 pp, Quality PB, 978-1-58023-318-7 **$14.99***

Jewish Holidays: A Brief Introduction for Christians *By Rabbi Kerry M. Olitzky and
Rabbi Daniel Judson* 5½ x 8½, 176 pp, Quality PB, 978-1-58023-302-6 **$18.99***

Jewish Ritual: A Brief Introduction for Christians *By Rabbi Kerry M. Olitzky
and Rabbi Daniel Judson* 5½ x 8½, 144 pp, Quality PB, 978-1-58023-210-4 **$14.99***

Jewish Spirituality: A Brief Introduction for Christians
By Rabbi Lawrence Kushner 5½ x 8½, 112 pp, Quality PB, 978-1-58023-150-3 **$12.95***

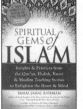

Spiritual Gems of Islam: Insights & Practices from the Qur'an, Hadith, Rumi &
Muslim Teaching Stories to Enlighten the Heart & Mind *By Imam Jamal Rahman*
6 x 9, 256 pp, Quality PB, 978-1-59473-430-4 **$16.99**

*A book from Jewish Lights, SkyLight Paths' sister imprint

Prayer / M. Basil Pennington, OCSO

Finding Grace at the Center, 3rd Edition
The Beginning of Centering Prayer
With Thomas Keating, OCSO, and Thomas E. Clarke, SJ; Foreword by Rev. Cynthia Bourgeault, PhD
A practical guide to a simple and beautiful form of meditative prayer.
5 x 7¼, 128 pp, Quality PB, 978-1-59473-182-2 **$12.99**

The Monks of Mount Athos: A Western Monk's Extraordinary
Spiritual Journey on Eastern Holy Ground *Foreword by Archimandrite Dionysios*
Explores the landscape, monastic communities and food of Athos.
6 x 9, 352 pp, Quality PB, 978-1-893361-78-2 **$18.95**

Psalms: A Spiritual Commentary *Illus. by Phillip Ratner*
Reflections on some of the most beloved passages from the Bible's most widely
read book. 6 x 9, 176 pp, 24 full-page b/w illus., Quality PB, 978-1-59473-234-8 **$16.99**

The Song of Songs: A Spiritual Commentary *Illus. by Phillip Ratner*
Explore the Bible's most challenging mystical text.
6 x 9, 160 pp, 14 full-page b/w illus., Quality PB, 978-1-59473-235-5 **$16.99**
HC, 978-1-59473-004-7 **$19.99**

Religious Etiquette / Reference

How to Be a Perfect Stranger, 6th Edition
The Essential Religious Etiquette Handbook
Edited by Stuart M. Matlins and Arthur J. Magida
The indispensable guidebook to help the well-meaning guest when visiting other
people's religious ceremonies. A straightforward guide to the rituals and celebra-
tions of the major religions and denominations in the United States and Canada
from the perspective of an interested guest of any other faith, based on information obtained from authorities of each religion. Belongs in every living room,
library and office. Covers:

**African American Methodist Churches • Assemblies of God • Bahá'í Faith • Baptist • Buddhist
• Christian Church (Disciples of Christ) • Christian Science (Church of Christ, Scientist) •
Churches of Christ • Episcopalian and Anglican • Hindu • Islam • Jehovah's Witnesses • Jewish
• Lutheran • Mennonite/Amish • Methodist • Mormon (Church of Jesus Christ of Latter-day
Saints) • Native American/First Nations • Orthodox Churches • Pentecostal Church of God •
Presbyterian • Quaker (Religious Society of Friends) • Reformed Church in America/Canada
• Roman Catholic • Seventh-day Adventist • Sikh • Unitarian Universalist • United Church of
Canada • United Church of Christ**

"The things Miss Manners forgot to tell us about religion."
—*Los Angeles Times*

"Finally, for those inclined to undertake their own spiritual journeys ...
tells visitors what to expect." —*New York Times*

6 x 9, 416 pp, Quality PB, 978-1-59473-593-6 **$19.99**

Struggling in Good Faith
LGBTQI Inclusion from 13 American Religious Perspectives
Edited by Mychal Copeland and D'vorah Rose; Foreword by Bishop Gene Robinson
A multifaceted sourcebook telling the story of reconciliation, celebration and
struggle for LGBTQI inclusion across the religious landscape in America.
6 x 9, 240 pp, Quality PB, 978-1-59473-602-5 **$19.99**

The Perfect Stranger's Guide to Funerals and Grieving Practices
A Guide to Etiquette in Other People's Religious Ceremonies
Edited by Stuart M. Matlins
6 x 9, 240 pp, Quality PB, 978-1-893361-20-1 **$16.95**

The Perfect Stranger's Guide to Wedding Ceremonies
A Guide to Etiquette in Other People's Religious Ceremonies
Edited by Stuart M. Matlins
6 x 9, 208 pp, Quality PB, 978-1-893361-19-5 **$16.95**

Sacred Texts—SkyLight Illuminations Series

Offers today's spiritual seeker an enjoyable entry into the great classic texts of the world's spiritual traditions. Each classic is presented in an accessible translation, with facing pages of guided commentary from experts, giving you the keys you need to understand the history, context and meaning of the text.

CHRISTIANITY

The Book of Common Prayer: A Spiritual Treasure Chest—
Selections Annotated & Explained
Annotation by The Rev. Canon C. K. Robertson, PhD; Foreword by The Most Rev. Katharine Jefferts Schori; Preface by Archbishop Desmond Tutu
Makes available the riches of this spiritual treasure chest for all who are interested in deepening their life of prayer, building stronger relationships and making a difference in their world.   5½ x 8½, 208 pp, Quality PB, 978-1-59473-524-0 **$16.99**

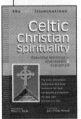

Celtic Christian Spirituality: Essential Writings—Annotated & Explained
Annotation by Mary C. Earle; Foreword by John Philip Newell
Explores how the writings of this lively tradition embody the gospel.
5½ x 8½, 176 pp, Quality PB, 978-1-59473-302-4 **$16.99**

Desert Fathers and Mothers: Early Christian Wisdom Sayings—
Annotated & Explained *Annotation by Christine Valters Paintner, PhD*
Opens up wisdom of the desert fathers and mothers for readers with no previous knowledge of Western monasticism and early Christianity.
5½ x 8½, 192 pp, Quality PB, 978-1-59473-373-4 **$16.99**

The End of Days: Essential Selections from Apocalyptic Texts—
Annotated & Explained *Annotation by Robert G. Clouse, PhD*
Helps you understand the complex Christian visions of the end of the world.
5½ x 8½, 224 pp, Quality PB, 978-1-59473-170-9 **$16.99**

The Hidden Gospel of Matthew: Annotated & Explained
Translation & Annotation by Ron Miller
Discover the words and events that have the strongest connection to the historical Jesus.
5½ x 8½, 272 pp, Quality PB, 978-1-59473-038-2 **$16.99**

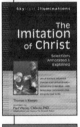

The Imitation of Christ: Selections Annotated & Explained
Annotation by Paul Wesley Chilcote, PhD; By Thomas à Kempis
Adapted from John Wesley's The Christian's Pattern
Let Jesus's example of holiness, humility and purity of heart be a companion on your own spiritual journey.
5½ x 8½, 224 pp, Quality PB, 978-1-59473-434-2 **$16.99**

The Infancy Gospels of Jesus: Apocryphal Tales from the Childhoods of Mary and Jesus—Annotated & Explained
Translation & Annotation by Stevan Davies; Foreword by A. Edward Siecienski, PhD
A startling presentation of the early lives of Mary, Jesus and other biblical figures that will amuse and surprise you.
5½ x 8½, 176 pp, Quality PB, 978-1-59473-258-4 **$16.99**

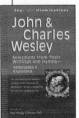

John & Charles Wesley: Selections from Their Writings and Hymns—
Annotated & Explained *Annotation by Paul W. Chilcote, PhD*
A unique presentation of the writings of these two inspiring brothers brings together some of the most essential material from their large corpus of work.
5½ x 8½, 288 pp, Quality PB, 978-1-59473-309-3 **$16.99**

Julian of Norwich: Selections from *Revelations of Divine Love*—
Annotated & Explained *Annotation by Mary C. Earle; Foreword by Roberta C. Bondi*
Addresses topics including the infinite nature of God, the life of prayer, God's suffering with us, the eternal and undying life of the soul, the motherhood of Jesus and the motherhood of God and more.
5½ x 8½, 224 pp, Quality PB, 978-1-59473-513-4 **$16.99**

Sacred Texts—continued

JUDAISM

The Book of Job: Annotated & Explained
Translation and Annotation by Donald Kraus; Foreword by Dr. Marc Brettler
Clarifies for today's readers what Job is, how to overcome difficulties in the text, and what it may mean for us. 5½ x 8½, 256 pp, Quality PB, 978-1-59473-389-5 **$16.99**

The Divine Feminine in Biblical Wisdom Literature
Selections Annotated & Explained
Translation & Annotation by Rabbi Rami Shapiro; Foreword by Rev. Cynthia Bourgeault, PhD
Uses the Hebrew Bible and Wisdom literature to explain Sophia's way of wisdom and illustrate Her creative energy. 5½ x 8½, 240 pp, Quality PB, 978-1-59473-109-9 **$18.99**

Ecclesiastes: Annotated & Explained
Translation & Annotation by Rabbi Rami Shapiro; Foreword by Rev. Barbara Cawthorne Crafton
A timeless teaching on living well amid uncertainty and insecurity.
5½ x 8½, 160 pp, Quality PB, 978-1-59473-287-4 **$16.99**

Embracing the Divine Feminine: Finding God through the Ecstasy of Physical Love—The Song of Songs Annotated & Explained
Translation & Annotation by Rabbi Rami Shapiro; Foreword by Rev. Cynthia Bourgeault, PhD
Restores the Song of Songs' eroticism and interprets it as a celebration of the love between the Divine Feminine and the contemporary spiritual seeker.
5½ x 8½, 176 pp, Quality PB, 978-1-59473-575-2 **$16.99**

Ethics of the Sages: *Pirke Avot*—Annotated & Explained
Translation & Annotation by Rabbi Rami Shapiro Clarifies the ethical teachings of the early Rabbis. 5½ x 8½, 192 pp, Quality PB, 978-1-59473-207-2 **$16.99**

Hasidic Tales: Annotated & Explained
Translation & Annotation by Rabbi Rami Shapiro; Foreword by Andrew Harvey
Introduces the legendary tales of the impassioned Hasidic rabbis, presenting them as stories rather than as parables. 5½ x 8½, 240 pp, Quality PB, 978-1-893361-86-7 **$18.99**

The Hebrew Prophets: Selections Annotated & Explained
Translation & Annotation by Rabbi Rami Shapiro; Foreword by Rabbi Zalman M. Schachter-Shalomi (z"l)
Makes the wisdom of these timeless teachers available to readers with no previous knowledge of the prophets. 5½ x 8½, 224 pp, Quality PB, 978-1-59473-037-5 **$16.99**

Maimonides—Essential Teachings on Jewish Faith & Ethics
The Book of Knowledge & the Thirteen Principles of Faith—Annotated & Explained
Translation and Annotation by Rabbi Marc D. Angel, PhD
Opens up for us Maimonides's views on the nature of God, providence, prophecy, free will, human nature, repentance and more.
5½ x 8½, 224 pp, Quality PB, 978-1-59473-311-6 **$18.99**

Proverbs: Annotated & Explained
Translation and Annotation by Rabbi Rami Shapiro
Demonstrates how these complex poetic forms are actually straightforward instructions to live simply, without rationalizations and excuses.
5½ x 8½, 288 pp, Quality PB, 978-1-59473-310-9 **$16.99**

***Tanya,* the Masterpiece of Hasidic Wisdom**
Selections Annotated & Explained *Translation & Annotation by Rabbi Rami Shapiro*
Foreword by Rabbi Zalman M. Schachter-Shalomi (z"l)
Clarifies one of the most powerful and potentially transformative books of Jewish wisdom. 5½ x 8½, 240 pp, Quality PB, 978-1-59473-275-1 **$18.99**

Zohar: Annotated & Explained
Translation & Annotation by Daniel C. Matt; Foreword by Andrew Harvey
The canonical text of Jewish mystical tradition.
5½ x 8½, 176 pp, Quality PB, 978-1-893361-51-5 **$18.99**

See Inspiration for *Perennial Wisdom for the Spiritually Independent: Sacred Teachings—Annotated & Explained*

Sacred Texts—continued

ISLAM

Ghazali on the Principles of Islamic Spirituality
Selections from *The Forty Foundations of Religion*—Annotated & Explained
Translation & Annotation by Aaron Spevack, PhD; Foreword by M. Fethullah Gülen
Makes the core message of this influential spiritual master relevant to anyone seeking a balanced understanding of Islam.
5½ x 8½, 336 pp, Quality PB, 978-1-59473-284-3 **$18.99**

The Qur'an and Sayings of Prophet Muhammad
Selections Annotated & Explained
Annotation by Sohaib N. Sultan; Translation by Yusuf Ali, Revised by Sohaib N. Sultan
Foreword by Jane I. Smith
Presents the foundational wisdom of Islam in an easy-to-use format.
5½ x 8½, 256 pp, Quality PB, 978-1-59473-222-5 **$16.99**

Rumi and Islam: Selections from His Stories, Poems, and Discourses—
Annotated & Explained *Translation & Annotation by Ibrahim Gamard*
Focuses on Rumi's place within the Sufi tradition of Islam, providing insight into the mystical side of the religion. 5½ x 8½, 240 pp, Quality PB, 978-1-59473-002-3 **$18.99**

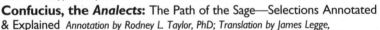
See Inspiration for *Perennial Wisdom for the Spiritually Independent: Sacred Teachings—Annotated & Explained*

EASTERN RELIGIONS

The Art of War—Spirituality for Conflict: Annotated & Explained
By Sun Tzu; Annotation by Thomas Huynh; Translation by Thomas Huynh and the Editors at Sonshi.com; Foreword by Marc Benioff; Preface by Thomas Cleary
Highlights principles that encourage a perceptive and spiritual approach to conflict.
5½ x 8½, 256 pp, Quality PB, 978-1-59473-244-7 **$16.99**

Bhagavad Gita: Annotated & Explained
Translation by Shri Purohit Swami; Annotation by Kendra Crossen Burroughs
Foreword by Andrew Harvey Presents the classic text's teachings—with no previous knowledge of Hinduism required. 5½ x 8½, 192 pp, Quality PB, 978-1-893361-28-7 **$18.99**

Chuang-tzu: The Tao of Perfect Happiness—Selections Annotated & Explained
Translation & Annotation by Livia Kohn, PhD
Presents Taoism's central message of reverence for the "Way" of the natural world.
5½ x 8½, 240 pp, Quality PB, 978-1-59473-296-6 **$16.99**

Confucius, the *Analects*: The Path of the Sage—Selections Annotated
& Explained *Annotation by Rodney L. Taylor, PhD; Translation by James Legge,*
Revised by Rodney L. Taylor, PhD Explores the ethical and spiritual meaning behind the Confucian way of learning and self-cultivation.
5½ x 8½, 192 pp, Quality PB, 978-1-59473-306-2 **$16.99**

Dhammapada: Annotated & Explained
Translation by Max Müller, Revised by Jack Maguire; Annotation by Jack Maguire
Foreword by Andrew Harvey Contains all of Buddhism's key teachings, plus commentary that explains all the names, terms and references.
5½ x 8½, 160 pp, b/w photos, Quality PB, 978-1-893361-42-3 **$14.95**

Selections from the Gospel of Sri Ramakrishna: Annotated & Explained
Translation by Swami Nikhilananda; Annotation by Kendra Crossen Burroughs
Foreword by Andrew Harvey Introduces the fascinating world of the Indian mystic and the universal appeal of his message. 5½ x 8½, 240 pp, b/w photos, Quality PB, 978-1-893361-46-1 **$16.95**

Tao Te Ching: Annotated & Explained
Translation & Annotation by Derek Lin; Foreword by Lama Surya Das
Introduces an Eastern classic in an accessible, poetic and completely original way.
5½ x 8½, 208 pp, Quality PB, 978-1-59473-204-1 **$16.99**

Sacred Texts—continued

MORMONISM

The Book of Mormon: Selections Annotated & Explained
Annotation by Jana Riess; Foreword by Phyllis Tickle Explores the sacred epic that is cherished by more than twelve million members of the LDS church as the keystone of their faith. 5½ x 8½ , 272 pp, Quality PB, 978-1-59473-076-4 **$16.99**

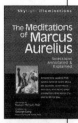

NATIVE AMERICAN

Native American Stories of the Sacred: Annotated & Explained
Retold & Annotated by Evan T. Pritchard These teaching tales contain elegantly simple illustrations of time-honored truths. 5½ x 8½, 272 pp, Quality PB, 978-1-59473-112-9 **$18.99**

STOICISM

The Meditations of Marcus Aurelius: Selections Annotated & Explained
Annotation by Russell McNeil, PhD; Translation by George Long, Revised by Russell McNeil, PhD Ancient Stoic wisdom that speaks vibrantly today about life, business, government and spirit. 5½ x 8½, 288 pp, Quality PB, 978-1-59473-236-2 **$16.99**

Hinduism / Vedanta

The Four Yogas: A Guide to the Spiritual Paths of Action, Devotion, Meditation and Knowledge *By Swami Adiswarananda*
6 x 9, 320 pp, Quality PB, 978-1-59473-223-2 **$19.99**

Meditation & Its Practices: A Definitive Guide to Techniques and Traditions of Meditation in Yoga and Vedanta *By Swami Adiswarananda*
6 x 9, 504 pp, Quality PB, 978-1-59473-105-1 **$24.99**

The Spiritual Quest and the Way of Yoga: The Goal, the Journey and the Milestones
By Swami Adiswarananda 6 x 9, 288 pp, HC, 978-1-59473-113-6 **$29.99**

Sri Ramakrishna, the Face of Silence *By Swami Nikhilananda and Dhan Gopal Mukerji; Edited and with an Introduction by Swami Adiswarananda*
Foreword by Dhan Gopal Mukerji II 6 x 9, 352 pp, Quality PB, 978-1-59473-233-1 **$21.99**

The Vedanta Way to Peace and Happiness *By Swami Adiswarananda*
6 x 9, 240 pp, Quality PB, 978-1-59473-180-8 **$21.99**

Vivekananda, World Teacher: His Teachings on the Spiritual Unity of Humankind
Edited and with an Introduction by Swami Adiswarananda
6 x 9, 272 pp, Quality PB, 978-1-59473-210-2 **$21.99**

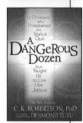

Sikhism

The First Sikh Spiritual Master: Timeless Wisdom from the Life and Teachings of Guru Nanak *By Harish Dhillon* 6 x 9, 192 pp, Quality PB, 978-1-59473-209-6 **$18.99**

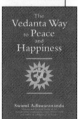

Spiritual Biography

A Dangerous Dozen: Twelve Christians Who Threatened the Status Quo but Taught Us to Live Like Jesus
By The Rev. Canon C. K. Robertson, PhD; Foreword by Archbishop Desmond Tutu
Profiles twelve visionary men and women who challenged society and showed the world a different way of living. 6 x 9, 208 pp, Quality PB, 978-1-59473-298-0 **$16.99**

Mahatma Gandhi: His Life and Ideas *By Charles F. Andrews; Foreword by Dr. Arun Gandhi*
Examines the religious ideas and political dynamics that influenced the birth of the peaceful resistance movement. 6 x 9, 336 pp, b/w photos, Quality PB, 978-1-893361-89-8 **$19.99**

Bede Griffiths: An Introduction to His Interspiritual Thought
By Wayne Teasdale Explores the intersection of Hinduism and Christianity.
6 x 9, 288 pp, Quality PB, 978-1-893361-77-5 **$18.95**

Spiritual Leaders Who Changed the World: The Essential Handbook to the Past Century of Religion *Edited by Ira Rifkin and the Editors at SkyLight Paths*
Foreword by Dr. Robert Coles 6 x 9, 304 pp, b/w photos, Quality PB, 978-1-59473-241-6 **$18.99**

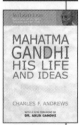

About SKYLIGHT PATHS Publishing

SkyLight Paths Publishing is creating a place where people of different spiritual traditions come together for challenge and inspiration, a place where we can help each other understand the mystery that lies at the heart of our existence.

Through spirituality, our religious beliefs are increasingly becoming a part of our lives—rather than *apart* from our lives. While many of us may be more interested than ever in spiritual growth, we may be less firmly planted in traditional religion. Yet, we do want to deepen our relationship to the sacred, to learn from our own as well as from other faith traditions, and to practice in new ways.

SkyLight Paths sees both believers and seekers as a community that increasingly transcends traditional boundaries of religion and denomination—people wanting to learn from each other, *walking together, finding the way.*

For your information and convenience, at the back of this book we have provided a list of other SkyLight Paths books you might find interesting and useful. They cover the following subjects:

Buddhism / Zen	Gnosticism	Poetry
Catholicism	Hinduism / Vedanta	Prayer
Chaplaincy		Religious Etiquette
Children's Books	Inspiration	Retirement & Later-Life Spirituality
Christianity	Islam / Sufism	
Comparative Religion	Judaism	Spiritual Biography
	Meditation	Spiritual Direction
Earth-Based Spirituality	Mindfulness	Spirituality
	Monasticism	Women's Interest
Enneagram	Mysticism	Worship
Global Spiritual Perspectives	Personal Growth	

Or phone, fax, mail or email to: SKYLIGHT PATHS Publishing
Sunset Farm Offices, Route 4 • P.O. Box 237 • Woodstock, Vermont 05091
Tel: (802) 457-4000 • Fax: (802) 457-4004 • www.skylightpaths.com
Credit card orders: (800) 962-4544 (8:30AM–5:30PM EST Monday–Friday)
Generous discounts on quantity orders. SATISFACTION GUARANTEED. Prices subject to change.

For more information about each book,
visit our website at www.skylightpaths.com.